How to Thrive as a Solo Librarian

EDITED BY
CAROL SMALLWOOD
MELISSA J. CLAPP

D0920764

THE SCARECROW PRESS, INC.
Lanham • Toronto • Plymouth, UK
2012

Published by Scarecrow Press, Inc.
A wholly owned subsidiary of The Rowman & Littlefield Publishing Group, Inc.
4501 Forbes Boulevard, Suite 200, Lanham, Maryland 20706
http://www.scarecrowpress.com

Estover Road, Plymouth PL6 7PY, United Kingdom

British Library Cataloguing in Publication Information Available

Library of Congress Cataloging-in-Publication Data

How to thrive as a solo librarian / edited by Carol Smallwood, Melissa J. Clapp.
    p. cm.
  Includes bibliographical references and index.
  ISBN 978-0-8108-8213-3 (pbk. : alk. paper) — ISBN 978-0-8108-8214-0 (ebook)
  1. Small libraries—Administration. I. Smallwood, Carol, 1939– II. Clapp, Melissa
J., 1977–
  Z675.S57H69 2012
  025.1—dc23   2011020786

∞™ The paper used in this publication meets the minimum requirements of
American National Standard for Information Sciences—Permanence of Paper for
Printed Library Materials, ANSI/NISO Z39.48-1992.

Printed in the United States of America

To the inspiring solo public librarians in northern Michigan
with whom I had the pleasure of working as a library consultant
—Carol Smallwood

To my mother, Sandy Shoop
—Melissa J. Clapp

Contents

Foreword

Valerie Nye

What is a solo librarian? Solo librarians are usually professional librarians running a small library within a larger organization or communities with limited populations. These librarians often run the entire library by themselves but may occasionally work with paraprofessional librarians, volunteers, or interns. Solo library jobs have been found traditionally in corporations, hospitals, churches, schools, law firms, museums, and within any organization where specialized research material is a required part of conducting business. In recent years, changes in the economy have forced organizations to reconsider spending priorities. In this new environment of shifting priorities, librarians may find themselves newly soloed in libraries that traditionally have had multiple employees.

The words "solo" and "librarianship" may bring to mind a quiet librarian working alone with little interruption in a small room surrounded by a special collection of books. This notion is far from the reality experienced by most librarians in this field. In many ways, solo librarianship demands more communication and collaboration than librarians might experience in larger multi-employee libraries. A librarian working alone is the primary advocate for library collection and all of its services. This advocacy requires ongoing connections with patrons and potential patrons so that the library and its services remain vital and relevant to the people it is intended to serve.

While some people aspire to work in solo positions, most librarians enter this unique field within librarianship without the specific career goal of running a library alone. Librarians who are interested in putting every level of their professional library skills to work on a daily basis may find solo job descriptions particularly attractive. The day-to-day work ranges from employing library skills such as shelving material and answering reference questions to high-level business skills such as creating policies and planning budgets. These diverse skills require that a librarian working in a solo position possess great organization skills and innate ability to prioritize and multitask.

Within the moments of busy activity of working in a library, a wise solo librarian will stand back and take note of all the things that one person can accomplish in a small library. Gratification comes when it is possible to observe all of the elements that a single person can put into action to provide service to a community with research needs.

The essays in this book paint a picture of the details required to run a successful library by oneself, and will inspire creativity in librarians who are working solo—but far from alone—within the various communities they serve.

Acknowledgments

Kim Becnel, assistant professor of library science, Appalachian State University, Boone, NC

James B. Casey, Ph.D., director of the Oak Lawn Public Library, Chicago, Illinois; recipient of the Illinois Library Association Librarian of the Year Award

Dorothea J. Coiffe, assistant professor, A. Philip Randolph Memorial Library, New York, New York

Tom Cooper, director, Webster Groves Public Library, Webster Groves, Missouri; *Writing and Publishing: the Librarian's Handbook* (ALA, 2010)

Wayne Finley, assistant professor/business librarian, Northern Illinois University Libraries

Larissa K. Garcia, assistant professor, National-Louis University Library, Lisle, Illinois

John Helling, director, Bloomfield-Eastern Greene County Public Library

James Lund, director, Red Wing Public Library, Red Wing, Minnesota; *The Frugal Librarian* (ALA Editions, 2011)

Rita Marsales, catalog librarian, Menil Collection Library, Houston, Texas

Aline Soules, library faculty, California State University, East Bay

Tom Taylor, continuing education coordinator, South Central Kansas Library System

Linda Burkey Wade, digitization unit coordinator, WIU Malpass Library, Macomb, Illinois

Kathryn Yelinek, reference librarian/coordinator of government documents, Bloomsburg University of Pennsylvania, Bloomsburg, Pennsylvania

Introduction

Carol Smallwood and Melissa J. Clapp

How to Thrive as a Solo Librarian is a compilation of twenty-six chapters by librarians writing from experience in order to help colleagues who must work alone or with very limited help. These previously unpublished chapters range between 3,000 and 3,500 words and they come to us from schools and colleges, special and corporate archives, public libraries, and seasoned LIS faculty across the United States and abroad who are familiar with the vigor, dedication, and creativity necessary for solo librarians. This book is intended for professionals and students in the field of librarianship. Valerie Nye, who wrote the foreword and is an experienced solo librarian as well as library manager, editor, and author, rightly noted: "In many ways, solo librarianship demands more communication and collaboration than librarians might experience in larger multi-employee libraries."

Despite the fact that most of these authors are currently working alone in their library or archives, they do not work in a vacuum. These energetic, organized, and resourceful librarians were eager to share their knowledge and experience for success with colleagues: the images of Superman and Superwoman often surfaced when reading their accomplishments.

These librarians were encouraged to submit three potential topics and to follow Gustave Flaubert's advice when writing their chapters: "Whenever you can shorten a sentence, do. And one always can. The best sentence? The shortest." The chapters are grouped into eight parts in the table of contents; the chapters are indexed by author, title, and subject with "see's" and "see also's" for ready access.

It has been a pleasure working with these dedicated librarians from many states across the country as well as abroad. The generous sharing of their experiences provides invaluable guideposts for other solo librarians.

Part I

TIME MANAGEMENT

CHAPTER 1

Solo Librarians as Jugglers

Roxanne Myers Spencer

The truth about juggling is that we all drop the ball some time, especially when the balls are different weights, shapes, and sizes. Accepting that we cannot keep all the balls in the air simultaneously, indefinitely, helps the solo librarian to approach managing time, tasks, and energy more efficiently.

The solo librarian or information specialist faces time and task management challenges daily. Demands on a medical, law, or business librarian vary from those on a public or school librarian, yet the effects are often the same: too many tasks, too little time; too much stress, too little support. We have become experts at juggling. Tough economic times have only increased our sense of urgency about getting everything done.

There are many resources for time and task management available in books, videos, and online. They can be useful—if we could only find the time to go through them! We know the essentials:

- prioritize responsibilities
- schedule important tasks first
- limit checking e-mail and returning phone calls

We are all doing more with less: more demands, more clients and patrons, less time, less money, fewer resources. The truth is we cannot manage time. We can only manage ourselves in relation to time.

So much of what librarians provide is service, whether reference, research, readers' advisory, homework, or community resources. In addition to public service, the solo librarian also manages most or all technical services and administration of the library or information center. To say no often induces feelings of guilt and a sense of failing to do your job effectively. We can get over the super-librarian mentality, especially important for those working in a one-person library, and still maintain our professional reputations and inspire confidence in our constituents.

What Can We Learn from Juggling? (Juggling and the Solo Librarian's Circus)

In *Lessons from the Art of Juggling: How to Achieve Your Full Potential in Business, Learning and Life*,[1] Tony Buzan and Michael Gelb use juggling as a metaphor for lifelong learning and success. Here are some of the principles and how they can be applied to solo librarianship:

- Set goals and visualize results: Choose one small, manageable task. Build on this success for more complex projects.
- Transform your attitude toward mistakes and failure: Everyone makes mistakes. This will never change. See mistakes and misguided attempts simply as minor detours along the way to success.
- Recognize and change limiting habitual patterns: Just because "it's always been done this way" doesn't mean that it's the only way or the best way. Re-examine task steps with a fresh approach.
- Re-attain your natural poise by cultivating the art of relaxed concentration: You accomplish more when you can go into the "zone" of calm, focused attention. Choose a task you enjoy and be mindful of your approach and mindset, and try to apply to other duties.
- Unleash your natural genius through the power of play: Take time to play a game or engage in an activity you enjoy. Let the "back burner" be inspired by your refocused attention.

In "Managing Multiple Projects, or the Art of Juggling,"[2] Hotchkiss says, "The consensus is that what juggling boils down to is focus, balance, and timing" which, in a nutshell, streamlines the processes of balancing numerous tasks and demands on your time. Hotchkiss goes on to summarize eight useful pointers from management literature to help the overwhelmed librarian.

Realistic Expectations/Perceptions (Even Master Jugglers Sometimes Drop the Ball)

It is important to recognize and remind others in your institution that you, as solo librarian, may be a one-person band, but you are not an orchestra. You can only accomplish so much—even with the best time management and organizational skills. Clarifying and negotiating reasonable expectations with your supervisor is a first step in successful juggling of multiple demands.

It is incumbent upon information specialists to define the parameters of their positions within the organization. This will vary with the library or information center setting. Without a clearly defined job description and expectations, solo practitioners will quickly find themselves over-whelmed—or worse, misunderstood and undervalued, which in any work environment can equate to becoming superfluous or redundant.

Each work environment differs in scope and function. Common considerations to keep in mind as a solo librarian:

- Anticipate change. Not that you necessarily prepare for the unknown, but expect that it will probably happen.

Are You Really Cut Out for a Solo Act?

With all the juggling solo librarians have to do, is a one-person library position really for you?

Ask yourself these questions, and answer yourself honestly:

1. Do you really enjoy being solely responsible for the collection, services, research of a solo librarian?
2. Do you prefer to work alone and control/manage all aspects of being a solo librarian?
3. Are you detail-oriented almost to the point of obsession?
4. Are you super-organized, so that you can point your finger or your mouse to exactly the resource needed in a matter of seconds?

If you answered "not sure" or "no" to any of the above, perhaps a career as a solo librarian isn't your best fit. Consider your needs for social interaction and work-sharing responsibilities for your best career options.

- Begin as you mean to go on, but be flexible, so you can change course in midstream.
- Say no without the guilt.
- Set realistic goals, revisit them, trim nonessentials.
- Know your role: limitations, capabilities, authority to decide and act.

Managing Time and Workload (Just How Many Things Can You Really Juggle At One Time?)

Time management requires active decision making and involves prioritizing, delegating (if possible), relegating (to the when-time-permits pile), and taking constructive action. To help the solo librarian cope with seemingly never-ending demands, consider the following process:

1. Identify priorities: Use the TF30 principle: Identify what must be done today, by Friday, what can be done within the next 30 days.[3] Break the must-do list into small chunks of time and tasks. Work in half-hour, even quarter-hour increments to make tasks manageable and to see progress.
2. Plan action: It may mean turning off your office phone ringer, putting your cell phone on silent, and refraining from opening your e-mail, until you have an action plan for a specific chunk of time.
3. Review essentials: Review your TF30 list daily and trim it to bare-bones essentials.
4. Do the most important tasks first: Don't be sidetracked by quick or easy-to-do tasks. It is too easy to get derailed and, ultimately, lose focus on the important tasks.
5. Accept that not everything will get done: This is a fact of life, but your "Done!" list will get longer if you focus on essentials.
6. Learn how to say no or, at least, "not now": This is a particular problem of people providing services. You can soften the hard edge of no without resorting to excuses and justifications: "I can't fit this in now, but I can make time for it next week," or "Let's look at the calendar, so I make this a priority."

Support: Using Networking Tools (There Is a Jugglers' Support System Out There!)

We live in an era of unprecedented opportunities for collaboration, peer support, and extended resources. We can poll potentially thousands of other practitioners with a simple post to an e-mail list, Facebook, or Twitter to get assistance with reference, cataloging, collection development, technology, and dozens of other aspects of our jobs. We often find ourselves with a surfeit of options and little time to indulge in the cornucopia of resources available to us at a keystroke. We seldom have time to catch up on RSS feeds, update our Facebook friends, follow the latest trends on Twitter—never mind respond to far-flung colleagues on e-mail lists.

Yet these are often the very tools that can lead us to possible solutions, excellent suggestions, and just the right information to complete a task, answer a stumper reference question, or make a dent in the backlog of cataloging stacked on the corner of the desk.

Making the best use of technology, rather than becoming enslaved by it, is our best bet for streamlining the workflow. By structuring our time online, we can make the most of professional development (webinars—in real time or archived), useful e-mail lists (suggest daily digests as less distracting), and latest news (keep the Twitter and Facebook time to fifteen minutes per day). We cannot possibly keep up with everything, so skimming the surface of essentials will keep us in the loop of ever-changing technology without drowning in information overload.

We subscribe to e-mail lists or RSS feeds because of a genuine interest or need for information yet find ourselves unable to keep up with the deluge of information. It's not a bad thing, initially, to subscribe to a few lists. The point is to monitor them well enough to know which ones will be most useful—the keepers—and know which ones really don't address our interests or informational needs well enough. Drop those that don't provide practical suggestions that improve your knowledge and skills.

Face-to-face networking is still an ideal worth pursuing. Making time for your own professional development among peers is important, despite the stack of arguments you amass against leaving the office for a couple of days. Chances are those in the profession your library serves pay attention to their own professional development—why should you value your career needs any less? Keep up memberships in organizations that provide the most salient information for your needs. In this way, you train your constituents to recognize your own dedication and professionalism. You have the right occasionally to swim in the bigger, broader waters of librarianship and information technology with far-flung colleagues. Even if you only manage to make the state or regional conferences, you give yourself the opportunity to exchange ideas and experiences and to learn new tools and skills. When traveling to a conference simply isn't possible, schedule time for webinars—either live or archived, as participant or presenter—to keep your hand in professionally.

Make technology work for you in other ways by utilizing the tools that organize and simplify a variety of tasks. For example, use Web 2.0 tools that help streamline collaboration and manage information:

- Use Google Apps to share work documents, spreadsheets, and presentations.
- Try Zotero (www.zotero.org), a Firefox browser extension, to organize and cite online research.
- Check out Zoho (www.zoho.com), among other applications with free plan levels, to develop an effective Personal Learning Network (PLN) or Personal Learning Environment (PLE) to manage a variety of tasks and tools.
- Determine which social networking sites are most relevant to you, and invest your time in a few choice sites.

Communicating Effectively (Playing to the Audience without a Net)

Use technology to communicate your services, policies, and new materials. Company intranets, private e-mail groups, lists, and social networks provide the means to get the word out to your constituents, whether they are lawyers, scientists, or elementary school teachers. List the basic procedures for research assistance, reserving materials, borrowing privileges, scope of services, and helpful resources in a simply designed, easily navigable for-

What if your organization expands or acquires and you are suddenly a solo librarian to many hundreds or thousands more personnel? How do you cope? What do you do to organize?

- Establish a start and an end to your workday, every day, and do not give in to temptation for "just another half-hour's work." By working unpaid hours, you send the message that you can handle the workload, even if it requires the addition of another position.
- Clearly establish what you can and cannot accomplish in serving an expanded clientele. Simply duplicating lesson plans, guidelines, or other handouts is not tantamount to managing an additional collection or meeting the reference and research needs of a worldwide sales force.
- Maintain professional development opportunities. You cannot effectively serve your new clientele if you do not keep up with changes in your field. Networking with colleagues at conferences or even attending webinars can give you fresh ideas for managing the increased workload.
- School librarians may be faced with serving two or more schools. Budget cuts could mean visiting two, three, four schools per week with hundreds more students. Duplicate lesson plans and upgrade/downgrade challenge level of assignments/lessons. Enlist volunteers from local communities. Simplify goals and activities.
- Monitor reference and materials requests diligently to see increase in usage and your time. Use chat or virtual library reference programs for worldwide library clientele. Consider the need for bilingual materials or materials in other languages and the cataloging needed.

mat. Follow the KISS principle, Keep it Short and Simple, in your design and messages. Sending monthly or weekly updates can be an effective and nonintrusive way to keep your constituents aware of library services. To manage the workflow, do updates on the same day each week or month. By maintaining an update schedule, you can focus on other priorities.

Solo librarians in institutional settings are often misunderstood by colleagues, being considered, erroneously, neither fish nor fowl. School librarians are usually certified teachers, law librarians often have law degrees, and medical librarians often have credentials in the health sciences fields. Exercise your communication skills, increase your visibility, and raise your professional profile by maintaining friendly, knowledgeable communications about your services and abilities.

Managing Workflow (How Many Balls *Should* You Keep in the Air at One Time?)

The solo librarian is often overwhelmed and overextended. The demands of patrons, supervisors, and resources management require flexibility and support, which must often come from outside sources and volunteers. Here are some considerations for managing the many ongoing tasks.

- Does your library vendor provide additional services such as catalog records, labels, dust jackets? The additional processing fee is worth your time, which can be better spent on more skilled activities.
- Is outsourcing technology, cataloging, or materials processing an option? If yours is a small, independent library, can you form an alliance with a local college or business for server space or technology upgrades?
- Is there a volunteer corps you can tap for clerical help? In school settings, library media specialists can recruit likely students, parents, or senior citizens for a few hours per week. In business settings, organizations such as AARP have connections to retired businesspeople who often volunteer to keep skills sharp.
- Is there a library consortium you can join to obtain discounted electronic research database resources? Regional, national, and international options may be worth pursuing. Networking advantages may be an additional benefit.

It's important to remember that streamlining and managing the workflow and workload is an iterative process (see figure 1.1). Special projects, new services, and other inevitable changes mean maintaining a flexible approach to managing and refining essential tasks.

Nurturing the Personal and Professional (Care and Feeding of the Complete Juggler)

Our responsibilities as solo librarians do not end with the workday or the workload. If we do not keep up with the changes in librarianship or in our specializations, we do a disservice to our clientele. It is a challenge to attend professional conferences because of the difficulties of closing the library

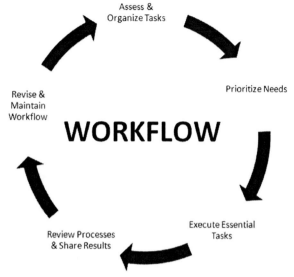

Figure 1.1

or, in the case of those fortunate enough to have help, leaving it in the hands of paraprofessionals. Where possible, webinars or other conference archives may be beneficial, but make the effort to attend the most relevant conferences to stay abreast of ongoing developments. This also serves to remind your supervisor and colleagues of the benefits of connecting with a large group of professionals in your field.

As important as professional networking and often neglected is the humble lunch hour or coffee break. Commit to at least a daily lunch and coffee break. Get outside the building and experience, even briefly, a change of scenery and fresh air. Ignore the guilt-gremlins that insist the time could be better spent reshelving or cataloging. Breaks are necessary to reinvigorate and refocus your energies. The patron requests and cataloging will be there when you get back. The competent juggler knows when to take a break!

Conclusion (Take Your Bow—You Deserve It!)

Juggling is a skill that requires practice, and perhaps no two jugglers approach the process in exactly the same way. Yet essential points carry through to applying principles of juggling to workload and workflow: a positive, can-do attitude; the ability to accept and learn from mistakes and failures; relaxed and focused concentration; and building on strengths and small successes. By using the right tools, building support systems, managing time effectively, and nurturing the personal as well as the professional, we can successfully navigate the many demands of solo librarianship.

Recommended Further Reading

Bryant, Sue Lacey. *Personal Professional Development and the Solo Librarian*. London: Library Association Publishing, 1995.

Gelb, Michael, and Tony Buzan. *Lessons from the Art of Juggling: How to Achieve Your Full Potential in Business, Learning, and Life*. London: Aurum, 1998.

Gordon, Rachel Singer. *The Accidental Library Manager*. Medford, NJ: Information Today, 2004.

Marler, Patty, and Jan Bailey Mattia. *Time Management Made Easy*. Lincolnwood, IL: VGM Career Horizons, 1998.

McElfresh, Laura Kane. "Cataloging and Classification in a Small Library: The Good, the Bad, and the Challenging." *Technicalities* 29, no. 4 (2009): 4–8.

———. "21st Century Collection Management and the Small College Library." *Technicalities* 29, no. 5 (2009): 4–5.

Siess, Judith A., and Jonathan Lorig. *The Essential OPL, 1998–2004: The Best of Seven Years of the One-Person Library, a Newsletter for Librarians and Management*. Lanham, MD: Scarecrow Press, 2005.

Notes

1. Michael Gelb and Tony Buzan, *Lessons from the Art of Juggling: How to Achieve Your Full Potential in Business, Learning, and Life* (London: Aurum, 1998).

2. M. A. Hotchkiss, "Managing Multiple Projects, or the Art of Juggling," *AALL Spectrum* (September 1998): 12–13.

3. Rick Carter, "Using Time Management to Aggressively Attack and Destroy Stress," April 9, 2009, goarticles.com/article/Using-Time-Management-To-Aggressively-Attack-And-Destroy-Stress/1530038/ (accessed November 1, 2010).

CHAPTER 2

Survive and Thrive as a Solo Librarian

Barbara Fiehn

Surviving and thriving as a solo librarian requires developing a mindset and following your plans. It is important that a solo librarian take control of the work environment as well as the workload. Achieving balance between conflicting aspects of their lives allows solo librarians to maintain an active life that can include work, family, and self. One way to do that is to clearly define the scope of your work life. Evaluate how you look at work. Where does work fit in your life? What are your work behaviors? The life patterns you bring to your work environment will be important in how you react to the good days and bad days at work.[1]

Keeping the balance between personal and professional roles is important in maintaining a healthy, vibrant life. Taking steps to contain the professional part of one's life within boundaries takes only some awareness and utilization of specific strategies. The librarian who allows the professional role to become consuming will find he or she is neither surviving nor thriving.

Mission, Goals, and Objectives

The Cheshire Cat in Lewis Carroll's *Alice in Wonderland* says, "If you don't know where you are going, any road will get you there." However, the solo librarian cannot wander aimlessly within their library environment. A solo librarian must have clear direction for their work. This direction comes from the mission and goal statements of the parent organization as well as the mission and goal statement of the library itself. The solo librarian controls the mission and goals of the library but makes sure they are aligned with those of the parent organization.

A mission statement defines who your organization is, whom it serves, how it does the job, and why the job is done. This is the overarching statement of why your organization exists.

Goals are written as long- and short-term specifics that must be accomplished. They are measurable and they direct the activity that leads toward fulfillment of the mission. Objectives are the small steps that must be taken in order to reach the goals. They are time finite, measurable, and provide the basis for the librarian's decisions.

Daily tasks can be linked to the goals and objectives. In every library, routine maintenance tasks keep the library operational. Beyond those maintenance activities, the solo librarian must make decisions about the use of time. The goals and objectives provide the basis for this decision making. If an activity does not move the objectives and goals forward, that activity likely should not be done.

Will or Will Not—Work Management/ Time Management

PEOPLE MANAGEMENT

The object and motivation of a librarian's work is concentrated on meeting the users' needs and expectations. Unfortunately, librarians are often frustrated by the disparity between what the library can do and what the users expect.[2] The misalignment of ability and expectation also frustrates the users because patrons often think of librarianship as a simple and uncomplicated occupation. This conflict sometimes results in requests that reside outside the scope of a library. Librarians generally do their best to fulfill patron requests and will often refer them to libraries more suited to the patron's needs. It is the librarian's responsibility to let patrons know when their requests cannot be met, which can be a hard, but necessary, job.

People other than patrons may also frequent a library. They have direct or indirect relationships with the library as "friends," county commissioners, deans, and so on. Their expectations of the library and of the librarian must also be managed. The solo librarian must be sure to protect her time from the requests of non-patrons while handling everyone in a professional manner.

HOW TO SAY NO

Saying no is not an easy task for service-orientated librarians. The first instinct is to say yes. Learning to say no is, however, a vital job skill for the solo librarian. Since the solo librarian has limited time to devote to the job, coupled with many different tasks to perform each day, managing time on task is important. Accepting tasks that are outside the scope of the solo librarian's job reduces the time available for completing daily work.

By reviewing the mission, goals, and objectives statements regularly, a librarian will be able to judge quickly the appropriateness of a request in relation to the scope of the job. It is reasonable to redirect a request to another person or library that is better equipped to respond.[3] The following phrases are reasonable ways to deflect requests:

- "Our library isn't equipped for dealing with that request. Please try . . ." Offering another library as a possible solution provides direction.
- "I'm sorry. I can't do this right now." Use a sympathetic, but firm tone.
- "Let me think about it and get back to you." This gives you a chance to review your schedule, as well as your feelings about saying yes to another commitment.
- "I can't do this, but I *can* . . ." and mention a lesser commitment that you can make.

Many people would rather not say no up front because they feel it is rude or might shut down future interactions. However, a clean yes or no is much better than a vague statement that leaves the questioner hanging. Many people will continue to ask you to meet their request until they get a firm no.

- "No, I can't do that right now; I have something already scheduled." You aren't saying that you will never help out again, just that you feel your schedule is as full as you would like now. Understanding your limits is a talent to be applauded.

- "No, I can't do that for you; our policy is . . ." If you cannot help out, offering another qualified resource is a valuable service. Make sure the resource you refer will handle the problem.
- "No, I have decided not to take on any more commitments until after . . ." Be honest if your schedule is filled. "Filled" doesn't have to mean really filled; know when you are scheduled as much as you are willing, and stop.
- "No, my current responsibilities do not allow me to do that." It doesn't matter what the commitment is. It can even simply be time to yourself or with friends or family; you don't have to justify—you simply aren't available.

Remember to be firm and polite. This gives the signal that you are sympathetic, but will not easily change your mind if pressured. Remember that there are only so many hours in the workday. This means that whatever you choose to take on limits your ability to do other things. So even if you somehow *can* fit a new commitment into your schedule, is it more important than what you would have to give up to do it?

BODY LANGUAGE

Nonverbal communication is very important for the solo librarian. Being aware of what your nonverbal communication says provides you with an advantage in communicating with others. Body language constitutes four elements:

- Facial expressions
- Hand gestures
- Posture, distance, touch
- Vocalizations of inflection, tone, volume, fluency, latency, and non-word sounds.

Nonverbal communication is open to misinterpretation and when used consciously must be aligned with verbalizations. Nonverbals are better at expressing attitudes and feelings than ideas.[4] An understanding of a few basic nonverbal behaviors can increase effectiveness in communicating with others. Caputo[5] contains an extensive chapter on using nonverbal communication; however, similar information can also be found in many of the books on body language or nonverbal communications. The following is an overview of these concepts.

- Facial expression: maintain a calm, pleasant expression; smile when appropriate.
- Eye contact: maintain eye contact particularly at the height of your message.
- Posture: maintain relaxed, comfortable posture; keep your head on level with other person.
- Distance: lean back when attacked, then lean forward to respond; lean back to listen.
- Non-words: use brief pauses with eye contact; nod as appropriate.
- Shake your head and use nonverbal assertiveness to underline your no. Your voice should be clear and direct. Maintain eye contact.

Time Management

Time is a villain for most people. Learning how to cope with limited amounts of time is a necessary skill if a librarian wants to thrive. Organizing your work life to maximize your time makes you highly productive and leaves you with a feeling of accomplishment. Here are some quick tips on time management:

- Plan each day. Planning your day can help you accomplish more and feel more in control of your life. Write a to-do list, putting the most important tasks at the top. Keep a schedule of your daily activities to minimize conflicts and last-minute rushes.
- Prioritize your tasks. Time-consuming but relatively unimportant tasks can consume a lot of your day. Prioritizing tasks will ensure that you spend your time and energy on those that are truly important to you and your function.
- Complete tasks. Increase the feeling of accomplishment by crossing off tasks from your to-do list as they are completed.
- Eliminate tasks. Always consider the relevance of a task. Is this task a duplicate of another task? Is the task obsolete? What would happen if it were not done?

- Delegate. Take a look at your to-do list and consider what you can pass on to someone else. Can it be done by a volunteer? Can it be passed on to another department?
- Say no to nonessential tasks. Consider your goals and schedule before agreeing to take on additional work.
- Take the time you need to do a quality job. Doing work right the first time may take more time up front, but errors usually result in time spent making corrections, which takes more time overall.
- Break large, time-consuming tasks into smaller tasks. Work on them a few minutes at a time until you get them all done.
- Practice the ten-minute rule. Work on a dreaded task for ten minutes each day. Once you get started, you may find you can finish it.
- Evaluate how you're spending your time. Keep a diary of everything you do for three days to determine how you're spending your time. Look for time that can be used more wisely. For example, could you take a bus or train to work and use the commute to catch up on reading? If so, you could free up some time to exercise or spend with family or friends.

Stress Management

Everyone experiences stress; it is part of daily life. Often stress isn't thought about until it becomes a major life issue. Understanding stress and the processes to deal with it allows a solo librarian to survive and thrive. Agrawal[6] describes stress as being both a physical and a psychological process caused by events that may be internal, external, or both and make demands on a person, which are beyond their coping ability. Without adequate coping strategies, it is easy to become overwhelmed by the many competing demands of being a solo librarian.

Call it burnout or techno-stress or overload; the names still revolve around stress. Stress among library professionals has been an ongoing area of research for many years as evidenced by Caputo,[7] Holcomb,[8] Steel,[9] and Taube.[10] The identified major stressors within the library profession are:

- Role ambiguity
- Conflict
- Overload
- Anxiety

- Frustration
- Isolationism
- Rapid technology change
- Abusive library users
- Role of the library
- Intellectual freedom
- Financial concerns
- Management concerns

Avoiding burnout, according to Jimenez,[11] is partly awareness. The signs of advancing burnout are noticeable. They often manifest as a lack of enthusiasm for going to work or doing the work. Other signs may be classic stress signs such as headaches and neck pain. It is important to evaluate your feelings and identify the root causes. Then identify things that can be changed and, if necessary, evaluate the need to remain in or leave the position.

STRESS AWARENESS

What does stress look like? For each individual, stress may look different. Common stress characteristics should be acknowledged and considered warning flags. Remember the stress talked about is primarily psychological and will often manifest as physical issues. This list is compiled using articles from Caputo,[12] Holcomb,[13] Mayo Clinic staff,[14] Steel,[15] and Taube[16]:

- Posture, changes in the way you sit or stand, unusual restlessness.
- Muscle tension, headaches, clenching teeth or fists, pain in neck or shoulders, low back pain, tightness in chest, general weakness.
- Sleep changes, wakefulness, tiredness, prolonged sleep, disturbed sleep.
- Medications and oral behaviors, increased use of sedatives, alcohol, stimulants, smoking, appetite increase or decrease.
- Emotional changes, increase in irritability, hyper-excitement, depression, impulsivity, crying, lack of concentration, anxiety, tension, overreaction, memory loss.

While awareness of stress or burnout is always a good precursor to actions, so is prevention. There is an abundance of research in the area of stress management. Prevention falls into two main categories: what to do to stay healthy and what to do to reduce stressors.

STAYING HEALTHY

The Mayo Clinic staff[17] suggests that altering your lifestyle choices contributes to improving all areas of your life. Choosing a healthy lifestyle can lead to an increase in efficiency at work and more energy for non-work activities. Part of living that healthy lifestyle includes:

- Sleep: healthy sleep habits promote a rested and restored body and mind.
- Healthy diet: following a medically accepted diet provides the body with adequate nutrients to function properly, thus promoting good physical and mental health.
- Exercise: regular exercise that includes aerobic movement strengthens the body and the mind.

However, staying healthy is only part of the equation for managing the stressful situations that confront librarians each day. Short of finding another, less stressful, career it is necessary to utilize strategies to reduce the effects of stress in the workplace.

STRESS REDUCTION

- Take time off to refresh and regroup.
  - Use your vacation time to revitalize your being.
  - Use your sick time to get well. Working when you are sick just spreads illness and you are not effective at work when you are ill.
  - Use professional development time to learn new ways to do your job and to refresh through sharing with other library professionals. It is good for the soul to know others are battling the same issues.
  - Take your lunch and break times. Many librarians skip breaks and eat lunch at their desk because there is so much to do. This only increases your body's reaction to stress. Use these scheduled times to regenerate your mind and relax your body.
- Take a short break when needed. Too much stress can derail your attempts at getting organized. Take a walk. Do some quick stretches at your workstation. You only need a minute to relax.

- Switch tasks. Look at the to-do list. Put away what you have been working on and do something different. You will return to the original task with more energy and be more productive.
- Revisit and renew your environment. Sometimes making a change in the environment gives you new energy. Change the decorations, move furniture, get rid of something you consider an eyesore, or just make something more efficient.
- Take a time management course. If your workplace doesn't have one, find out if a local community college, university, or community education program does.
- Establish friendships within the library community. Having a friend you can call or e-mail is helpful. Another librarian will be able to empathize with you. Friends in the profession may have a solution you haven't discovered.

RELAXATION

There is abundant research to support the use of relaxation as a counter to stress and anxiety. The Mayo Clinic staff[18] recommends the following:

- Exercise: Yes, exercise will help you relax. The endorphins created by exercise create a feel good effect in the brain. A workout will recharge your energy levels.
- Relaxation techniques: These techniques slow heart and breathing rates, lower blood pressure, increase blood flow to major muscles, reduce muscle tension and chronic pain, improve concentration, reduce anger and frustration, and boost confidence to handle problems.
  - Meditation: Take a stress-reduction break wherever you are.
  - Yoga: Tap into the many health benefits.
  - Tai chi: Discover the many possible health benefits.
  - Positive thinking: Reduce stress, enjoy life more.
  - Massage: Get in touch with its many health benefits.

Another relaxation tool to remember is laughter. Like regular exercise, laughter allows the release of healing endorphins and increased blood flow to the heart and the brain. Among the numerous benefits to mental health, regular laughter is believed to reduce stress, elevate mood, and improve job performance.

Most importantly, put yourself first. What is most important, you or the job? Without you the job will be filled by someone else. Therefore, it is crucial you put yourself first. Of course, you will do the job to the best of your ability, but you cannot let the job rule. Put the job into its place within your life. Take the time needed to discover what stress reducers work for you. Make the time you need to follow through on your stress reduction plan.

Conclusion

Surviving and thriving as a solo librarian takes organization and planning. It means accepting that not everything will be done. Surviving means understanding that to focus the job, the mission and goals statements need to drive the activities to be undertaken. Thriving means learning to say yes to requests that are appropriate but no to those that are not.

The surviving and thriving strategies will be different for everyone. Try different strategies. Take classes or get a trainer for relaxation and exercise strategies. Do what is necessary to keep yourself healthy in body and soul so that you will continue to love your job.

Notes

1. Rita Jimenez, "Change Is the Only Constant," *Oregon Library Association Quarterly* 12, no. 3 (2006): 4–5.

2. Lisa A. Ennis, "The Evolution of Technostress," *Computers in Libraries* 25, no. 8 (2005): 10–12.

3. Judith A. Siess, *The OPL Sourcebook: A Guide for Solo and Small Libraries* (Medford, N.J.: Information Today, 2001).

4. Ronald B. Adler, Russell F. Proctor, and Neil Towne, *Looking Out, Looking In*, 11th ed. (Belmont, Calif.: Wadsworth, 2004).

5. Janette S. Caputo, *The Assertive Librarian* (Phoenix: Oryx, 1984).

6. Rita Agrawal, *Stress in Life and at Work* (Thousand Oaks, Calif.: Response Books, 2001).

7. Caputo, *The Assertive Librarian*.

8. Jean M. Holcomb, "Battling Burnout," *Law Library Journal* 99, no. 3 (2007): 669–74.

9. Anitra Steel, "Flying with the Phoenixes: Avoiding Job Burnout as a Librarian and a Manager," *Children and Libraries* 7, no. 3 (2009): 51–52.

10. Mortimer Taube, "Realities of Library Specialization," *The Library Quarterly* 12, no. 2 (1942): 246–56. www.jstor.org/stable/4302934 (accessed November 29, 2010).

11. Jimenez, "Change Is the Only Constant."

12. Caputo, *The Assertive Librarian.*

13. Holcomb, "Battling Burnout."

14. Mayo Clinic staff, "Time Management: Tips to Reduce Stress and Improve Productivity." www.mayoclinic.com/health/time-management/WL00048 (accessed November 29, 2010).

15. Steel, "Flying with the Phoenixes."

16. Taube, "Realities of Library Specialization."

17. Mayo Clinic staff, "Time Management."

18. Mayo Clinic staff, "Stress Management Basics." www.mayoclinic.com/health/stress-management/MY00435 (accessed November 29, 2010).

Part II

COMMUNITY INVOLVEMENT

CHAPTER 3

Building Partnerships

Julie A. Evener

Some of the most rewarding relationships to cultivate as a solo librarian are those with other departments at your institution. While you may be alone at your library, you are almost certainly not alone at your organization, whether it is a school, college, corporation, or county. Partnering with other departments can help fill the gaps in your own knowledge, streamline your responsibilities, and serve your patrons more effectively.

Building and maintaining a partnership can be challenging, particularly for an information professional accustomed to working alone. Unlike large libraries, we can't hire special liaison librarians who have already developed the specific skills necessary for collaboration—flexibility, communication, reliability, interpersonality, patience, ingenuity. If we don't already possess these skills, we must nurture them in ourselves.

Best practices for business partnerships are well documented throughout the literature for that field, and much of the knowledge gained in the business arena transfers to our libraries. Dr. Robert W. Keidel, a business management expert, wrote the following in his book *Seeing Organizational Patterns*: "A commitment to collaboration means neither going off on one's own nor dutifully taking orders. Rather, collaboration means continuously looking for opportunities to assist others—in different jobs, functions, divisions, or locations."[1] In a profession that revolves around assisting others, partnering cannot be far from our minds. Indeed, partnering is an organic outgrowth of our traditional, valued responsibilities.

As librarians, and particularly solo librarians, we need to know how to create, build, and sustain partnerships. This chapter provides tips and advice to that end.

Benefits of Partnerships

Why partner with others? The short answer is that a successful partnership will help you better meet the needs of your patrons—the predominant goal of most every library. Specifically, partnerships are:

- Efficient. Libraries can accomplish more with less. Pooling resources, knowledge, money, and so on can provide goods or services to your patrons that you could not have offered alone. Often, partnerships help you reach out to your patrons where they are, rather than waiting for patrons to find you.[2]
- Interdependent. Sharing responsibilities means that you are not shouldering them alone—a relief to solo librarians used to doing so. Interdependency also increases the chances that the departments with which you partner will partner with you again.
- Strengthening. Collaboration between departments can increase the feeling of community and involvement within an organization. Rather than separate departments competing for budgetary allocations, you and your partner are allies under the flag of your organization.[3]
- Learning experiences. Partnerships broaden your horizons. They give you the opportunity to learn and to discuss the insights of others. As often happens in collaboration, ideas spark other ideas until everyone walks away with something new.[4]
- Successful. With the world growing smaller through technological advances, your organization is shrinking, too. The business world regards strategically formed partnerships as necessary for success. Companies can focus on areas in which they excel and partner with other companies with different strengths. Everyone wins, especially the customer. We can view our libraries as companies and follow this same model.

Types of Partnerships

Partnerships can take many forms. They can be big, project-based collaborations with written objectives and weekly team meetings or a simple commitment to lend a hand when needed. They can be based around providing a service or sharing knowledge. A partnership with the mailroom or shipping department, for example, would be service-based, while collaborating with teachers or faculty is knowledge-based. Partnerships with IT departments or management/administration could be either or both.

Throughout the literature, various authors use different terms to communicate the idea of partnership, including collaboration, integration, alliance, teams, and so forth. It can also be called "embedded librarianship" in some cases. Though each of these terms varies slightly in meaning or connotation, for the purposes of this chapter, we'll consider them synonyms. All center on the basic concept of two or more entities working together for a common goal.

A partnership can incorporate more than two departments, but the larger the group, the more complicated the project can become. For larger groups, be more formal with your agreements and communication. Set out your objectives in writing, as well as the roles or responsibilities each member of the group will have. Make sure everyone has a copy of these objectives and maintain constant communication through e-mail or periodic meetings to ensure that everyone is on the same page.

The types of partnerships in which you engage will depend largely on your library's goals, the culture of your organization, and the partner with whom you're working. For example, a corporate librarian in a formal environment may want to draw up an official contract for each person in the group to sign. A manager or other bigwig may need to approve the contract in an official capacity. On the other hand, a librarian at an academic library in a small college or university may prefer more casual agreements if the culture of the school supports such informality. An e-mail or short meeting may be all the partners need to form their alliance.

Get to know the climate of your organization and determine what steps you should take to form a partnership with another department. Check procedure or policy manuals for rules specific to your organization. When in doubt, discuss your plans with your supervisor to ascertain whether you're following the proper protocol.

Common Challenges to Partnerships

Just like any worthwhile endeavor, forming and maintaining a successful partnership will have its roadblocks. The specific challenges you face will differ depending on the situation, project, and people involved. Here are four common ones:

- Personality. Whenever people gather, differing personalities can conflict. In a working environment, these clashes may result from varying work styles or temperaments. For example, an organized, "everything in its place" worker will almost certainly collide with one who needs a little bit of chaos to think. A procrastinator will inevitably butt heads with an early bird.
- Practical. In an ideal world, everyone would have enough time, space, money, and motivation to work together successfully. In the real world, however, this is rarely the case. In any department or organization, time is a valued and scarce commodity. Space for meetings may be limited. Budgets may not stretch far enough to incorporate a new idea. The project, or the library in general, may not be a high enough priority for your partner to warrant the time and effort.
- Perceptual. Specifically, misperceptions can prevent a partnership. Other departments in your organization may not realize all the library has to offer. Some people still think of libraries as rooms filled with dusty books and librarians as shushers who spend their days stamping due dates and reading. That picture offers little opportunity or reason for partnership. And the stereotyping works both ways. We might also harbor misguided ideas about our potential partners.
- Institutional. Your organization may have procedures or policies in place that make partnering with other departments more difficult. In a school or university, for example, even if teachers are willing to work with the library, their curriculum requirements may not allow it. Often, you may need your management or administration's approval to partner for a new project, particularly if you are signing an official contract.[5]

Getting Started

Once you've decided to try partnering with other departments at your organization, you can take several steps to increase your success.

- Know your library's goals/overall mission. A key component in partnering with others is first knowing what purpose the library serves in your organization. Any partnership you form should align with those overarching goals. Read and understand your library's mission statement. If your library doesn't have a mission statement, create one.[6]
- Improve existing partnerships. You may already be partnering with other departments in your organization—school librarians may collaborate with classroom teachers, academic librarians may work with faculty, and so forth. Making those partnerships better will make other departments more willing to work with you.[7]
- Develop a friendly rapport. Be friendly, considerate, and helpful, both inside the library and out. Always show respect and courtesy for everyone around you. People will not think twice about working with you if they know it will be pleasant. Furthermore, your friendly attitude will help develop trust, a key factor in collaborative relationships.[8]
- Identify potential partners. The specific departments that will benefit your library depend largely on the type of organization of which you are a part. The potential allies of a corporate library, for example, will immensely differ from the potential allies of an elementary school library. To recognize potential partners in your institution, identify "hot initiatives" (objectives or programs that are most important to your organization) and ask yourself: "How can the library help this initiative to succeed?"[9]
- Be proactive. Don't wait for other departments to come to the library for help. Instead, search out opportunities to partner with other departments.[10] Become more visible throughout the organization. Join committees, participate in information fairs or orientations, e-mail monthly newsletters, and so on.
- Suggest mutually beneficial partnerships. Nobody wants to do extra work for nothing. The ideas you present to potential partners should clearly benefit each department involved. With a vested interest and the promise of benefitting from the collaboration, partners will be more willing to get involved and see the project through.[11]

Building a Partnership

Once departments agree to partner, the real work begins. According to John R. Katzenbach and Douglas K. Smith, "The essence of a team is common commitment. Without it, groups perform as individuals; with it, they become a powerful unit of collective performance. This kind of commitment requires a purpose in which team members can believe."[12] Balancing schedules, responsibilities, and ideas can be difficult. Here are some more suggestions for making the task more palatable:

- Communicate. Have agreements (formal or informal) based around what each department will do and the overall goal of the partnership. The formality of your agreements will differ depending on the culture of your organization and the nature of your collaborative project. In the corporate environment, a written contract might be desired. For less formal partnerships, a discussion at a committee meeting or the exchange of e-mails may suffice. Either way, constant and clear communication may be the most significant step in creating a successful partnership.
- Be available. Make the partnership a priority and make yourself available when your partners want to plan or discuss the project. As media specialist Toni Buzzeo says, "Above all, the key to successful collaboration is constant, willing, and cheerful availability."[13] This should not, of course, be at the expense of your other responsibilities, but realize ahead of time that the partnership will take a lot of time.
- Be reliable and trustworthy. Always do what you say you'll do. Your partners will trust you more if they know they can depend on you. Picking up another group member's slack is never fun.
- Shift your thinking. In a partnership, perspectives need to change from "me" to "us."[14] Be aware of how your actions will affect the group. Be considerate of their time, ideas, and perspectives.
- Be flexible. Partnering with others means that everything is not your decision. As solo librarians, we sometimes become accustomed to making unilateral decisions. This type of decision making has no place in a partnership.[15] Discuss decisions with your partner and be willing to compromise.
- Share your perspective—and hear the perspectives of your partner. The faculty you work with might not understand how the library world works, but you might not understand how their lesson plans work. Learn the "language" in which your partner communicates, in other words, the terminology prevalent in his or her field.[16] If you are working with an IT department, for example, familiarize yourself with some

technology terms relating to your project. Learning the language will not only help you understand your partner better, it will also demonstrate competence and credibility, fostering respect and trust.

- Be equitable. Partners must work as peers to accomplish true collaboration. One person bossing the other is not a good partnership. Come to the table prepared to listen to ideas, rather than just proposing your own.
- Capitalize on your strengths. Working equitably does not mean partners all have to do the same tasks. Instead, let each person use his or her own strengths and unique skills to contribute to your project. That way, you'll produce the best possible results.

Sustaining a Partnership

Your partnership is up and running, or you've completed the project for which you created the partnership in the first place. You still have some work to do:

- Assessment. Is what you're doing working for your clients or patrons? In a more formal, long-term project, the need to assess is high. Consider developing benchmarks or "outcome indicators" at the beginning of the project, and then take the time to discuss whether or not those objectives have been met.[17] If not, what adjustments do you need to make? If your partnership is not one with a specific beginning and end, try assessing your progress throughout the project at predetermined and consistent intervals.
- Patience. The fruits of a partnership are not always immediately evident. If you're implementing changes at your organization as a part of your collaboration, it may take time for your patrons and your organization as a whole to accept them. If the partnership truly brings forth a better product, service, or environment for your patrons, you will succeed in the end.
- Continuous communication. Never stop communicating with your partner. A lapse in communication can send an unintended message: you've lost interest in the project; you're too busy to devote time to it; you no longer want to include your partner. Additionally, a partnership not stoked with communication will burn out.

Suggested Partners for . . .

Academic Libraries
* Faculty
* IT department
* Athletic department
* Writing center
* Reading center
* Student services
* Career services

Special Libraries
* IT department
* Legal department
* Day care center
* Professionals

School Libraries
* Teachers
* PTA/PTSA
* Art department
* Athletic department

Public Libraries
* Unemployment/welfare office
* Supervisor of elections office
* Public schools
* Museums, parks, community center

For more ideas, browse association publications, library news outlets, scholarly journals, listservs, blogs, and so on.

Putting the Tips to Work: Real-Life Partnerships

ACADEMIC LIBRARY

At the University of Denver, the library worked with faculty, the campus bookstore, information services, Blackboard staff, and the university's Center for Teaching and Learning for a solution to the confusing and disconnected process of finding course-related content and disseminating it to students, either in print or online. The library had expertise in accessing information materials and copyright laws, and the other departments involved knew about the course requirements, the technological environment, and the needs of the students and faculty.

Working together, the group simplified the course-related materials find-and-disseminate process and made plans to integrate even more. In their collaboration, the team eased the frustrations of the two primary library patron groups: students and faculty.[18]

Though this scenario takes place in a large university library, the idea can easily be adapted for a one-person college or university library. Who are the stakeholders at your institution? How could the library help to streamline the course-related materials or course reserves process?

PUBLIC LIBRARY

The Enoch Pratt Free Library in Baltimore, Maryland, formed a unique partnership with another city department, the Baltimore City Health Department, and a local supermarket to give their inner-city patrons better access to healthy, fresh foods. The neighborhoods the Enoch Pratt Free Library serves lack major supermarkets, so it's often difficult for the people in those areas to buy groceries. With the partnership, patrons order their groceries online at the library with help from health department employees, pay for the groceries at the library, and pick the groceries up from the library the next day.[19]

Each stakeholder in the collaboration gains from this arrangement. The supermarket increases sales, the health department helps citizens eat healthier, and the library demonstrates its worth as a community center while getting patrons in the door. Once there, patrons may find other programs, services, or resources they can use.

Solo librarians in public libraries are more likely to be in rural than urban areas, but the lessons of the Baltimore scenario still apply. What community problems can your library help address? What organizations or departments in your city/county/local government are already working on those problems?

SCHOOL LIBRARY

The school librarian at Elkton Pointe Middle School in Roswell, Georgia, partnered with a remedial reading teacher to improve the reading comprehension and vocabularies of ten students in the remedial reading class. Working together, the librarian and the teacher analyzed the test scores of the students and identified their weak points, and then planned an interactive lesson tailored specifically to those areas.

The team engaged the students in the preparation and performance of a "readers' theater" version of the short story "The Masque of the Red Death" by Edgar Allan Poe. As a result, the students understood the characters and their motives in the story better than if they had simply read it silently, or even aloud, to themselves. They added new words to their vocabularies and had a good time in the process.[20]

With what subjects or classes do the students at your school struggle? How can the library get involved in teaching students in new, fun ways?

SPECIAL LIBRARY

Jill Stover Heinze, the research analyst at Affinion Loyalty Group in Richmond, Virginia, recently joined forces with the company's Brand Communications Unit to keep them better informed of market trends and research findings. The company decided to embed Heinze in this unit—physically moving her desk to that department, placing her in a high traffic area of the marketing department.

As a result of this partnership, Heinze could more easily share information with the Brand Communications Unit, which allowed them to keep up-to-date on the latest promotional best practices. In return, the Brand Communications Unit helped Heinze market her researching services to other areas of the company, increasing her visibility and significance. Heinze credits their successful partnership with "helping [the] organization weather the economic upheaval."[21]

What departments at your organization could most benefit from your research expertise? How could that partnership help your company? No matter what kind of library you run, forming partnerships with others can vastly increase your visibility and better serve your patrons. However, partnering with other departments within your organization is not an endeavor to take lightly. Successful collaboration involves specific skills such as "negotiating, being able to see tradeoffs, and being comfortable sharing control."[22] As solo librarians, we may not be accustomed to using these talents. It is equally important for us, however, to hone our people skills and work in collaboration with others. If we do so, we can enrich the lives, learning, and livelihood of our patrons or clients.

Notes

1. Robert W. Keidel, *Seeing Organizational Patterns: A New Theory and Language of Organizational Design* (San Francisco: Berrett-Koehler Publishers, 1995), 55.

2. Ilene F. Rockman, "Establishing Successful Partnerships with University Support Units," *Library Management* 23, no. 4/5 (2002): 192–93.

3. James Cory Tucker, Jeremy Bullian, and Matthew C. Torrence, "Collaborate or Die! Collection Development in Today's Academic Library," *The Reference Librarian* 83/84 (2003): 224.

4. Rockman, "Establishing Successful Partnerships with University Support Units," 192–93.

5. Bullet points adapted from: Monty L. McAdoo, "Be the Bridge," *American Libraries* 2009, americanlibrariesmagazine.org/features/11232009/be-bridge (accessed October 25, 2010).

6. For help creating mission statements, see Charles Curran and Lewis Miller, *Guide to Library and Information Agency Management* (Lanham, Md.: Scarecrow Press, 2005), 2–8.

7. Deborah Tenofsky, "Teaching to the Whole Student: Building Best Practices for Collaboration between Libraries and Student Services," *Research Strategies* 20 (2007): 290.

8. Tami Echavarria, "Collegiality and the Environmental Climate of the Library," *ALKI* 17, no. 3 (2001): 23.

9. Patricia Iannuzzi, "Faculty Development and Information Literacy: Establishing Campus Partnerships," *Reference Services Review* (Fall/Winter 1998): 99.

10. Tenofsky, "Teaching to the Whole Student," 289.

11. Roger Guard, "Musings on Collaboration and Vested Interest," *The Journal of Academic Librarianship* 3, no. 2 (2005): 89.

12. John R. Katzenbach and Douglas K. Smith, "The Discipline of Teams," *Harvard Business Review* 83, no. 7/8 (2005): 165.

13. Toni Buzzeo, "Teaming Up with Teachers May Be Difficult, but It's Not Impossible," *School Library Journal* 2002, www.schoollibraryjournal.com/article/CA240062.html?display=searchResults&stt=001&text=collaboration (accessed November 3, 2010).

14. Kristin Antelman and Mona Couts, "Embracing Ambiguity . . . or Not: What the Triangle Research Libraries Network Learned about Collaboration," *C&RL News* 70, no. 4 (2009): 231. Available at crln.acrl.org/content/70/4/230.full.pdf+html (accessed November 1, 2010).

15. Valerie Wildridge, Sude Childs, Lynette Cawthra, and Bruce Madge, "How to Create Successful Partnerships—A Review of the Literature," *Health Information and Libraries Journal* 21 (2004): 8.

16. Martha K. Heyman, "Speaking It, Staying a Librarian: Building Successful Relationships with the Information Technology Organization without Losing your Identity as a Librarian," *Inspel* 34, no. 3/4 (2000): 159.

17. Wildridge et al., "How to Create Successful Partnerships," 9.

18. Bethany Sewell, "Course-Related Materials at the University of Denver," *C&RL News* 68, no. 8 (2007): 514–17. Available at: crln.acrl.org/content/68/8/514.full.pdf+html (accessed November 3, 2010).

19. Jennifer T. Ries-Taggart, "Baltimore's Virtual Supermarket @ Your Library," *Public Libraries* 49, no. 4 (2010): 7.

20. Toni Buzzeo, "Strength in Numbers: Data-Driven Collaboration May Not Sound Sexy, but It Could Save Your Job," *School Library Journal* 2010, www.schoollibraryjournal.com/slj/printissue/currentissue/886879-427/strength_in_numbers_data-driven_collaboration.html.csp (accessed November 3, 2010).

21. Jill Stover Heinze, "Leveraging Internal Partnerships for Library Success," *Information Outlook* 14, no. 1 (2010): 14.

22. Antelman and Couts, "Embracing Ambiguity . . . or Not," 232.

CHAPTER 4

A Guide to Recruiting and Retaining Volunteers of All Ages

Tatum Preston

Aside from helping you—the only librarian on staff—get more done with less cost, volunteers provide a way for you to stay connected to your community, they help you continue to learn and grow, and they bring your library's mission to a broader audience.

This chapter outlines the best practices I have learned for recruiting and retaining volunteers at a museum library. With careful forethought and planning, you can use these tactics to start a volunteer program at your library or to enhance your existing program.

The most important thing to keep in mind, both as you develop your volunteer program and as it grows, is that the relationship between your library and the volunteer must be beneficial to both parties. Yes, you seek free labor and help with the tasks that you don't have time to complete, but you also provide the volunteer with something in return: perhaps a sense of giving back, college course credit, real-world experience, or camaraderie. Volunteers give their time for various reasons. For your program to succeed, you must determine what each volunteer hopes to gain from the experience and create an environment where these needs are met. Also keep in mind that while volunteers' motivation for working with you is often different from that of paid employees, you should apply the same professionalism and attention to detail to the process of recruiting and retaining volunteers that you would to employing and evaluating a paid employee.

What Will Volunteers Do?

The first step in establishing and running a successful volunteer program is to decide what you want volunteers to *do*. Think about these two questions: what you need the most help with and what tasks are appropriate for volunteers. In your mind, the answer to what you need help with may be, "Everything!" Your program will be more successful, though, if you explicitly define the areas where you need the most help. I have found it helpful to divide potential volunteer work into two categories: day-to-day tasks and special projects. Day-to-day tasks include shelving books, filing, covering and creating spine labels for new books, and greeting library patrons. Special projects are more involved and better suited to volunteers who can commit to volunteering more time: for example, sorting and creating a finding aid for a new archive or creating reading lists and subject bibliographies. Think about your needs and what would help your library run more efficiently and smoothly.

Once you've established the list of things you need help with, decide what tasks are appropriate for volunteers. Consider the specialized skills, such as computer proficiency, needed to complete a task. Are there physical requirements, such as being able to lift a certain amount of weight, required for a task? Remember that as a general rule, volunteers should not be asked to help with tasks that involve handling money, budgeting, or sensitive information, such as personnel records or information housed in a closed archive.

Write Job Descriptions

Once you've established a list of potential tasks and projects for volunteers, creating job descriptions is the next crucial step. The job description can be used in four ways: to assist with recruiting, to help you match your needs with volunteers' interests and skill sets, to lay the foundation for the volunteer's schedule and tasks once he or she is on the job, and to provide a barometer to measure a volunteer's performance. Each job description should provide a brief overview of your library, its mission, and the population it serves. Describe the tasks or projects a volunteer will be expected to complete, and list any special skills needed. Specify the hours you would like the volunteer to work. Some job descriptions may be very general; others may be specially written for a specific project. A quick Internet search yields examples of good job descriptions from other libraries.

Recruiting

Once you've drafted job descriptions, it's time to start finding volunteers. While volunteers can come from all walks of life and bring a plethora of backgrounds and experiences to your library, I have found a few groups that are especially good to target in recruitment efforts.

GRADUATE STUDENTS

Many graduate programs in library and information science encourage students to complete internships for course credit. Graduate interns are typically required to work 150 hours during one semester, or about ten hours per week. Schools often have an internship coordinator or listserv where you can advertise your volunteer opportunities. Graduate students in advertising and public relations, communications, education, or other fields may also be interested in internships, depending on the projects available at your library.

FEDERAL WORK-STUDY STUDENTS

The U.S. Department of Education sponsors the Federal Work-Study Program, which provides part-time employment to students at over 3,400 colleges and universities. The program is administered through each school's financial aid office. You can submit your volunteer opportunities to the financial aid office, often through their website. Institutions who hire work-study students are sometimes asked to pay a portion of the student's hourly wage (in my experience, less than $3 per hour). Many private schools cover the entire salary for their work-study students. Undergraduate students typically work eight to ten hours per week, around their class schedules.[1]

HIGH SCHOOL STUDENTS

Some high schools also give students course credit for volunteering. Juniors and seniors at the International Baccalaureate high school in Birmingham volunteer every Monday afternoon. Other students seek less formal resume-building, college admissions–enhancing volunteer opportunities. Boy Scouts need leadership service projects to attain Eagle Scout honors.

SENIORS

In 2009, 9.1 million adults 65 and older (23.9 percent of this demographic) dedicated 1.6 billion hours of service to communities across the country.[2] Retirees often look for ways to stay active within their former employment field. Retired librarians make excellent volunteers, as do professionals from other fields. Their time is usually flexible and their experience is invaluable.

PEOPLE SEEKING EMPLOYMENT EXPERIENCE

Recent graduates seeking practical work experience are a great source of volunteer labor. They are full of the latest best practices and are eager to apply what they've learned in the classroom to a "real-world" setting. The promise of receiving a good letter of recommendation or job leads from you upon completing a project well can be a powerful motivator for recent graduates.

There are many free or low-cost venues to advertise your volunteer opportunities, including:

- Classified ads in your local newspaper, or a free listing in your local city paper
- Open houses or other events at your library
- Volunteer fairs at area colleges
- Your website: Look at other libraries' websites for examples of well-designed library volunteer web pages. Include any necessary qualifications, your job descriptions, and an online application if possible. Ask website visitors to help you spread the word that you are seeking volunteers.
- Online library internship posting services
- Internship rosters on professional association websites: I recently got a fantastic graduate student intern from out of state through a free roster posting on the Art Libraries of North America (ARLIS) website. Other professional associations offer this service as well.
- Social media sites such as Facebook: Issue a call for volunteers on your library's Facebook page or Twitter account. When possible, include images of your library and of current volunteers in action.
- Word of mouth: Any time I am asked to speak to a class, museum docents, our board of directors, or any other group, I always mention at

the end that I am constantly seeking new volunteers before handing out my business card.

- Referrals from other volunteers: Happy volunteers may be your best source of new ones. Create a flyer that current volunteers can share with their friends or colleagues who may be interested in becoming more involved with your library.

Screening Potential Volunteers

Once you have identified a potential volunteer, is it important to follow several steps to ensure that he or she is a good fit for your library and that the relationship between your library and the volunteer will be mutually beneficial.

1. APPLICATION

Create a basic paper or online application for the potential volunteer to complete. Applicants should list previous volunteer or paid work experience, references, and emergency contact information.

2. INTERVIEW

An interview can be completed over the phone, but ideally you should meet with the potential volunteer in person. Ask the applicant why he wants to volunteer and what he hopes to gain from the experience, and make your expectations and goals clear as well. Discuss his previous work, volunteer, and educational experiences and skills. Describe your potential tasks or projects, and determine where the applicant's interests lie. Using the information gathered during this discussion, establish what the applicant will be working on, if accepted. If meeting with the applicant in person, show him your space and try to give him an idea of the atmosphere where he'll be working.

3. BACKGROUND CHECK

As soon as possible after the interview, conduct a background check. At the very least, contact the references your applicant has listed. Some libraries perform formal background checks on volunteers. If the volunteer will be working with children, a background check is essential. Consult your human resources department for more information and direction on conducting background checks.

4. CONTRACT

Some organizations require volunteers to sign a contract committing to a specified time period or number of hours of service. Having volunteers sign a contract reinforces professionalism and creates a tangible agreement between the library and the volunteer. The contract can be used in conjunction with the job description to make sure the volunteer has a clear understanding of his duties and to review the volunteer's work. It also gives you the option to terminate a volunteer who isn't fulfilling his responsibilities.

Training

Once you and a volunteer have agreed upon his or her job and hours, schedule the first volunteer session. Make sure this first session occurs at a time when you can devote your full attention to the new volunteer. Prior to the volunteer's first day, be sure he knows basics such as where to park and appropriate attire.

When the volunteer arrives, orient him to your physical space. Point out the location of bathrooms, water fountains, and the break area or refrigerator. Create a handbook for volunteers that you can review together. The handbook should include basic information about your library such as hours, directions, and key phone numbers. Detail basic procedures you wish volunteers to follow, such as how to sign in upon arrival, how to greet library patrons, or who to contact in case of an emergency. If volunteers will access specific databases or subscription services, provide URLs, login usernames and passwords, and step-by-step instructions for using the databases. Include directions for walking to nearby coffee shops, restaurants, or other attractions that either volunteers or library patrons may want to visit. Introduce the new person to existing volunteers and let them describe the tasks or projects they are working on.

Reiterate the mission of your library and how the volunteer will be contributing to its fulfillment. Review the volunteer's job description and show him how to complete the tasks in it. Explain each task clearly and make it clear why this task is important. Tasks that seem routine to you may be new to volunteers. For example, if a volunteer is wrapping books in Mylar covers, explain that these protect the books. Helping volunteers understand how their tasks fit into the big picture and mission will help them to be more invested in what your library aims to accomplish. Make sure the volunteer is comfortable with the assigned tasks and ask if he has any questions. Set clear goals and expectations, using the job description as a guide. Check on new volunteers frequently to make sure they still understand their assignments and are fitting in to your environment.

Also, be sure to share your core values. I always stress to new volunteers that I care more about things being done correctly than finished quickly, and emphasize that each library patron should be greeted and assisted in a friendly manner. Sharing core values helps volunteers better understand your library and its mission and makes it easier for them to help you with the fulfillment of this mission.

Retention

As you think about how to retain volunteers, keep the mutually beneficial relationship between your library and its volunteers in mind. By creating an environment where volunteers interact, learn, and feel appreciated, you will ensure that volunteers stay happy and continue to support your library with their time.

Foster relationships between volunteers. Once you have completed a volunteer's initial orientation, let volunteers train each other whenever possible. This both saves you time and provides a structured activity where volunteers can interact.

Some volunteers are content with performing the same tasks repeatedly; if this is the case, continue to assign these. However, many want to learn new skills or deepen their involvement with the library. Vary tasks for these volunteers to maintain their interest. As volunteers become more knowledgeable about the library and its day-to-day operations, increase their level of responsibility and assign more detailed tasks.

Don't frustrate volunteers by assigning tasks that they lack the time or skills to successfully complete. If a graduate student signs up for a semester-long, 150-hour internship, give him a project he can realistically finish. If a volunteer lacks computer skills, do not ask him to complete a complicated technology task, and do not ask a volunteer with mobility or stamina issues to do things that require a great deal of physical activity.

When possible, allow volunteers to work creatively. Often graduate students come to the library with fresh ideas and more recent knowledge than you possess, and retirees bring expertise from their former career field. Any new volunteer can contribute a fresh perspective on how tasks are accomplished, and volunteers offer an opportunity for a mutual learning process. Try to strike a balance between mandating that tasks be completed in the same or traditional way and being open to new ideas. Encourage volunteers to be innovative when appropriate, but maintain time-tested ways of completing tasks when you know what works best.

When planning volunteers' schedules, be as accommodating as possible. This is especially important with work-study students, who may have school assignments or tests to study for, and whose class schedule will change each semester.

Help volunteers feel vested in the organization. Show them behind-the-scenes areas that the general public doesn't get to see, share information about your library and its accomplishments, and keep them engaged by inviting them to library events. Some organizations send regular communications to volunteers through e-mail. If you e-mail your volunteers, be mindful of keeping them connected and informed without overloading their inboxes with too many messages. Introduce volunteers to other staff members. If you have a parent organization, ask its director to stop by and say hello to volunteers periodically.

Maintain a sign-in book to log each volunteer's hours. Periodically calculate the number of hours worked by both individual volunteers and by the group. Share these statistics with volunteers, your staff and board of directors, and the public, and make it clear how vital volunteers are to your library.

Assessment and Recognition

As your program grows, you must evaluate both your program and volunteers. Periodic assessments ensure that volunteers are having a positive experience, and that you are getting the most benefit from their efforts. Begin by reviewing your list of tasks and job descriptions. Remove completed or obsolete tasks, or those that have proven better suited for you to complete rather than a volunteer, and add new projects.

Regular conversations with and evaluations of volunteers also provide valuable feedback. Some sample questions to ask include:

- What did you expect from your volunteer experience? How has your actual experience compared?
- How would you describe your volunteer experience to someone who was curious about volunteering at the library?
- What have you learned from your volunteer work? What else would you like to learn?
- What do you think you have contributed? What else would you like to contribute?[3]

When a student completes a formal internship, his school may ask you to complete a performance evaluation. I typically share this evaluation with the student, and, if the student was a good intern, offer to provide a professional reference in the future.

Assessment also allows you to recognize your volunteers' achievements. Volunteer recognition inspires pride in a job well done and also allows you to let others know about the valuable work volunteers do.

Thank volunteers as often as possible. Let them know how much you value their contributions and acknowledge the impact they have. I frequently tell people that I could not do what I do without the help of volunteers. There are many free or low-cost ways to tangibly show your appreciation. Small gestures, such as making coffee for a volunteer who loves java or remembering birthdays with a card, go a long way. Small gifts, such as candy or pencils, are another way to show your gratitude. My museum also holds an annual volunteer appreciation party and honors a Volunteer of the Year with a prominently displayed plaque. Again, a quick web search yields lots of simple, cheap ideas for thanking volunteers.

Another excellent way to both thank volunteers and recruit new ones is to profile them on your website, in your newsletter, through social media outlets, or with a newspaper article. Give background on the volunteer and what led him to your library, or quote him on what he most enjoys about or has learned from volunteering. Be sure to provide information on how readers can get involved.

Finally, make sure your supervisor, director, board of directors, other governing entities, and donors understand the contributions volunteers make. Regularly report the number of volunteers you have, their backgrounds, how they help you, the number of hours they contribute, and the monetary value of their contribution.

A Final Note: Dealing with Problem Volunteers

Despite your best planning, screening, and training efforts, you may eventually encounter a volunteer who is just not a good match for your library. Problems with volunteers fall into two categories: skill set and behavior. A lack of needed skills, such as how to use a computer, or negative actions, such as interacting with the public in a rude way or frequently missing scheduled shifts, may limit a volunteer's ability to contribute to your library.

Whether the problem is skill or behavior related, it should be dealt with directly and immediately. Speak with the volunteer privately to see if a resolution can be reached. If the problem is the lack of a certain skill, suggest other tasks for the volunteer. If the problem is behavioral, clearly explain why the volunteer's behavior is not in keeping with the policies of your library and volunteer program. Refer to the job description, contract, and your volunteer handbook if needed. Listen to any feedback or comments the volunteer may have. While this discussion may be awkward, it is better in the long run for both the volunteer and the library to get problems out in the open to see if they can be remedied.

If the problem cannot be resolved, you must dismiss the volunteer. You may choose to simply state that the relationship is not working out or that there is no more work available for the volunteer. Again, use the job description, contract, and handbook as concrete support for your decision.

With a little thoughtful planning, thorough preparation, and regular evaluation, you can create a volunteer program that meets both your needs and those of your volunteers. You can save time and money, your library can run more smoothly and efficiently, and you can balance the responsibilities of all those hats worn by solo librarians more effectively.

Notes

1. For detailed information on federal work-study, visit the U.S. Department of Education Federal Work-Study Program, www2.ed.gov/programs/fws/index .html.

2. "Volunteering in America," created by the Corporation for National and Community Service, www.volunteeringinamerica.gov/.

3. Ellen Horzy, *Transforming Museum Volunteering: A Practical Guide for Engaging 21st-Century Volunteers* (Washington, D.C.: American Association for Museum Volunteers, 2007), 59.

CHAPTER 5

Simple Programming Strategies to Enhance Libraries

Cassandra Jackson-Ifie

Embrace Your Community

When I first started working at the library as a paraprofessional, I remember one of my managers stating, "The library does not belong to us; it belongs to the community." The first real lesson I learned as a solo librarian is that I was a part of a community that included students, staff, faculty, and alumni. I learned to ask for help and embrace my community. I am a passionate librarian, and I feel my most important role is to encourage scholarship and lifelong learning among students. Many librarians may find this issue challenging. How do you implement initiatives to attract students when your budget is being slashed and your resources are limited? It is especially difficult if you are a solo librarian and you also have instructional and committee responsibilities. To make struggles more complex, *you* seem to be the *only* advocate for the library. My students, mostly millennials (young people born between 1980 and 2000), are my biggest assets. My students come to campus extremely tech savvy and culturally sophisticated. They inspire me to forgo tradition, eliminate budget worries, and get more in tune with my creative energy. The results shared in this essay will include programming, instructional ideas, and faculty connections that have increased library visits and improved the library's image on campus!

I sincerely want students to have a voice in library programming and operations. As campus librarian, I feel their input is extremely important.

I have developed a survey to gather information on student demographics as well as their suggestions for library improvements. The survey results have proven to be extremely informative. Results reveal 90 percent of my students are millennials. Research suggests millennials share such characteristics as impatience and being experiential and exploratory learners. They read less, tend to be digital natives, and are obsessed with gaming.[1] Awareness of these behaviors has helped significantly with developing new programs and library initiatives.

Faculty Connections

FACULTY FESTIVAL

Let's face it, faculty can make or break library attendance. They assign the research assignments that bring students into your library. In the academic library world, you want to make as many faculty friends as possible. It is imperative you spend time sending e-mails updating faculty about library news and resources. A significant amount of time should be spent mingling, connecting, and being extremely visible on your campus. Your library program will not be successful without collaborating with faculty. Faculty members can be instrumental in assisting with library programs, subject-based collection development, instruction, and increasing the number of students who visit the library by assigning research-based projects. In the past, I have connected with faculty by creating an event called Faculty Festival.

Faculty Festival has a carnival theme. I convince two work-study students to personally deliver each faculty member an invitation in clown costumes. On the day of the carnival, each faculty member in attendance is greeted by the same clown-costumed students and presented gift bags. The gift bags contain small items such as pens, notepads, and Post-its, and a few had gift cards to local restaurants. Faculty members select their own bags located on a table. The event was held in a large conference room. Tables are set up to separate the various sections. Sections include new acquisitions, express database tutorials, upcoming library programs and lectures, and course reserve registration. Most importantly, all faculty members leave the event with a brochure highlighting how to effectively collaborate with librarians as well as an overview of all library services.

FACULTY PROFESSIONAL DEVELOPMENT

When you work as the sole librarian in an academic environment, you have to keep your colleagues aware of current trends as they relate to the library and the curriculum. Many times faculty members need and desire ideas on *how* to effectively work with the librarian. Solo librarians have to be aggressive when it comes to faculty outreach because faculty members can significantly increase library visits and circulation statistics. One way I have decided to reach out to faculty is by volunteering to do a session focusing on information literacy during a faculty in-service day. By introducing faculty to concepts of information literacy, I hope to motivate them to assign more research-based assignments.

I introduce the concept by giving faculty a historical overview and explanation of the term. Throughout the year, I usually work with an English instructor presenting various sessions to help students with research-based assignments. I present sessions on accessing the databases relevant to literature. Also, I prepare a session introducing students to statistical references sources in print. The instructor infuses information literacy skills in his courses heavily. I chose to invite this faculty member to co-present during the session. I felt presenting the session with another faculty member would be beneficial because audience members could easily identify with a colleague who shares their daily classroom challenges. Administrators are also invited to attend the session. During the session, faculty also participates in an activity. They are given a subpar research-based assignment and an effective research-based assignment. They are divided into groups and each group has to choose the best assignment for students. They are also asked to discuss whether or not they would use the assignment in their classes. Faculty leave the session motivated and eager to send students to the library by assigning more research-based projects. A great deal of effort during a few semesters set the standard for greater student and faculty involvement in semesters to come. For solo librarians, one project sometimes must take priority over others when considering the future of the library.

Library Programming

FLASHBACK LISTENING LOUNGE

My library has a diverse music collection containing many rare LPs. Many of my students have never seen or used an LP or record player. The "Flashback Listening Lounge" was created to introduce students to resources in our music collection and highlight various artists with whom students may not have been familiar. To pique student interest, the featured artist always includes an artist in our LP collection combined with someone who is currently popular on the music charts. An example would be Joni Mitchell meets Norah Jones or Ella Fitzgerald meets Lalah Hathaway or Usher meets Otis Redding. Usually, I will hire a student to serve as DJ for the evening and one of the library conference rooms would be set up like a club setting. An alternate idea for librarians who lack resources to hire a student is to advertise for a student volunteer. Students who are interested in music or are studying mass communication would enjoy the opportunity to add a "gig" to their resume. Light refreshments are served and a discography for each artist is prepared in a brochure. Simple decorations such as books related to the artists that students could check out take the place of costly store-bought decorations. I display pictures or articles about each artist on the wall. The room is usually also filled with music CDs or DVDs of music documentaries available for checkout.

FACEBOOK READING GROUP

Nearly all of my students have Facebook accounts. Facebook is an extremely popular social networking site. After a failed attempt to create a traditional book club, I decided to encourage students to participate in an online reading book club via Facebook. The Facebook Reading Club currently has forty members. Each month a member of the book club serves as facilitator. He or she leads an online discussion and suggests a book for members to read. The facilitator introduces the book and manages the discussion. Each quarter I suggest a book for members, and we meet at a local restaurant to bond and discuss books! At first, I hesitated to take the reading circle outside of the library. However, the reading group flourished outside the library and I found that students who would not normally join a book club joined the reading circle. The diversity of the group resulted in interesting discussions. The experience of the Facebook Reading Group also taught me a valuable lesson about solo librarianship: sometimes thinking outside the box means taking your library services outside the library. Librarians should consider planning activities such as this one outside of the physical library building as a tactic to attract traffic back into the library. Once people who hesitate to visit the library get to know the librarian they may be more likely to enter the library and take a look around.

GAME TIME

Every quarter the library offers game day as a stress buster for students. Students are required to RSVP because we serve refreshments. Generally, we provide popcorn, hot dogs, sodas, and cookies. We dedicate two rooms to game tournaments. Students rotate to each game. Featured games include chess, checkers, Scrabble, and Monopoly. Also, we usually feature a Wii room. We hire an inexpensive DJ to play music and announce winners. It always is a great opportunity to turn the library into something other than the library!

For some reason even older folks get a kick out of being able to talk a little louder than usual in the library. At the end of each semester, we prepare game day for faculty and staff. The event serves as a thank you for their support and collaborative efforts during the semester. Faculty game day is without students and includes an upgraded menu. The faculty's menu includes pizza, sandwiches, and various salads along with an assortment of beverages. I am not sure who had the most fun, students or faculty. The DJ would add excitement to the game day experience by playing random songs. Faculty would have to guess the artist and year. Also, faculty karaoke was always popular as is our version of "Name That Tune." Events like this one are great opportunities to turn the library into something other than the library in order to attract visitors and create lasting memories with colleagues.

FIRST FRIDAY BREAKFAST SOCIAL

Solo librarians need to take advantage of ideas that result from everyday coincidences. For example, I was preparing a book review on a book that discusses the status of black leadership in America.[2] That evening, the local news channel reported on issues relating to our local black community leaders. The idea occurred to me that the book could be a great backdrop to discuss local issues. Shortly thereafter, the First Friday Breakfast Social was born. Each month, on the first Friday, I would facilitate a discussion about a hot topic. Topics included everything from Obama's health care plan to how social networking has changed the way we communicate. A library book would always serve as the backdrop for this discussion. Usually, the featured selection would be a new acquisition, and sometimes a guest speaker visits. In the case of the social networking topic, I invited a local social media specialist to speak to the group. This program was also inexpensive to host. Doughnuts, fruit, and juice is the usual breakfast fare. After the session, students are able to browse and check out books displayed relevant to the topic.

Instructional Initiatives

FRESHMAN SCAVENGER HUNT

Freshman orientation is usually skipped by many of the freshman students. The traditional tour and lecture is not appealing to my students. I revamped orientation by offering two sessions. The first session lasts thirty minutes. It provides a basic overview of the library and library services. I also show students how to access resources such as the catalog and databases. During the second session, each freshman faculty member has to bring their students to the library. Students are given worksheets with questions relevant to the card catalog, electronic resources, special collection, print journals, and other library resources. Students are required to access and locate resources using the library catalog, databases, and print journals. In some instances, prizes are hidden near some of the resources. In other cases, the first students to access material are given a prize. This process keeps students motivated and interested in completing the worksheet. Once the worksheet is completed, students are able to find a book in the library, access electronic materials, and choose print journals related to their assignments or subject preferences. The scavenger hunt is all totally hands-on and requires students to use most of the library's resources. The activity has proven to be an engaging and practical learning assignment for students.

HIP-HOP CURRICULUM CONNECTIONS

Hip-hop music and culture is popular among my students. A faculty member requested I introduce his class to APA style citations and plagiarism. I decided to incorporate a plagiarism case involving a popular hip-hop artist into my lesson plan. As students enter the classroom, I usually play the song involved in the plagiarism case on low volume. I open the session with a discussion about the artist and his case and connect it to classwork and the academic setting. I discuss the consequences of plagiarizing with students and we move on to methods of plagiarism prevention. I present a brief PowerPoint on basic APA formatting, then students are divided into groups. Each group has to collectively cite a series of sources, and to make it competitive, the session was timed. Whichever team completes the most correct citations wins the challenge. It is important librarians stay connected to popular culture when working with students. The aforementioned lesson plan, "Bibliographic Barbecue," is published in *The Library Instruction Cookbook* edited by Doug Cook and Ryan Stittler.[3] Opportunities to connect popular culture into lesson plans increase student interest and offer memorable library lessons.

LUNCH AND LEARNXPRESS SERIES

It has been documented that many of today's students enter college tech savvy but not information savvy.[4] Students are able to design web pages and access social media, and they possess advanced Internet search skills. However, students lack the necessary skills to access and analyze information appropriately. Most of the time, I provide an overview of the databases in our collection during my classroom presentations, but the sessions are also usually combined with instruction relevant to the research process. As I began observing student needs regarding research, I wanted to offer sessions on specific databases such as LexisNexis, ProQuest, JSTOR, and EbscoHost. I felt these types of sessions would be beneficial throughout their college careers. My goal was to dedicate time to each database, highlighting special features and access points. Each Lunch and LearnXpress series is an hour. The sessions include forty minutes of hands-on instruction. We eat lunch the final twenty minutes and students are able to ask questions relevant to the presentation. I suggest ways the databases can be useful in specific courses or while completing certain assignments. The series gives students the opportunity to explore databases on their own outside of the classroom. I focus on one database per month. I offer sessions on various days and alternate lunch times. Students leave the session with pointers presented during the lecture as well as search tips. The overall goal is to develop better student researchers by introducing them to databases that will assist them at preparing higher-quality research assignments. It is also an attempt to show students alternatives to Internet resources. Solo librarians should take every opportunity to offer hands-on instruction using research resources. We spend a great amount of time purchasing these resources for students and faculty. We should also invest time ensuring our campus community is getting optimal use out of these resources.

Space Design

In an effort to personalize library visits and make students comfortable, the library is divided into various sections. The main floor is for students who desire to surf the Net or study. It is the quietest level. The second level has study rooms and practice/presentation rooms. The second floor is a larger space and can accommodate group study or small class sessions. The spaces are designed with the frame of thought that students will enter for different reasons, and we want to ensure that each student has a space conducive to their needs. We publicize the newly created spaces and encourage students to practice their presentations in the practice rooms or meet with a study group on the second floor. We find that our efforts work and students visit the library for these purposes. The library is one of the few places on campus that has areas to support group study or enclosed practice rooms.

In addition to space accommodations, the lighting is also updated on each floor. Bold and vibrant-colored contemporary furniture has been purchased to modernize the library and provide a "hip" appearance for students. The decision to modify the space to a more user-centered environment has definitely enhanced the library's reputation on campus. It is known as a "cool" place to hang out.

Revamp Results

As a solo librarian, your work environment can sometimes become overwhelming. *You* are the library committee, the circulation clerk, the reference librarian, and the senior research project instructor all at the same time! Most days it is easy to lose sight of what is important and why you were *really* hired. At the end of the day, you are responsible for providing a library environment conducive to the academic needs of the students and institution. Your priorities should never waver from this purpose. I do not think library school prepares you for solo librarianship! You have to have passion for the profession and creativity. In addition, you have to network and make wise use of the resources you do have in your possession! The practical advice below may be helpful for solo librarians interested in revamping their library program.

- Stay current with popular culture. Tune into VH-1, MTV, or BET every now and then.
- Do not take anything personally.
- Your students can teach you many things.
- Do not be too proud or stubborn to take advice or constructive criticism from colleagues.
- Always lean on the positive side!

My library program has become something that has made me extremely proud. Students have started to see the library as something other than a brick and mortar building with books. They have started to "check us out," and they have found hip programming, insightful instruction, and amazing acquisitions geared toward their interests and research needs. I have learned the valuable lesson: an excessive budget doesn't necessarily guarantee a successful library program; sometimes you have to put your heart in the matter and tackle things solo!

Notes

1. Janet McNeil Hurlbert, *Defining Relevance: Managing the New Academic Library* (Westport, Conn.: Libraries Unlimited, 2008), 8.

2. Cynthia Griggs Fleming, *Yes We Did? From King's Dream to Obama's Promise* (Lexington: University Press of Kentucky, 2009).

3. Doug Cook and Ryan Stittler, eds., *The Library Instruction Cookbook* (Chicago: Association of Colleges and Research Libraries, 2009).

4. Rob Salkowitz, *Generation Blend: Managing Across the Technology Age Gap* (Hoboken, N.J.: John Wiley and Sons, 2008), 96.

CHAPTER 6

The Solo School Librarian
CREATING A CONSTELLATION OF COMMUNITY SUPPORT

Jess deCourcy Hinds

When I started a new secondary school library in 2008, I began with an empty room, empty bookcases, and a forbidding mountain of donated, uncataloged books. I only had one summer to create a warm, inviting, organized library. So I learned to do something new: I learned to ask for help. Without a constellation of support, I would not have been able to create an automated library of seven thousand volumes in one summer. Without the talents of the school and larger community, I would not have been able to build a library program for 550 patrons.

Other school librarians often ask with envy in their voices, "How do you attract so many volunteers?" Recruiting volunteers through e-mail is the easy part. The real challenge is sizing up the people who walk through the door, figuring out how they are, and assessing what they want to get out of the volunteer experience. The next hurdle is to match them to a task or project that is as fulfilling to them as it is helpful to you. Building relationships with volunteers can sometimes be so time-consuming that we wonder if we're better off alone. We aren't. This article offers tips about how to draw support from all corners of a school library community.

Sizing Up a Volunteer in Under Five Minutes

When someone asks, "Do you have volunteer opportunities?" you should always respond with a big smile and extra-enthusiastic, "Yes! Thanks so much for asking!" even if your mind draws a blank and you can't think of single volunteer job offhand. Don't let the person walk away without scheduling their first volunteer session and learning three essential things:

1. What unique skills does the volunteer bring?
2. What new skills do they want to learn?
3. How much time do they have to give? Do their schedules mesh with yours?

Coordinating Volunteer Work

"Now you know how to run an army!" my dean quipped when she saw me overseeing dozens of volunteers the summer we created the library. It was challenging to orchestrate volunteers. But I managed to find jobs for people of all ages and skill levels: from the five-year-old daughter of a graduate student (who loved alphabetizing—and had a high school volunteer check her work) to the ninety-year-old retired teacher (who sorted books on a table while her college student friend ferried boxes of books back and forth for her).

The summer library launch was a success because people cared deeply about building a library and worked long, hard, cooperative hours. Skilled volunteers took leadership, trained others, and helped me supervise. This was especially helpful because people showed up for training and work at all different times of day. I could have insisted that everyone report for duty at 8 a.m. so I could assign everyone to different tasks and train them in groups, but that rigidity would have discouraged too many people. So I suggested that we start at 10 (it was summer vacation time, after all) and welcomed everyone warmly whatever time they arrived. Some working parents could only donate an hour between 3 and 4 p.m. Sometimes I had to stay late, until 8 p.m., because volunteers could only work after 6 p.m. At times when I was exhausted and tired of not having a personal life (I was also planning my own wedding that summer), I resented that volunteers were actually making my day longer. At the same time, I knew I couldn't build a library without them. I welcomed any volunteer who came in the door and any skill level. Ninety-nine percent of the time, the volunteer contributed something valuable to the library, making worthwhile all the effort of training them and the bleary-eyed twelve-hour days.

How do you match volunteer jobs to people? When I asked my congenial volunteers what they were interested in, they often said, "I'll do anything—I don't care!" However, I have always found that volunteers actually do care, and it is important to match people well. So I give them choice of two activities. "Do you want to learn to catalog books using Destiny software, or would you rather do something more hands-on, like shelf books or pot plants?" People almost always have a strong preference, and during the day, I can observe the nuances of their relationship with technology, Dewey decimals, or fiction. When a volunteer comes in a second day, I often have a special job customized for them—one that shows that I have paid attention enough to tailor an activity to their interests and skills. This is as simple as asking a woman who is a published poet to catalog poetry, inviting a bird-watcher to shelve ornithology books, or encouraging a basketball player to organize the sports section of the library. "This is so fun I don't want to go home!" is something I hear a lot.

To keep volunteers coming back, I try to take care of them, being attentive to their needs—even just for a few minutes a day. It would seem that this is an obvious point, but it is actually quite difficult when you are supervising children and volunteers at the same time. This is why it is often useful to have two volunteers working together; they can help each other and keep each other company.

Setting Up Library Projects for Others to Supervise

Last summer, my principal asked if I could manage fifty volunteers from a bank who were doing community service hours for a day. Unfortunately I was unavailable that day, but I spent a couple hours setting up a structure so the project could run smoothly in my absence. I came up with a list of volunteer tasks like dusting bookcases, scrubbing tables, covering books in clear plastic, and inserting anti-theft devices in books. I left a detailed explanation about how to do tasks and trained my dean and principal so they could train school support staff, who then trained the volunteers from the bank. The project was a complete success; we got more than one thousand books covered and five thousand books secured with anti-theft devices.

It is richly rewarding to design a project that can be accomplished with— or without—your presence on the day it takes place. Although it is heartening to coordinate volunteer projects, sometimes you want to reserve your energy for working with your young students. This means that others can step in. Who can you invite to come to your library after hours, or on a weekend or holiday? Are there corporate groups who want to do a daylong community service project? Is there a nonprofit devoted to school improvement? (New York Cares is an example of an organization in my area.) Are there religious communities? A Parent Teacher Association? Students needing community service? Simply type up instructions and train the project supervisor. Then plan an hour-by-hour itinerary of how the volunteer day would proceed and pay for pizza or simple bagged lunches for the team. And voila! Magical transformations will happen in your library while you stay home, designing informational literacy lessons—or taking a well-deserved nap.

Student Volunteerism

ADOPT A SHELF

My school's dean proposed that I invite students to share responsibility for shelving books. So I created the "Adopt a Shelf" program. In my poster and e-mail advertising, I described it as "similar to adopting a cat or dog. You give and get love, but it's less work—and free!" It's also like adopting a highway. I decided to assign students to a single shelf rather than a full bookcase because I wanted students to have a manageable task to which they could commit for a full school year.

"What's your favorite subject? Math? Music?" I ask students. If they don't have a favorite Dewey section, they get to choose their favorite alphabet letter in fiction or biography—their name or friend's name— which makes the activity seem personalized and fun.

To Adopt a Shelf, a student must:

- Check that the books are straight—two times a week.
- Check the Dewey order or alphabetization—two times a week.
- Agree to have his or her name on the shelf, which gives him or her a sense of pride and helps the librarian assess who's caring for their shelves well.

MAINTAINING PHYSICAL SPACE AND TECHNOLOGY

When I first announced the "Adopt a Shelf" program, students asked if they could adopt areas instead, like the computer area or Media Room. One student asked if he could help do an inventory of the DVDs. Two students split the job of cleaning up stray papers around the computer area and helping me maintain the computers.

Computer-area caretakers are invested in the tech-user experience. For example, one boy regularly makes suggestions like this one: "Can we put the Microsoft Word icon on the desktop of every computer so it's easier to access?" I also ask students to help implement my projects that promote research, like designing posters that explain how to use databases.

Recommendations for supervising tech volunteers include:

- Don't give students administrative access to computers (which might open the floodgate to downloading viruses).
- Don't ask students to handle printer jams (printers can get surprisingly hot and even burn fingers).
- Don't ask students to lift heavy equipment. Even carrying two laptop computers at once may be too much.

In general, student volunteer activities that involve alphabetizing or mundane activities should be completed in less than fifteen minutes each day. These tasks should be springboards for more intellectually demanding, enriching activities, like reader advisory.

What Else Can Students Do?

- Make Dewey Decimal signs using PowerPoint or Microsoft Publisher.
- Design posters with compelling quotes about libraries, books, and authors.
- Create book displays for "Banned Books" week, African American history month, or holidays.
- Write book reviews and post them beside bookshelves.
- Evaluate sections of the library to ensure that there are enough study aids or interesting books for that student's grade level, and then create a book wish list using Strandbooks.com or Amazon.com.
- Weeding: Although the librarian makes the final call, students can vote on which books to weed from the collection and which to keep.

HOW STUDENTS CAN SHARE IN READER ADVISORY

I keep a notebook in the front of the library with the words "What Books Should the Library Buy?" on the cover. Students record their wishes for purchases; if they have a lot of requests, I ask students to make an online shopping cart on Strandbooks.com (an excellent second-hand independent bookseller with a library department that does cataloging and labeling and ships to libraries for free). If we lack money for purchases, I ask students to write me one or two paragraphs about why they want the books, which helps me write grants on DonorsChoose.org, an online educational charity in which donors of modest means team up with philanthropists like Bill Gates. The grants funded most quickly are in the $100 to $400 range. Only teachers—and not students—are permitted to apply for these grants. But students help me understand their reading preferences, and the rationale for the grant, by writing an enthusiastic paragraph, and my grants are more compelling when I capture students' voices. Students' involvement in grant writing, even on the very basic level, can yield exciting rewards. When a box of shiny, new books comes through the door, a student will be extra enthusiastic to read them—and proud knowing that he or she helped obtain those books.

Faculty Library Committees

When I first envisioned starting a faculty library committee, I imagined us all around a boardroom table, with myself at the head of the table. This image filled me with dread. I much prefer meeting with faculty individually and brainstorming over coffee, and meeting as a large group only once or twice a year. How does a library committee work? Each committee member designs a project based on their interests. For example, one English teacher wanted to develop the graphic novel section with literary titles like *Persepolis* and *Fun Home*. She has helped me make book lists and write grants to support our collaborative graphic novel units. Another teacher likes hands-on organizing projects, like maintaining equipment and organizing my "Books to Be Cataloged" area. He set up shelves where students can browse donated books before they were cataloged.

HOW TO ORGANIZE A GREAT COMMITTEE

1. Choose one representative from every department. Each department representative is in charge of being the liaison between the department and the library. If more than one person volunteers from the same department, make sure that these people all have diverse viewpoints or expertise.
2. Communicate your expectations early on. Faculty members love the idea of helping the librarian spend book money, and many of them will be clamoring to join. Purchasing new books is only one element of the committee's work. The library committee may also collaborate with the librarian and faculty to write grants, organize fund-raisers, and solicit book donations. The committee should be as enthusiastic about bringing in money as they are about spending it.
3. Get to know each committee member. Spend time with each person, learning about his or her passions. Typically, the library committee member wants to improve the library holdings for her classes and her academic specialty or niche. This is great, as long as the committee member is also thinking more broadly about the needs of the department he or she represents.

BEFORE ASKING FACULTY MEMBERS FOR HELP, ASK YOURSELF

Is this a small, manageable task? The first time we ask a teacher or library committee member for help, start with a job that takes fifteen to thirty minutes. If the faculty member accomplishes the task quickly and easily, she will feel good about it and be more willing to help again. If you give her an hour-long task that she does not finish, she will walk away thinking that library work is something she doesn't have time for.

Am I meeting the teacher more than halfway? If you want a history teacher's help coming up with a book list for the library, you are less likely to get results with an open-ended e-mail asking for a list. Instead, obtain the teacher's syllabus (or curriculum) and make the list yourself. Then show the list to the teacher and ask him to comment on it, revise, and add to it. Once you have established a strong working relationship with a teacher, you can send bigger or more open-ended requests.

Does the task benefit the faculty member? Teachers should ensure that a job they do to assist the librarian is appropriate and relates to their role as a teacher in the school. For example, teachers sometimes like sitting at the front desk of the library so they can be available to tutor students. One teacher sat at the desk all afternoon the day before a test and gave twenty students extra help. This was helpful to me because it allowed me to catch up on shelving and cataloging. It would be unfair to ask a teacher to take the desk if he or she did not also benefit from the experience.

Faculty Activities to Improve the Library

- Recruit guest speakers and authors to visit the library. Advertise around school with posters, and bring in a larger audience of students.
- Send the librarian book purchase recommendations.
- Cowrite grant applications through DonorsChoose.org, an online educational charity that is particularly welcoming to amateur grant writers.
- Evaluate the current library collection and help with weeding.
- Cover the desk during my lunch break.
- Coordinate spending of the state money book purchase; serve as a liaison between their department and the librarian.

Internships

Graduate students, undergraduates, and young people wishing to gain experience are a great resource. I have worked with a wide variety of interns, from library science students to English literature MA and creative writing MFA students to an adolescent psychology Ph.D. student. All interns put in shifts at the front desk greeting students and checking out books, but each person also embarks on special, individualized projects based on their career interests. Interns help with collection development, grant writing, cataloging, designing library programs, and teaching.

TYPES OF INTERNS

When looking for student interns, it is useful to learn about your local college and graduate school requirements for what makes an internship and what an internship supervisor must do. In New York state, library science students completing library media specialist certification must complete one hundred hours of "observation hours" or "fieldwork hours," which should be light volunteer work (usually in their first year). In their second year, they need 120 hours of student teaching in an elementary school and 120 hours in middle or high school. Student teaching is more demanding and often requires that the intern teach his or her own class. The supervising librarian must also communicate regularly with the graduate department head and, in some cases, write reports evaluating the intern. A librarian can supervise observation hours even if she herself is not school-certified, but she cannot supervise student teaching until she has held her certification for a minimum of three years.

I have been certified for only two years, so I haven't had a student teacher yet. But I have had four or five interns every semester, usually one or

Library and Teaching Internship at Bard High School Early College Queens

Our innovative school—a college and high school hybrid—is looking for creative, energetic individuals interested in gaining experience in education, literacy, technology, community building, youth work, and libraries.

Interns can design their own schedules around a M–F 8:30–4:30 schedule, completing shifts of three to four hours or full days. The internship begins the first week of October. Although experience with teaching is not required, enthusiasm for those between ages fourteen and eighteen is required.

All interns help with book circulation, administration, and readers' advisory.

Interns can choose to focus on one of the following:

Teaching: Workshops may include "Poetry Writing," "Study Skills," and "Grammar Boot-camp."
Tutoring: Writing Center one-on-one tutoring.
Grant Writing: Learn to research and write winning grant proposals.
Community Building: Organize events that will inspire and unite the school community.
Technology Development: Set up a new computer lab; improve technology throughout the library.

Interns will receive extensive training and guidance in their area(s) of interest. It is an unpaid internship, but there is a possibility of growth into a paid position through substitute teaching. Those with special skills may also be invited to receive stipends to lead workshops/trainings as well. Interns will complete independent projects that they can use as samples of their work in professional or teaching portfolios.

If interested, please submit a letter of interest and resume to Jess deCourcy Hinds, Library Director, jhinds@emailaddresshere.edu.

two per day. To recruit so many interns, I had to advertise on various library listservs and invite people outside the school library community to apply. For example, one intern was in the general library science program training to become a public young adult librarian. He didn't receive any academic credit or certification through the internship. He was just eager to bolster his resume with young adult library experience. Another intern was a career-changer in her 40s who wanted to switch from real estate to library work.

WHERE TO ADVERTISE FOR INTERNS

- Post to school library listservs and graduate library science listservs.
- Visit graduate school websites and e-mail department heads of any programs that might plausibly have internship opportunities.
- Advertise on websites like Idealist.org, a website for nonprofit, charity, and arts organizations, which includes volunteer opportunities, internships, and paid work.
- E-mail library school and education graduate school faculties, asking them to communicate with their students directly.

A Final Note about Building Community Support

The most useful advice I could ever give a solo librarian is that saying thank you goes a long, long way. You can never say thank you too much or write thank you notes that are too effusive. I give volunteers quotations about libraries on beautiful stationery for framing. The quotes remind the volunteer about the value of giving one's time to the library. For example, one thank you note template includes this quote by Cicero: "A room without books is like a body without a soul."[1] Inspiring our volunteers is our duty. After all, it takes a village to raise a library, and it takes a librarian with vision to create a village.

Note

1. J. Geary, *Geary's Guide to the Great Aphorists* (New York: Bloomsbury USA, 2007).

CHAPTER 7

Teen Volunteers to the Rescue!

Cindy Welch

Did you get your share of the 4.4 million?

Teen volunteers, that is. If you are running a library by yourself or with only minimal staff, your scarcest commodities are time and money. Everything is a trade-off between helping patrons and doing all else necessary to keep the doors open. Then, for some libraries, there is the expectation of regular programming, particularly for children, and often patrons need time-consuming technical help opening e-mail, filling out an online job application, or simply finding information in a database.

One answer to the solo librarian stretch is to add teen volunteers to the mix. The 2010 *Volunteering in America* report issued by the Corporation for National and Community Service indicates that in 2009 teens (ages sixteen to nineteen) donated 389.5 million hours (mostly) to educational, religious, and social services organizations in their communities.[1] These statistics only tell part of the story because they don't account for the middle school set (ages twelve to fifteen). Unless you work in a retirement village, every community has teens; the question is how you perceive them, and the fact is that they fall or rise to the level of our expectations of them. Teen volunteers, given the right support and training, can be a boon to a busy library.

Implementing a teen volunteer program can be time consuming, as can any good volunteer program, but for every single hour of training you provide, they can give back countless hours in programming, computer training, decorating, shelving, and other tasks specific to your situation. The keys to a successful teen volunteer program are:

- Knowledge of teens and their developmental needs;
- An understanding of how they view volunteerism and why they do it;
- A (flexible) plan for making it happen.

What's in it for you? In addition to the opportunity to increase programming, get more done, and improve your library environment, teens have a unique take on the world and their presence can bring fresh energy and enthusiasm. They tend to move in herds, so once they have invested in you and your library, you may discover the library has acquired some "street cred" with their peers. This investment in the library as place can potentially lead to fewer incidents involving acting out or vandalism in or around the library itself. You also have the means and the way to influence your community's view of teens, to move them from "problem" to "possibility."

Teens as Volunteers: What You Need to Know about Teens

Since the early 1980s various groups have been involved in studying American adolescents and their behavior. First it was the Center for Early Adolescence in Chapel Hill, North Carolina, who derived a set of what they called "developmental tasks." These tasks represented opportunities that would help teens move more easily through adolescence into a healthy adulthood. Next, the work of the center migrated north to Minneapolis, where the Search Institute expanded the earlier research and created forty "assets" (www.search-institute.org/developmental-assets/lists), again, opportunities for youth to essentially practice adult skills with a safety net. The third wave of research, since the mid-1990s, is brain research, during which we've learned that different parts of the brain develop at different times, essentially from the back of the head to the front.

The outcome of all this research is that we understand now that teens act as they do for good reasons. They are going through an identifiable process, a revolution in both body and mind. In fact, their level of brain development, from ages eleven to thirteen in particular, is second only to that of babies.

They need as many varied types of experience as possible so that the hard wiring in their brain circuitry during this second great wave of development leads to the widest array of talents they can take forward into adulthood.

This is interesting theory, but what does it have to do with teens volunteering at your library?

Table 7.1 relates the developmental needs to volunteerism, and knowledge of these needs gives you the keys to understanding why teens would volunteer for/with you and how to keep them engaged. It comes down to the relationship they develop with you and your staff, and whether they feel their work contributes to something meaningful.

Teens are perceptive and they have learned to expect disrespect and dismissal, so be authentic, respectful, and sincere in your dealings with them. This extends to how you think about their help. One useful tool for evaluating your intentions is Hart's Ladder of Participation, first developed in 1992. As you can see from table 7.2, adult-teen cooperation can be anything from lip service (on the part of the adult) to meaningful interaction and even teen-led activities. It is important that as much as possible teens see their value to the library, and know that they are contributing in a real way to the work of the organization.

Librarian, Know Thyself: Getting Started Means Getting Organized

The first step in any volunteer initiative is to take a moment to think about how best to use your extra help. One of the keys to working with teens is to try to match a teen's talents and interests with the task, whenever possible. If you've done your homework ahead of time, you'll be better able to articulate your needs and get the right person(s) on board. This will also help you keep your free help, since job variety can reduce boredom. Having an ongoing list of volunteer tasks/opportunities may also help you attract and manage adult volunteers as well. One other point on this topic: don't merely save the drudgery for your volunteers. Whether they are teens or adults, no one likes to spend all their time on boring things. However, one person's boredom is another person's joy, so check in with them on a regular basis.

Consider how many teens you can use, and what you'll do if you have more applicants than spots. Perhaps you've already seen a flood of interested teens trying to fill service learning or community service graduation

Table 7.1. Developmental Needs and Their Relationship to Teen Volunteerism in Your Library

Need for:	Description	Tasks, Rationale
Structure and clear limits	Teens are seeking boundaries, and they are also testing the need for those boundaries.	Set a regular work schedule for your volunteers. Designate a locker or other personal space for them to use. Clearly communicate expectations and consequences. Then, follow through.
Self-expression	Teens are exploring their identities culturally, socially, and emotionally. This is why they often switch friends, change their appearance, become obsessed with their ethnic roots.	When you have a task that has some degree of latitude, ask their input. Perhaps they have ideas for arranging the space, designing flyers, or engaging with different groups.
Physical activity	Teens need time for physical activity as well as times for their bodies to be at rest.	Mix physical and mental tasks.
Creative expression	Teens are testing their abilities through writing, art, fashion, reading, music. This is an extension of their search for identity and an attempt to understand their own individual talents.	Mix in opportunities for self-expression and creative expression. Consider asking them to help create displays, nametags for programs, or decorations or even put together a program on a hobby.

Positive social interaction with peers and adults other than family members	Teens are learning the social ropes, so the more opportunities to practice social interaction (outside their family confines) the better!	Mentoring is a natural part of having a teen volunteer, so keep communications lines open and check in regularly with teens. Consider having them work in teams or pairs.
Meaningful community involvement	Teens need to see that their work matters, that it isn't trivial or busy work. That doesn't mean they won't shelve books; they just need to understand how even routine jobs make a huge difference to an organization.	Connect the tasks they are asked to do with the results for patrons or for running the library; make sure they know that they are making valuable contributions. Include meaningful tasks, not just work you prefer not to do.
Competence and achievement	They are often told they are "in the way" or "problems," so they need chances to prove that they are capable and that they can follow through.	Celebrate their successes—in an authentic way. Consider a certificate, letter from the mayor, posting their names somewhere, mentioning them in a newspaper article on the library, etc. Say thank you often.

Planning for Teen Volunteers

- What would you do with a volunteer or volunteers if you had them? How would you use them?
- What tasks need doing?
- Are the tasks done daily, weekly, seasonally, or occasionally?
- What do you dream of doing if only you had the time?
- What attributes would be a good match for the task(s)?
- How much time can you carve out to work with them in the early stages?
- How will you manage more than one? What if they want to work as a team? As a group?
- Would you consider using volunteers as part of a class project?

requirements, or who are trying to pad their college applications. If you find yourself in this situation, consider the long-term benefits of volunteer teams. One of the most effective teen volunteer programs I ever saw was in a Chicago Public Library branch, where the children's librarian took the time to train teens and was able to retain them with the promise of job growth, so that in a year or two, the teens completely ran her entire summer reading program. There were teams of teens, complete with team captains and the opportunity to advance! When funding was available, the team captain roles became paid summer jobs. Remember, they need the opportunity to demonstrate competence and achievement, to be part of something that makes a concrete contribution to their communities.

Table 7.2.   Roger Hart's Ladder of Participation

8. Child-initiated, shared decisions with adults
7. Child-initiated and directed
6. Adult-initiated, shared decisions with children
5. Consulted and informed
4. Assigned but informed
3. Tokenism
2. Decoration
1. Manipulation

Note that 1–3 indicate nonparticipation and 4–8 indicate degrees of participation.

Once you know your needs and your capacity (how many volunteers you can reasonably handle), you're ready to think about recruitment. This is where your knowledge of the community comes in handy. Middle and high schools are great sources of volunteer applicants, and it is important to consider all the options within the school. Is there a library club or are there library aides (who are already trained to a certain extent), who might want to work all or part of the year with you? Perhaps guidance counselors know of teens who are seeking unpaid jobs, and reading and English teachers may know teens who already believe in what libraries do. If your needs are clerical in nature, consider consulting with the business education teacher.

In addition to schools, consider already established after-school programs. YMCAs, Key Clubs, even church youth groups can be sources of teens. By tapping into these resources, you're able to talk with adults who have knowledge of the teens' talents and abilities, and you're also able to connect with any youth development groups in your town. Just remember that you must talk to the teens, too, not just the adults.

The easiest way to develop a corps of volunteers is to simply ask current teen patrons. Ironically, the reason teens usually give for not volunteering is that they have simply not been asked. If they use the library, they may already be invested in it and may only be waiting for the chance to be more involved. Sometimes you've watched these teens grow up, which means you know a great deal about them already. Or, if you have been able to have teen programming, you may know something about their interests, as well.

You need to decide if you will accept everyone who volunteers or if you prefer teens to apply. There are benefits and drawbacks to both methods: accepting everyone means that you may need to weed out the less serious volunteers, while an application process doesn't guarantee a good worker. If you decide to go the application route, Diane Tuccillo's *Teen-Centered Library Service* (Libraries Unlimited, 2010) and Kellie Gillespie's *Teen Volunteer Services in Libraries* (VOYA, 2004) both have great examples of applications, task lists, and timekeeping systems.

On Your Mark, Get Set, GO: Planning and Implementation

Just as general pre-planning is important, so is planning ahead of time how you will train and manage your volunteers. You can think of your volunteer army as a long-term teen program, or you can think of it in terms of new employees. However you choose to view it, take it seriously, and be prepared to invest the time and attention required to get it started and keep it going. Depending on your volunteer pool and how often you need to or decide to recruit, you may do a volunteer orientation once every school semester or perhaps only once a year.

Create notebooks that detail routine tasks, so you can occasionally supplement individual training with clear and concise instructions for simpler jobs. The most important thing is to take it seriously, not just point your teen(s) toward shelving and go back to what you were doing before they arrived. Don't forget to get other library volunteers or workers on board with the program. Your attitude and that of your colleagues can make or break any interaction with teens.

This Isn't Working, Or Is It?

Think in terms of gradual development. Trust must be built between you and your teen volunteers, and an early failure to meet your expectations may not mean you need to send them away. Realize that this is a learning experience for them and for you, and that often this is their first foray into the world of work. Tolerance, not taking things personally, patience, and a sense of humor will go a long way toward successfully working with the younger generation. Here's a brief checklist of things to have ready the first day of "work":

- Have a place for teens to put their "stuff."
- If possible, carve out even a small workspace they can call their own.
- Decide ahead of time how you will keep track of their hours, and have schedule sheets and sign-in sheets ready when they arrive.
- Develop a brief list of acceptable behavior guidelines; for example, no cell phone/texting during volunteer hours, ask friends to respect the work, dress code (e.g., unripped jeans are okay, plain T-shirts or button-downs, closed-toed shoes protect feet from falling books).
- Have an ongoing list of tasks so that if they finish something early they can be a little autonomous in their work.
- If you have a nametag, they should, too.

Make sure you have cleared time to talk to them about your expectations and the nature of the work. You may decide to limit their hours in the beginning so that they don't burn out and so that you can pace yourself as well. Suggest that they bring a copy of their school/sports/extracurricular activities schedule(s) during the academic year so that you can work out the best volunteer times for you both. Be sure to ask them what they would like to get from this experience; two-way conversation builds the relationship that is key to their continued involvement with you and your library. Check their work but don't make it the Grand Inquisition. If something needs improvement, tell them simply and without heat or condescension. They'll likely get it the next time.

What Can They Do?

The only limitations are those set by you and your teens. More traditional ways to use teen volunteers:

- Scenic improvements: displays, decorations, bulletin boards
- Program-related help: setting up chairs/furniture before or after programs, pre-cutting children's program materials, making nametags
- General tasks: shelving/shelf-checking, shifting books and materials, labeling books and other materials
- School related: tutoring, reading with/to younger children

    Fresh ideas for teen volunteers tap into our developmental understanding and encourage teen input in the planning and execution of many different types of task:

- Teen advisory board
- Conducting or even creating programs for their peers or for the general public
- Training adults to use computer applications such as e-mail or eBay
- Conducting story times or craft programs for children
- Creating videos or podcasts as publicity for the library or its materials

Breaking Up: Reevaluation and Change

As with any job, there may be times when things aren't working out with your teen volunteer. This is another place where pre-planning can pay off. Being clear from the beginning about expectations and tasks gives prospective volunteers the freedom to walk away if the fit isn't there; and it gives you a basis for times when the match between your library and your teen isn't ideal. Give the situation time to develop, remember that mentoring goes along with having teens as volunteers, and put yourself in the teen's place before jumping to the conclusion that you can't make this relationship work. But if you've done everything you can, then be as clear and gentle as possible as you suggest that the teen seek opportunities elsewhere. You don't want to lose a library advocate simply because they aren't the ideal volunteer, so try to speak from the facts and explain fully why you think it best they move on.

Working with teens can be a rewarding experience, if you have planned ahead, created a mix of tasks, identified necessary talents and skills, and built in opportunities to get their feedback. Be patient, allow for early missteps, be clear and consistent about expectations, and help them feel like an important part of your staff. They will rise to your expectations and may even become lifelong advocates for your library.

Further Resources for Working with Teen Volunteers

Gillespie, Kellie. *Teen Volunteer Services in Libraries*. Lanham, Md.: VOYA Books, 2004.

Shoemaker, Kellie. "Top Ten Myths and Realities of Working with Teen Volunteers." *VOYA* 21, no. 1 (April 1998): 24–27.

Tuccillo, Diane. *Library Teen Advisory Groups*. Lanham, Md.: VOYA Books, 2005.

Tuccillo, Diane. *Teen-Centered Library Service: Putting Youth Participation into Practice*. Santa Barbara, Calif.: Libraries Unlimited, 2010.

Great Articles about Successful Teen-Led Programs and Volunteer Experiences

Bolan, Kimberly. "Bridging the Gap: Proactive Approaches for Adults Working with Teens." *Young Adult Library Services* 4, no. 4 (Summer 2006): 32–34.

Colvin, Sharon. "Story Teens: Putting Teens to Work in the Children's Room." *VOYA* 33, no. 2 (June 2010): 130–31.

Gallo, Erminia M. "A Year in Volunteering at the Library." *Young Adult Library Services* 8, no. 2 (Winter 2010): 17–19.

Tadhg, Camden. "Bending Circuits and Making Music: Teen Tech Week in Downtown Minneapolis." *Young Adult Library Services* 8, no. 2 (Winter 2010): 20–22.

Note

1. Corporation for National and Community Service, Office of Research and Policy Development. *Volunteering in America 2010: National, State, and City Information,* Washington, D.C., June 2010. Available online at www.volunteering-inamerica.gov/assets/resources/IssueBriefFINALJune15.pdf (accessed October 27, 2010).

Part III

PUBLIC RELATIONS AND MARKETING

CHAPTER 8

Advertise the Library? Horrors!

Laurie Selwyn

Everyone knows libraries exist and everyone knows anyone can use them so why expend the time, effort, and expense to market your library? In reality, libraries are virtually invisible to approximately 30 to 50 percent of the American population. According to WSAW-TV's website, approximately 40 percent of Wisconsin's residents, for example, do not have a public library card.[1] Moreover, the Maine State Library's 2006 annual report indicates that 40 percent of their public library service population is also card-less[2] and these two states are not anomalies. A 2006 Gates Foundation–funded study indicates that nationally 27 percent of Americans do not use the library at all while another 26 percent use the library less than ten times a year.[3] With figures this low, the truth is you cannot afford not to market the library.

Why Market Your Library?

One advertises a product, service, or business to create a consumer need or improve the relationship between the product, service, or business and one's target audience. According to the *Concise Oxford American Dictionary*, "marketing" is another term for advertising or promoting something or someone[4] while "public relations" is either "the state of the relationship between the public and a company or other organization" or "the professional maintenance of a favorable public image by a company or other organization."[5] Every time you or your volunteers interact with a patron, employee, supervisor, board member, or potential patron, you and they perform some type of public relations, advertising, or marketing action. Everything you and your volunteers do, say, or fail to do or say reflects on you and your library. Something as fundamental as having a bad day, dealing with an obnoxious patron, or dressing down can project the wrong or right image. While that impression may be neutralized with a justifiable reason or another, more recent, action, some issues can escalate unexpectedly into full-blown controversies. The way you deal with a negative image or outright controversy becomes a form of public relations and marketing.

All organizations, including public, academic, school, and special libraries, need to market themselves and their services. A law library may have a legal mandate to provide resources to government officials and employees, local Bar Association members and their employees, the local jail, and those laypeople living in a specific jurisdiction. A public or school library may face an enormous uphill battle at every budget request due to its lack of visibility. An academic library may find itself fighting with one or more academic departments for enough money to provide adequate services to its clientele. A special library faces the same difficulties if the appropriate administration, managing partners, or library board is unaware of the library's services to the organization. Failure to get out the word to these intended constituencies could result in the library's receiving a smaller budget and fewer resources than it needs despite a well-organized and expertly presented request. All this makes marketing your library critical in today's tight money environment and a key component to your library's success.

The more people using the library, the more important the library becomes to the community or organization, the more successful your budget requests and the easier it will be to raise funds outside the budget process. While money is the most obvious reason to market your library, other reasons exist including:

- Ensuring your constituency knows the library exists;
- Educating your community on what services are available;
- Ensuring your library maintains a life as a community resource despite today's electronic 24/7 global community;
- Enabling the library to grow as an organization;
- Encouraging donations;
- Counteracting negative press.

Make sure your constituency knows the library exists. If the community does not know the library exists, you have very little justification for the continuation of its life—and ultimately, your job. Marketing spreads the word of the library's existence, its hours and available services while public relations sets the tone for the library's relationship with other people and organizations in the community.

Educate your community on what services are available. Never assume that everyone knows what a library is and what it does or does not provide to its patrons. Just because some people in the community are familiar with the library's service hours, address, and telephone number does not mean marketing is unnecessary. Some reasons for disuse include a lack of awareness of what the library offers. Do new parents know about the weekly "Toddler Story Time" program? Do those instructors and volunteers involved with the local ESL program know they can work with the library to introduce their students to additional resources? Attorneys in a large law firm may be unaware of the expensive resources their library has access to both in-house and through inter-library loan. Other reasons for low library use might be incorrect assumptions that the library is available only to people in certain income levels or with certain job titles. Maybe a potential patron believes that the services needed or desired are not available at a particular facility or the library's staff/volunteers do not present a welcoming demeanor. Others may still believe the library is a place where only bookworms and nerds go and where Shhhhh! is the operative word.

Despite today's internet 24/7 global community, it is possible for the library to remain a valuable community resource; however, the library's staff and volunteers must work to present and validate this image. Over the past decade, numerous articles and blogs have posited the question and posted comments declaring that "everything" is available via the Internet, making libraries passé. While that is far from the truth, it has put librarians on the defensive with many believing they have to prove "everything" is not on the Internet or that Internet information is incorrect. Academic librarians have seen a need to add a component on web veracity to their bibliographic instruction, library introduction, and research classes.

There are many ways to turn the library into a community resource. Some are as inexpensive as providing a centralized location for the community or company to post announcements and documents such as minutes from the latest council meeting or distribute local, state, or company forms. Public libraries routinely provide income tax forms. Some small public libraries provide a centralized coupon or pattern exchange site for their communities. An academic librarian might work with colleagues in other departments or institutions to provide the faculty and students access to resources beyond their specific department or within the larger off-campus community. A special librarian may find herself supervising the organization's records retention or knowledge management program or serving as the in-service training location for the organization's employees.

Marketing and public relations enable the library to grow as an organization. If the community is only peripherally aware of the library, there is no reason for it to grow and a very good reason for it to die when it comes down to saving the parent organization money. While physical growth is the most obvious visual picture of organizational growth, it is not necessarily the answer. Again, the more people utilizing the library and the more support shown by patrons, the stronger your justification for a larger budget, larger space, grants application assistance, or special program. The public librarian's goal should be to see the library become one of the community's major departments rather than an afterthought. The special librarian's goal should be to work the library into the heart of the organization so that the next time new interns or associates are hired, their supervisors automatically send them to the library instead of handing over that expensive individual database password with instructions to try Google, Yahoo!, Blekko, or Yippy before killing the organization's research budget with expensive database charges. Academic and school librarians' goals should be to attain the reputation of the library as the go-to place for faculty, staff, and students in need of educational and informational resources.

Library budgets are never large enough to meet all the library's needs and wants. Often donations, which make up the difference, come about as a side effect of effective marketing and good public relations. People like to give to an organization that makes them feel good or honors something or someone they feel strongly about, so making the library's constituents aware of the library's existence and needs is to the library's advantage. Once word gets out that so-and-so gave the XYZ Library a badly needed public access computer or assisted with the expense of the library's first OPAC, others become interested in making an occasional donation.

No one likes negative press, particularly an institution or organization that is dependent on someone else's money. Besides being a downer negative press does an excellent job of convincing people with money that the library is not worth funding—or that the library is merely another problem. This is where marketing and public relations join forces to correct incorrect or negative messages and impart accurate information to the library's current and potential patrons. If a public library faces the incorrect impression that it is providing child sex offenders a home away from home, marketing and public relations activities begin as soon as the librarian sets the record straight concerning the library's policies relating to children, public access computers, and problem patrons. Are your patrons aware of the unattended children and supervision of minors policy? Is the public access computer policy being enforced when a patron accesses an inappropriate site? Is the library's problem patron policy enforced fairly? Most importantly, are all three policies known to the library's staff, volunteers, and patrons?

Negative press is not limited to public libraries. An academic librarian with a disgruntled academic department may need to show faculty members that the only way she can purchase more materials in their disciplines is if they help identify the materials—or demonstrate that nothing is currently available that is not already represented in the collection. A special librarian might learn the library is scheduled for replacement with individual password database subscriptions for each professional employee and the space used for additional clerical offices.

Targeting Your Audience

Review your library's mission statement, goals, and objectives to determine exactly which groups make up your library's constituency. A public library has the broadest range of clientele in age, interests, education and personal background, and social and economic status. An academic library is usually responsible only to the institution's students, faculty, and staff. A school library is responsible to the immediate school system—often limited to the building in which the library is physically located and the staff and students therein. While most special libraries are only concerned with service to the parent organization, be it a law firm, a hospital, or a government agency, some special libraries, such as a public law library or a historical society library, have a dual mandate to provide service to non-members.

Identify the reasons you are trying to reach this audience.

- Is the library so new, small, or insignificant that no one knows it exists?
- Has it moved recently?
- Have the services changed in some way? Expanded? Decreased?
- Has the library's mission, goals, or objectives changed?

Once you have determined who your audience is and why you need to provide information to your patrons, determine which information you want to share and the best format in which to present that information. Areas to consider include:

- Reason for the communication,
- Budget,
- User education levels,
- User attention span.

Those special and academic libraries responsible for serving a wide range of patrons may want to devise two different sets of marketing materials. In the example below, both public law library bookmarks provide the library's logo, name, location and contact information, access hours, and a brief list of major resources available to library users. Beyond these basics, each bookmark is customized to a specific group's needs.

The major differences between these two sample bookmarks include jargon, fax number, applicable loan policy, and the state law citation giving the layperson permission to use the public law library. The bookmark intended for legal professionals, government officials, and government employees provides the library's fax number, uses legal jargon, refers to specific vendor resources, and includes the appropriate circulation policy. The layperson's bookmark excludes the fax number (as the librarian has no need to receive faxes from the general population) and avoids legal jargon such as "WESTLAW," "case law," "statutory law," and vendor specific resources. Since this particular library has a limited circulation policy in which only local attorneys, government officials, and government employees have weekend circulation privileges, the layperson's bookmark states all materials are for in-house use. Although many laypeople are unsure of their welcome in a law library and may even receive a "stay out; you're not allowed here" impression from local legal professionals, a state statute grants the layperson the authority to use the library's resources.

Public law library bookmarks for legal professionals and government officials/employees should differ from bookmarks intended for all other users. Notice the different services advertised for specific audiences.

Judge Cleo Smith Law Library
Jason County Courthouse
2nd Floor
123 N. Acorn Dr.
Smithville, USA 78421
Phone: (888) 555-1212
Fax: (888) 555-2121
Library Hours
M–F 8:30–12:00, 1:00–5:00
Sat., Sun., County Holidays:
Closed
Resources
50 State Public Access Lexis-Nexis, WESTLAW
State Case Law
State Statutory Law
Matthew-Bender Resources
CD-ROM Resources
Limited weekend loans available upon request to local attorneys, county officials, and county employees.

Judge Cleo Smith Law Library
Jason County Courthouse
2nd Floor
123 N. Acorn Dr.
Smithville, USA 78421
Phone: (888) 555-1212
Library Hours
M–F 8:30–12:00, 1:00–5:00
Sat., Sun., County Holidays:
Closed
Resources
State Case Reports
State Laws
Electronic Databases for all 50 States
Forms
Criminal Law
Civil Law
All materials are for Library Use Only.
Per state law (29 V.U.C. 261.195.8), the library is available to any Jason County resident.

Marketing on a Budget

Review your daily tasks and try to fit them into broader categories. For example, does your library offer:

- Inter-library loan
- Telephone reference
- Bibliographic instruction or database training

- Library tours
- In-house reference

As a special librarian, do you provide:

- Research services
- Programs such as CLE courses
- New hire or new associate training

Chances are your library is providing some form of just about every-thing already mentioned. Let your constituency know that your medical library offers medical professionals and hospital administrators research services as long as they ask in a timely manner. As a public librarian, get the word out to schools and day care centers that you would love to have them bring their students for a visit. An academic librarian might publicize bibliographic instruction opportunities to the faculty.

In order to keep the library's publicity and marketing efforts on track and within budget create a road map or marketing plan. In its purest form, a marketing plan is a detailed document setting out the intent and reasons for marketing the library to specific groups of people. It includes specific steps, procedures, actions, goals, objectives, and evaluation meth-ods. While a small library will not have the financial and staff resources a detailed marketing plan requires, the librarian can substitute a policy statement outlining the organization's reason for marketing the library and general guidelines on the type of information to be included and identify-ing those people with the authority to approve marketing efforts prior to carrying them out. Below is a sample marketing policy.

Marketing Suggestions

FREE RESOURCES

- Make use of local media PSAs (public service announcements).
- Encourage the local media to periodically spotlight an activity or service in an article or blurb.
- Submit press releases for newsworthy events such as author visits or advance registration for the next story time program.
- Create a website.

XYZ Public Library, Smalltown, USA, Marketing Policy Statement

Based upon the library's stated mission to provide educational, informational, and recreational resources to residents of Smalltown, USA, the XYZ Public Library's head librarian will publicize, direct, and support all efforts to make the library's presence known in the community.

Ultimately responsible for all marketing activities to ensure that the publicity meets the library's intended purpose, the head librarian will receive assistance from the Library Board, town officials, and members of the Friends of the Library. With the exception of routine program announcements, flyers, general brochures, bookmarks, weblog entries, and general media articles, marketing efforts must be approved in advance by the Library Board at its regular monthly meeting or by the head librarian's immediate supervisor. Friends organization activities must be cleared with the head librarian in advance. When the head librarian deems it necessary for board or supervisor approval, the librarian and a Friends representative will consult with the appropriate person.

Marketing methods include but are not limited to bookmarks, flyers, brochures, press releases, media articles, website, library programs, PSAs, and annual reports. All documents will include the library's logo, name, full address, telephone number, and service hours. Promotional materials for library programs and special activities such as book sales will include additional information specific to the program or activity. A professional demeanor is expected at all times regardless of the format or the person handling the situation, presentation, or promotional activity.

- Create a blog.
- Use social media (Facebook, Twitter).
- Encourage the friends organization to assist through book sales, community talks, and so on.
- Host meetings. These do not have to be library meetings. School board meetings could be held in the school library; a small public library might double as a community room for town council meetings or the annual community Halloween party.
- Attend community or regional meetings specific to your target audience. A public law librarian might attend an occasional local Bar Association meeting; an academic librarian an occasional departmental faculty meeting; a public librarian, an ESL board meeting.

- Provide a centralized location for the dissemination of community forms or information.

INEXPENSIVE TO IMPLEMENT

- Write an annual report. (See chapter 18.)
- Customize bookmarks.
- "Brand" your library with a log
- Create a basic quarterly or semi-annual newsletter.
- Create brochures and flyers.
- Hold a Library Snapshot Day.

EXPENSIVE TO IMPLEMENT

- Create a glossy quarterly or semi-annual newsletter.
- Celebrate significant library events such as National Library Week, Banned Books Week, and Gaming Day (fee-based library programs).
- Create paid advertisements.
- Outsource public relations and marketing activities.

Conclusion

Marketing your library can be as expensive and time consuming as you choose to make it. For a solo, the biggest marketing challenge is deciding where to put one's limited resources in order to obtain the biggest bang for the effort. The suggestions in this chapter are intended to provide a starting point. There are many library public relations and marketing resources available in print and digital formats and a small selection of those titles appears below.

Additional Resources

BOOKS

Flowers, Helen F. *Public Relations for School Library Media Programs: 500 Ways to Influence People and Win Friends for Your School Library*. New York: Neal-Schuman, 1998.

Reed, Sally Gardner, and Beth Nawalinski of Friends of Libraries USA. *Even More Great Ideas for Libraries and Friends.* New York: Neal-Schuman, 2008.

Russell, James D. *Public Relations and Marketing for Archivists: A How-To-Do-It Manual.* New York: Neal-Schuman, 2011.

Walters, Suzanne. *Library Marketing That Works!* New York: Neal-Schuman, 2004.

Wolfe, Lisa A. *Library Public Relations, Promotions, and Communications: A How-To-Do-It Manual for Librarians,* 2nd ed. New York: Neal-Schuman, 2005.

ARTICLES

Claggett, Laura. "Identify Your Brand, Before You Market." *Information Outlook* 6, no. 11 (November 2002): 12–15. site.ebrary.com/lib/slaioarchives/docDetail.action (accessed November 15, 2010).

Fuller, Ronald, Meredith McNett, and Ross McPhail. "One Moment in Time." *AALL Spectrum* 15, no. 2 (November 2010): 14–15, 18. www.aallnet.org/products/pub_spectrum.asp (accessed November 15, 2010).

Layne, Ashley. "Branding @ Your Library." *Special Libraries Handbook* (May 8, 2007). www.libsci.sc.edu/bob/class/clis724/SpecialLibrariesHandbook/SpecialLibrariesHandbooks2007/LayneAshley.htm#Bib (accessed November 15, 2010).

INTERNET RESOURCES

LisNews. www.lisnews.org/taxonomy/term/89 (accessed November 8, 2010). This weblog provides access to a wide variety of library topics.

Ohio Library Council. Marketing the Library. www.olc.org/marketing/4image.htm (accessed October 30, 2010). Presents a series of broadly written training modules for all size public libraries and budgets.

ProQuest. Library Marketing Toolkits. www.proquest.com/en-US/utilities/toolkits/default.shtml (accessed November 15, 2010). Provides some free downloadable marketing materials for all library types.

WebJunction.org. www.webjunction.org/marketing (accessed October 30, 2010). Provides several excellent documents specific to small libraries, rural communities, and branding and marketing to Spanish speakers that can be used for training.

Notes

1. Casey O'Halloran, "Library Popularity Growing," WSAW-TV, news release, September 18, 2010. www.wsaw.com/home/headlines/103209254.html.

2. Maine State Library, "Maine Public Library Statistics FY 06," annual report July 2007, unpaged, 63 pages long. www.maine.gov/msl/libs/statistics/paststats/fy2006/statsrpt06.pdf.

3. Public Agenda, *Long Overdue: A Fresh Look at Public and Leadership Attitudes About Libraries in the 21st Century*, 2006, 69. www.publicagenda.org/files/pdf/Long_Overdue.pdf.

4. *Concise Oxford American Dictionary*, s.v. "marketing" (New York: Oxford University Press, 2006).

5. *Concise Oxford American Dictionary*, s.v. "public relations" (New York: Oxford University Press, 2006).

CHAPTER 9

Public Relations

PROMOTING YOURSELF AND LIBRARY RESOURCES WHEN NO ONE ELSE WILL

Andrea Wilcox Brooks

Librarians who work alone must find a balance between performing tasks at their desks and actively engaging with patrons and colleagues in their organization. Choosing to work at your desk all day isn't necessarily wrong and it's unlikely one would lose one's job over it, but a librarian who rarely surfaces from behind the computer screen will not gain many new patrons and certainly does nothing proactive to benefit the library. Services and resources will go unnoticed. Communication and promotion are arguably the most important aspects to effective service and library usage, especially in solo-run libraries. In these libraries, one person has knowledge of a library's potential. If that person doesn't market what the library offers, nobody else will. Without adding public relations to the job role, the library and the librarian risk fading into the background.

Public Relations, Marketing, and Publicity

"Public relations" is a concept connected with many other terms, including marketing, promotion, publicity, and communication. The literature provides many examples of these definitions, including Judith Siess's *The Visible Librarian*, a book on marketing and advocating a small library.[1] Call it what you will, as a solo librarian the bottom line is you need to communicate your value to your community, and public relations is the key to accomplishing that goal. Incorporating some proven marketing and publicity concepts will only help your cause. It's OK if you don't have a background in or experience with public relations or marketing. I didn't. Chances are, as a solo librarian, you will pick up many roles you never imagined you would take on. Many PR techniques can be implemented with an outgoing personality and a vision to increase your library's value.

Pick up the PR Role

When I began my position as the head librarian at Brown Mackie College, a career college located in Northern Kentucky (BMC–NKY), I quickly realized little, if any, attempt at library promotion had taken place in the past several years. The library was just an extra room in the building that housed computers. The library had no web presence, a Microsoft Excel spreadsheet substituted for the library catalog, and other than a ten-minute tour of the one-room facility, no bibliographic instruction was provided to students. Circulation statistics were low each month and usage statistics showed that students did not log on to the subscription databases. One flyer in the library displayed the log-in information for online database access. Before starting the position, I observed a student library tour and noticed the database subscriptions weren't mentioned to the group.

An exchange with a coworker further opened my eyes to how obsolete the library had become on campus. It occurred when an employee, who worked in a different department, stopped in the library to introduce himself. During the conversation, I mentioned I was working toward my master's degree. He commented that my job in the library was perfect. After all, I could sit at my desk all day and complete my assignments. I was shocked at this comment and wondered if that was really what he thought I did all day. I had a to-do list longer than the number of lines in my notebook. It hadn't occurred to me that my coworkers didn't know what I did. I now realized I not only had to convince students of the library's value, but also the staff on campus. I opened a new page in my notebook and added library public relations to my laundry list of new duties.

The good news is that public relations can be incorporated into many existing job responsibilities. For example, every time you give a presentation to a group of students, you are plugging the library. When you add signs to the stacks, you are creating promotional material. At BMC–NKY, my public relations efforts were very simple, using print and online tools. I learned that when developing relations with the library's community, seemingly small efforts resulted in big differences. The key is to be visible and involved. If you're persistent with these efforts, then public relations will flow naturally into place.

Be Visible

When you accept a solo librarian position, immediately make yourself visible on campus. Start by taking a walk around campus or your organization's building every few hours. Take the proactive approach and let your coworkers and potential users see your face. If you are concerned about leaving the library unattended, find out if anyone else in the building can provide some relief. At a college, work-study students are perfect in this situation. If you are in a position where you have no access to extra help, keep your walks short. Unless you are mandated to never leave the library, taking a five-minute breather isn't going to hurt anything. I started doing this at BMC–NKY and met a lot of instructors and staff in different departments. After a couple of months, other employees and students began to stop me in the hall to ask a question or request a service. You cannot count on students or instructors to come to the library every time an information need arises. Sometimes, seeing your face reminds them of their need. It is unfortunate but true that many small libraries suffer from the habits of students and faculty—the habit of *not coming* to the library. Proving that you are visible on campus or within your company shows that you care about the organization, the library, and the people whom the library serves. When you actively engage with your community, students and faculty members become more involved in the library, even if it means simply speaking with you in the hallway.

One public relations advantage many solo librarians have is supporting a small community. For example, at BMC–NKY, the faculty pool is much smaller than at a large university. Spreading messages to forty or fifty faculty members at a career college is easy compared to thousands at a university. At BMC–NKY, full-time and adjunct faculty members are required to attend faculty meetings every month. These meetings are held to ensure all faculty members receive information about campus news, events, and changes to their classroom responsibilities. Once you feel comfortable on campus, expand your visibility by attending these meetings, whether it's faculty meetings or all-staff meetings. These gatherings provide the perfect forum for librarians to market resources. The first time I addressed the faculty at a meeting, I unveiled the library's new website and briefly highlighted some of the online databases available to them and their students. In the months following this meeting, I noticed usage statistics rising and more instructors requesting information about the library and its services. After the initial presentation, I continued to use the faculty meeting as a public relations platform to make announcements about anything related to the library.

Orientations provide another opportunity for solo librarians to be visible and promote the library. Most colleges provide new student orientations, and many employers provide orientations for new staff. At BMC–NKY, the library has a presence at new student orientations. Student orientations include a meet-and-greet session with staff and faculty. I attended this session each month to meet with students in an informal setting and briefly highlight the library's value. At a minimum, students left knowing where the library was located and that I was a resource. Involvement in student orientations could get more in-depth depending on what level you are capable of presenting. For example, solo librarians can host their own orientations in the library. Advertising on the university's or company's website and utilizing a student or employee listserv would attract attendees. Librarians could also host subject-specific orientations that outline resources and research methods for one particular subject or career, in my case.

Make the Library Visible

Not only is it important for the librarian to be visible on campus, but the library needs to be visible too, inside and outside its walls. This can be done with print and online resources. If you're new to the position, it's easy to feel overwhelmed with the need to incorporate public relations into your job responsibilities because there are many tools to choose from, including social networking, e-mail, newsletters, and blogs. I'd recommend starting with the basic, old-fashioned flyer as an easy and effective way to begin communication. A flyer on bright yellow paper announcing a new online resource or extended hours is going to capture someone's attention. Most public places on campuses have a bulletin board where you can post announcements and information. You should target student and employee lounges, restrooms, and lobbies. If your library doesn't have a bulletin board, request one.

Get creative and don't be afraid to ask for items that will make your library better. As a solo librarian, I was forced to get creative when I realized my library did not have a receipt printer to provide patrons with a due date reminder upon checkout. This meant a lot of books were not getting returned. I created bookmarks. The bookmarks not only acted as a solution to this problem but also as a communication tool. At the top of each colorfully designed bookmark a line was added to write in a patron's due date. The rest of the bookmark was used as advertising space. New bookmarks were designed every few months to announce library news, promote the library's online resources, highlight recent additions to the collection, and provide research tips.

Due Date: _____

*If you need to renew your book, stop by the library

Join the BMC–Northern Kentucky Library Book Club! The club is currently reading *The Kite Runner*, a novel by Khaled Hosseini. Share your thoughts and enjoy some baked goods at one of our upcoming meetings:

- Monday, May 24th @ 1:00
- Tuesday, May 25th @ 5:00

Stop by the library to check out a copy of the book or suggest a future book club read. Students, staff, and faculty are welcome to join! More information is available at www.librarybmc.com.

Create a newsletter. Instead of creating a "library newsletter," focus the newsletter on a larger group. At BMC–NKY the newsletter centered on the Academic Department. This got more people involved and gave a broader range of information to the student body. The newsletter contained information about upcoming events and meetings for students. It highlighted outstanding students, staff, and instructors. Since I was the editor, I made sure to leave room for a "Library Corner" where I could place information about new databases, book reviews, or upcoming services. The newsletter was distributed in print format to each class at the end of every month. One important tip to remember is that solo librarians need to capitalize on opportunities to collaborate and partner with other groups whenever possible. This newsletter appeals to a broad audience because it covers many topics from various groups while giving the library promotional space at the same time.

Paper is an effective and easy way to start, but with new technologies, promotional tools have greatly expanded and even librarians working alone or with very small staffs can combine these tools with their paper-based communications tactics. Virtual communities accompany many libraries and public relations efforts should expand into the online world. More often libraries are using Twitter accounts and Facebook pages to connect with users. Harry Glazer writes that after posting on Facebook information about music databases available to students at Rutgers University, the student newspaper ran a front page story about the resources.[2] Such a tool has its advantages; however, check with campus administrators before creating a Facebook page. Many organizations prefer to keep Facebook pages under the control of a wider communications department.

Two online tools I recommend are GoogleSites and WorldCat Lists. My library did not have a web presence. There was no central location to place links to subscription databases or the online catalog, when it was acquired. In addition, there was no way to provide online reference help in the form of tutorials or research guides. GoogleSites offers a free and easy tool to create a website and provide all those necessary links and information services. Plus, the website provided a platform to post announcements and promote the library. I used Yahoo! domains to purchase our own domain name. The address, www.librarybmc.com, was a much easier URL for students to remember than the URL assigned by GoogleSites. I used flyers, word-of-mouth, announcements at faculty meetings, and instruction sessions to promote the website to students and faculty. I also used a label maker to create stickers with the website's URL. The stickers were placed on the frame of all the computers in the library.

I used WorldCat Lists to highlight new titles added to the collection. I created five lists, each one divided by subject area. When new books arrived, I added the title to one of the five lists. Library users can connect to the lists at any time from the library website. Users can also subscribe to an RSS feed to instantaneously receive those updates, although only a few users chose to do this. To ensure instructors knew about these lists, I sent out e-mail blasts every couple of months providing links to the lists. The e-mails also reminded faculty that the lists were available to view anytime via the website.

Get Involved

If you're visible and the library is visible, the next step is to get involved. This includes getting involved with areas of your campus or company that don't directly relate to the library. For example, I sat on the Continuing Student Review Committee (CSR). This committee focuses on student retention trends and develops strategies to keep students in school. CSR has representatives from all departments on the committee. Sitting on the committee increased my visibility with other departments and gave me the opportunity to showcase the library's value in terms of student retention. Joining this committee also gave even more members of my community the chance to get to know me better, which makes them more likely to approach me and the library when they would like my assistance.

Near the end of my first year on campus, I formed a Library Advisory Committee. The committee is made up of full-time and adjunct instructors. These instructors advise librarians on collection development and service development. The committee only meets twice a year, but in between meetings, the members serve as "Library Ambassadors" and continuously provide feedback on the library. They also advocate use of the library to students and other instructors.

Of course, involvement in and creation of committees won't happen overnight. Seek out committees where your talents could be utilized and where you see an opportunity for advancing the library's value. Also, make yourself aware of campus-wide goals. At BMC–NKY, administrators wanted to see more student involvement in professional organizations and clubs. I formed a book club to provide one avenue for students to participate in an extracurricular activity. Participation in the book club was open to students, faculty, and staff. About fifteen to twenty students and staff would read each selection. This wasn't an overwhelming number, but costs were minimal so the club continued. Admission representatives even started using the book club display as a promotional tool when giving potential students a tour of campus.

Make a Plan

Before you start creating promotional materials and building relationships, take a moment to think about what you would like to promote in your library and the goals you would like to accomplish. Do you want to increase circulation? Do you want to increase awareness of information literacy? Perhaps you want to highlight a new service or resource in your library. Determine what it is you want to promote and who should receive the message. As a solo librarian, it may not be feasible to draft a lengthy marketing plan, but outlining a few goals and outcomes can help you focus your PR efforts and estimate a timeline of events to reach your goal.

Seeing Results and Keeping Statistics

I started my position at BMC–NKY in August 2008. I began tracking usage statistics almost immediately. I had access to past circulation records, making it possible to tabulate some statistics for the entire 2008 year. I saw growth in circulation and an increase in library instruction in the first six months. After formalizing a library orientation session, increasing my visibility, and getting involved on campus, I saw a more significant increase in usage across the board after just one year.

Prior to August 2008, library instruction sessions were not provided on a regular basis and consisted only of a library tour. In the first six months, I focused on building a library orientation that centered on information literacy skills. In 2009, fifty-five instruction sessions were held. Of those fifty-five classes, seventeen were non-orientation sessions. Bibliographic instruction had not been provided in the past, and I mainly credit public relations efforts aimed at faculty for the successful launch of library instruction on the campus. As of September 2010, forty-eight instruction sessions had been held and nineteen were non-orientation sessions.

Information literacy sessions provided an opportunity to provide public relations to the student body. Circulation records showed that in 2008 an average 19.5 books were checked out each month. In 2009, the average increased to 69.5 books each month. Looking at the first six months of 2010, that number had increased to 103 books each month. One factor to consider when looking at these numbers is that student population did increase by about 250 students during this time period. However, circulation multiplied at a much higher rate than the student population did and is likely more closely correlated to the increase in instruction sessions than the increase in the population.

Database usage statistics were also tracked. From August 2008 to June 2009, about 1,000 people logged in to the databases. The majority of those occurred in the latter half of the fiscal year. From July 2009 to June 2010, more than 5,500 people had logged in to use the databases.

The above statistics are meant to show you the difference between a librarian who places an emphasis on promotion and one who does not. Simple steps can go a long way. Make your presence known and be involved in as much as your workload can afford. Be transparent. Make sure your colleagues know what projects you're working on and when you have completed them. If you build relationships across your community and effectively communicate the library's value, then a successful, highly used library should fall into place.

Notes

1. Judith Siess, *The Visible Librarian: Asserting Your Value with Marketing and Advocacy* (Chicago: ALA, 2003).

2. Harry Glazer, "Clever Outreach or Costly Diversion? An Academic Library Evaluates Its Facebook Experience," *College and Research Libraries News* 70, no. 1 (2009): 11–14, 19. Retrieved from WilsonWeb (200900103836004).

CHAPTER 10

Public Relations as Relationship
SAYING YES!

Rhonda Taylor

It is ironic that individuals most in need of time management are the very individuals without the time to devote to it! Similarly, it falls to the librarian in a one-person setting to coordinate public relations, seemingly in addition to the many responsibilities that are distributed among several staff members in other libraries. However, there are six strategic steps that can assist the solo librarian, regardless of the type of library, in being an effective public relations manager. Being that manager starts with an understanding of what public relations really is.

Step 1: Understanding Public Relations (PR)

Public relations are best characterized as public relationships. The term "relationships" assumes three things:

- that there is commitment,
- that there is communication, and
- that the relationship is clearly, consistently part of an identity.

And, most importantly, relationships are with people, people whom one can actually identify. People are the "public" aspect of PR.

COMMITMENT

No one would say: "Yes, I have a relationship with my [fill in the blank: family, friends, coworkers] but only [fill in the blank: on Tuesday, every other month, twice a year]." Nor would one say, "Yes, my relationship with [fill in the blank] is only when I'm at home." And, yet, public relations[ships] are too often seen as either one more add-on to pressing responsibilities or something that will be tackled in the far distant future. So, the first step in public relations is to start thinking in terms of a relationship. PR as a relationship means that it is ongoing and an important part of every day's activities and not restricted by the four walls of the library building.

COMMUNICATION

The classic communication model is circular. Someone (the sender) has a message. She or he sends the message through some sort of delivery system, which might be simply speaking directly to another individual or group (in person or on a cell phone) or sending an e-mail or texting and so on. Then, the recipient (receiver) of the message must not only have received the message but actually understood it. This is the step that can be the most challenging. It is easy to make a very long list of ways that the message can go astray or be misunderstood. Those errors range from a poorly constructed message, to a message put in terms not easily understood by the recipient, to choosing the wrong delivery system for the recipient, to the recipient's misinterpretation of the message.

In communication it is important to remember that simply sending a message is not, repeat not, communication! Sending the message is simply telling someone something. As everyone who works with children clearly understands, "telling" does not mean that there is either understanding or acceptance of what has been said. The same is true of every other age group as well. Communication is a loop. Once the recipient receives the message, then the recipient's response/acknowledgment of the message is returned to the sender. Next is the step that is often totally overlooked, both in everyday communication and in public relations. The original sender must use the feedback from the recipient to determine how to respond back to the recipient. This step of continuing the communication completes the circle.

CONSISTENCY: RELATIONSHIPS AND IDENTITY

People in a committed partner relationship openly exhibit indications that there is a relationship. Perhaps those signs are in the form of a wedding ring or a name change or a shared home address. Those cues, some subtle and some more obvious, help others to understand the nature of the relationship. At the same time, people in a committed relationship understand their own roles, including their responsibilities. And a good relationship is consistent over time; the relationship is transparent to all. Public relations is also a committed relationship, one that mirrors the identity of the library.

These three characteristics of relationships (commitment, communication, and consistency) provide a model both for understanding what is meant by public relations and for proceeding with enhancing PR. Improved public relations must be the goal because the reality is that every library already has public relations. However, those relationships have not necessarily been planned. People within the library (the librarian, volunteers, etc.) and outside of the library (people who use the library, people who don't use the library) already have ideas about what the library is, does, and ought to do. Those ideas were shaped by all the encounters that they have had with the library, including just checking out books. Those ideas were also built on encounters that they have not had, such as lacking knowledge of what the library offers.

Step 2: Yes, It Is about Planning!

The one step that means the difference between effective and ineffective public relations is the step that often makes busy professionals groan: planning. However, nowadays one does not start on a trip to an unfamiliar location without first consulting a roadmap or a web mapping service or using the car's GPS—in other words, planning. One does not want to waste time being lost, being ineffective. It is equally important to plan public relations. The good news is that such planning should not be an "extra" task. Remembering the three Cs of public relations (commitment, communication, consistency) means public relations planning is integrated into planning that is already happening.

One "plans" collection development, programs, outreach, literacy instruction, and other library activities, from the initial ideas through implementation through evaluation. Public relations is simply part of the list for what needs to be done for all library activities. A well-made patchwork quilt has many pieces sewn into a distinctive pattern. Similarly, good public relations is sewn into every library undertaking, no matter how small. It is not "tacked on" as some sort of out-of-place addition after, for instance, a program's planning is already done. In other words, one is committed to effective public relations and does not ignore it.

Step 3: Starting with What's Already There

Launching an effective public relations campaign means starting with basic planning documents that the library already has: vision, mission, and goal statements. After reviewing those "maps," one should clearly understand what the "point is" for the library and its undertakings and who the library is supposed to serve. In other words, the librarian then knows the "destination" of the trip. With that understanding, one is better prepared to explain it to others.

THE ELEVATOR SPEECH AND RECRUITMENT

There are two simple approaches that are great tools for starting to add public relations to every encounter. The first one is the well-known one-minute elevator speech (although it is sometimes explained as a two- to three-minute speech). Individuals in education and business fields are often advised to think of what one would say to a stranger in an elevator if one were going to talk about one's work.

What would you say in one to three minutes if you had to "explain" the library? There are many audiences who provide the opportunity to use this speech one on one: seatmates on mass transportation, strangers at social receptions, newcomers to the community, one's hairstylist . . . the list is infinite. Why bother? The first reason is communication. Communication starts with a message. The message has to be delivered to have any impact. These informal occasions are great opportunities for making the telling into communication, one on one. What is the reaction? Did you learn something about what people know/don't know about the library? Did the person have questions? How can this new knowledge be merged into longer messages about the library for more formal occasions and in delivery systems to larger audiences, such as presentations to community groups, the library's website, newspaper articles, library card brochures, and so on? These and other opportunities, including those one-on-one conversations, provide the chance to recruit people to the library. And public relations is always about recruiting. One is always recruiting library customers and support, both now and for the future. Those potential customers are possible attendees for a library program, applicants for library cards, members for a library friends' group, and so forth. Their support can be donations for a library friends' book sale or future votes for bond initiatives.

VIRAL PUBLIC RELATIONS

The second reason to always have the elevator speech ready is the viral nature of public relations. Sometimes in restaurants and other retail establishments there is a sign that says if you are satisfied, tell your friends; if you're not satisfied, tell the management. Regardless of the sign, the customers/patrons will tell people within their circles (family, friends, work, even strangers) about their positive and negative service experiences—the message goes viral (spreading like a virus, person to person). The Internet and social networking have simply accelerated the rate and spread of message distribution. The librarian needs to be proactive in spreading the library's message.

The person-to-person spread of messages is another reason why each transaction within the library should trigger quick evaluation of PR. It doesn't matter if the transaction is a reference question answered, a DVD circulated, or a patron's search of the OPAC or library website. Each one should have the librarian asking, "If I had been the customer/patron, what would I think about this encounter—what would I share with my friends?" Public relations start here, at the one-on-one encounter, even if it is virtual.

Step 4: Who's in This Relationship?

Shaping the elevator speech and practicing it and starting to think about how to expand it are basic actions leading toward building good public relationships. This effort continues with being intentional about PR in all library activities. Here are ways to ensure that commitment:

A. Review the public face of the library and compare it to your elevator speech. Is it a match? The public face is everything encountered by the public (the library's customers). Think about experiences with stores where you shop in person. You want to shop at a store that says "welcome" and "we're here for you, you as an individual, and we know what you want." Here are some ways that you "read" that message:
   • Curb appeal: You gauge the store before you ever enter the door, based on everything from landscaping to signs on the door to seasonal decorations.
   • Accessibility: How easily can you get in the door, especially if you're physically challenged?
   • The human factor: Everyone working in the store represents the store. Are they visible? Are they friendly and knowledgeable and yet not intrusive? You as the solo librarian must meet this standard, but training ensures that any volunteers and temporary or part-time workers in the library are also good representatives. Do they know the elevator speech?
   • Help!: If you need assistance while in the store, is it clearly available?
   • Arrangement: Is the store's arrangement logical and easy to navigate? Does it say "welcome"? Is it easy to find what you're seeking? Is signage available, and is it attractive and easily read and understood?
   • Other factors that matter to you as customer: If you shop online, you make these same evaluations, but you're judging a virtual store. Think about those virtual stores visited on the web. How do the retail store criteria (above) apply there? Now think about the library building and the library's virtual presence and what the customer is seeing.
B. As every activity (whether buying a resource or creating a web page or writing a book review or considering a program) is planned by the library, consider this checklist for building PR:
   • Who do you want to serve with this activity? Are there people you want to reach with this activity who are not already library users?
   • Are there people or organizations or institutions who could be your partners in this activity? Does the library already have a relationship with them? How will you build on an existing relationship, or start

to form a new one, to "recruit" people to this effort, as partners in making this activity happen and/or as participants?

- What information delivery channels are most often accessed by these groups of people that you want to reach with a message about this activity? Those channels could be everything from flyers to newspaper articles to television and radio public service announcements to Twitter tweets to web page banners. If you're not sure, start by asking several people from this group!

- Post-activity, gauge how well the enhanced public relation activities worked. What would you change next time around with this type of activity? Take the data generated from evaluation efforts such as user surveys or patron suggestions and consider how the information can be used for better PR. Evaluation and reflection are ongoing aspects of healthy relationships.

C. Keep relationships continuing. The reason that retailers want your e-mail address is because they are trying to connect with you repeatedly, post-sale. They want a relationship. The especially savvy retailer encourages customers to bring in others—think of those magazine offers that provide inexpensive renewal to customers if they also subscribe for a friend. The library's relationship with its customers and potential customers has to be maintained beyond one encounter. One must stay in communication, repeatedly and appropriately, using those information channels that reach various groups of customers. However, remember to target the message and don't overload the customers with too much information.

Step 5: Don't Reinvent the Wheel!

Having a good grasp on the message to be delivered, and having identified the target audience(s) for the message, it's time to look at specific ways to reach out to the audiences. Be efficient and don't reinvent the wheel. Many librarians have already been down this path, and you can benefit from their sharing.

A. Engage in continuing education/professional development. While it is hard for the solo librarian to get away for conferences and workshops, look for those opportunities, offered by local, state, regional, and national library associations, that will provide more guidance in PR. They need not be in person. Increasingly there are online learning offerings through webinars. One example is the American Library Association's (ALA) Library Leadership and Management Association programs, which frequently cover aspects of PR: www.ala.org/ala/mgrps/divs/llama/conted/index.cfm.

B. Don't forget that other professional organizations than those for librarians (such as educational, business, etc.) also offer continuing education opportunities about PR. Similarly, don't forget that such organizations, as well as professional library associations, can be good venues for presentations about your library. Such presentations are another way to build PR for your library, both within the professional organizations and back home when you publicize this involvement. And consider going to a conference that is attended by many of your patrons. For instance, if you're an academic librarian, consider a professional conference attended by college faculty. This is a great way to learn about your users' information needs and to build those relationships.

C. Network, network, network. People still go to professional conferences in person for many reasons, one of which is the chance to network one on one. That networking means sharing of ideas and building potential partnerships, both of which are particularly valuable for the solo librarian. For how-to guidance on networking, take a look at this *Public Libraries Briefcase* overview of "Networking for Business Librarians," with advice that works for any type of library: www.ala.org/ala/mgrps/divs/rusa/sections/brass/brasspubs/publibbrief/no231q2010.cfm.

D. Take advantage of credible materials and resources freely offered. Examples:

American Library Association's (ALA) "PR Tools and Resources." Included is an article on eight "Principles and Practices for Effective Multicultural Communication." Especially helpful are the full-text offerings of *Communications Plan Workbook, Speaking Up for Library Services to Teens, Toolkit for Academic and Research Libraries, Toolkit for School Library Programs, A Small but Powerful Guide to Winning Big Support for Your Rural Library, Kids! @ Your Library Campaign Toolkit,* and *A Communications Handbook.* Also provided are public services announcements, downloadable artwork/photos, and many other tools. www.ala.org/ala/issuesadvocacy/advocacy/publicawareness/campaign@yourlibrary/prtools/prtoolsresources.cfm.

ALA's Office for Literacy and Outreach Services (OLOS) provides links to "OLOS Toolkits." Toolkits include *How to Serve the World @ Your Library: Serving Non-English Speakers in U.S. Public Libraries, Keys to Engaging Older Adults @ Your Library, Guide to Building Support for Your Tribal Library*, and other titles. www.ala .org/ala/aboutala/offices/olos/index.cfm.

ALA Webliography of annotated links to "PR Resources and Other Relevant Links" from state library associations. Resources offered include PowerPoint Presentations, newsletter content, brochures, posters, etc. www.ala.org/ala/issuesadvocacy/advocacy/advocacy university/coalitionbuilding/resources/index.cfm.

ALA's Advocacy University, "Making Budget Presentations." It's easy to overlook the fact that the library needs a good public relationship with its board and other advisory/supervisory groups and individuals and with elected officials. This online resource provides guidance in making budget presentations (yes, the budget process is part of public relations!). www.ala.org/ala/issuesadvocacy/advocacy/ advocacyuniversity/budgetpresentation/index.cfm.

E. Learn from the examples of others. When browsing the professional literature or your favorite library-centered blog, be alert to PR activities that others have undertaken. For instance, the Public Relations and Marketing Section of ALA's LLAMA highlights its John Cotton Dana Awards winners on its web pages: www.ala.org/ala/mgrps/divs/llama/ publications/llandm/llmhome/23n3/web_exclusive/index.cfm

F. Grow a circle of colleagues, not necessarily just those in one-person libraries and not necessarily those in the same type of library, with whom you can have hallway chats, virtually and at conferences. Talk about PR activities and ideas. Learn from each other.

G. Take advantage of newer technology outlets for reaching customers. Familiarize yourself with ones that are the most popular among customers and look for ways to use them for PR. Look among volunteers and the friends group of the library for helpers to assist in using these tools. Or consider having an instructional program in the library taught by someone else, so you can be a student, too. Read this *Public Libraries Briefcase* article on "A Few Social Networking Tools Not to Miss" for an easy-to-understand look at these tools, with links: www.ala .org/ala/mgrps/divs/rusa/sections/brass/brasspubs/publibbrief/no22 winter2009.cfm.

Step 6: Wait, Is This Marketing?

So, if public relations is about relationships, where does marketing come into play? At one time, the distinction between public relations and marketing was fairly clean, especially for profit organizations. Then, marketing equated with selling, and public relations supported selling. Increasingly, the distinction has blurred even for profit organizations. For nonprofits (such as libraries), marketing and PR are very much intertwined, since building relationships is the goal. Bottom line: Don't worry overly much about the distinctions. Do take advantage of resources tagged as library marketing, since they will be helpful in your public relations program. One example is the ALA Association of College and Research Libraries' "ACRL Marketing Minute," with biweekly postings on Facebook: www .facebook.com/marketingminute.

Along the same lines, resources for advocacy are also useful in the PR program. For a variety of links offering assistance with advocacy efforts, see ALA's "Advocacy Clearinghouse," on the ALA website.

Conclusion

Public relations is about building relationships. It requires being proactive, since no one ever grew a successful relationship by simply waiting for someone else to take the initiative. However, for the solo librarian, the good news is that PR means reaching out as a regular part of all library activities, keeping current relationships active, and looking for new ones to cultivate.

CHAPTER 11

Tips for Solo Librarians
DEALING WITH PATRON PROBLEMS

Sandra O. Stubbs

Librarians functioning solo are tasked, in spite of this human resource constraint, with providing excellent customer service to expectant and often demanding patrons. They must provide facilities and services in keeping with the highest industry standards to ensure that the clientele served is kept happy. Librarians functioning alone in libraries as the single staff member or only professionally trained library staff are forced to develop unique coping strategies for handling patrons.

Customer Attitudes and Expectations

In the Caribbean experience, patron expectations and demands of academic libraries are fueled by varied factors. These include the reputation of the institution, services provided by competitors, and the economic pressure of tuition fees. Similarly, Peter Hernon and John R. Whitman[1] found that it is logical to assume that customer expectations regarding library services will be influenced by other service providers with whom they interact. Such service providers would include courier services (speed and accuracy) and bookstores (operating a café along with browsing and reading, thus combining reading and leisure). To this end, they suggest that librarians monitor other service providers to see what services exist that they should try meeting or exceeding.

In Jamaica as well as the United States, there is a prevailing environment of rising costs and reductions in government subsidies for higher education. Colleague librarians at the University of the West Indies, Mona Campus, Cheryl Kean and Faith McKoy-Johnson, accurately describe the stressful financial situation faced by some of our students. These students enter university with financial challenges, and some have to face the stress of balancing work and study. Kean and McKoy-Johnson point out that some students will even "continue their university life uncertain of how future tuition fees will be paid and daily expenses met."[2]

In this context of stress on both service provider and patron, attempts to improve the overall customer service experience for students sometimes involve pacifying impatient, intolerant, and economically anxious students. A number of students may employ the attitude that whatever tuition fees they have been made to pay should accord them all rights and services on demand. The solo librarian, therefore, has to deal both with patron problems and problem patrons. The strategies and tips that follow have been learned from customer service practice over many years and re-enforced by practitioner experience at the Western Jamaica Campus (WJC) library at the University of the West Indies (UWI).

Solo at the Western Jamaica Campus Branch Library

WJC is part of the Mona Campus. Situated in Montego Bay, Jamaica's second largest city and tourist capital, it commenced operations in 2008 with approximately 250 students. The campus has grown steadily and enrollment as of February 2011 was just under one thousand students. WJC benefits from close collaborations with faculty and staff on the Main Campus. Most WJC pioneer members of staff, including the librarian, served previously at the Mona Campus location. The WJC library began offering services in support of all campus programs at inception in August 2008, with the librarian as sole staff member in the library. The WJC library collections include print and electronic resources concentrated in the following subject areas: hospitality and tourism management, management studies, public relations and mass communication, psychology, banking and finance, management information system, law, nursing, medicine. As you can see, this solo librarian has a wide variety of subjects to serve.

Coping Strategy 1: Get Help

In the beginning, I had to rely heavily on the help of volunteers, namely colleagues in other departments who would sit in the library briefly to allow me to carry out other duties that would take me outside of the physical space of the library. In such instances, my mobile phone was always on so that I could be contacted and recalled as necessary. Among the first order of business, while setting up physical resources and awaiting the completion of others, I recruited and trained a team of student assistants in order to offer services from 9 a.m. to 9 p.m. daily. I was able to assemble an adequate team of paid student assistants because UWI, Mona has a culture of creating opportunities where possible for students to earn income while studying.

However, while student help has proved extremely valuable, at times of assignments and exams their help becomes unreliable. During these times in the semester, the library's student assistants have the same academic pressures as the patrons they serve. Therefore it is critical for the assistants to learn to separate their stress from their job at the library. Another source of help possible for solo librarians in academic libraries is students doing fieldwork or an internship. Some interns work free of cost. Others are given a stipend or paid competitive rates depending on the financial resources of the host institution. Whoever helps in the library, all staff members must be trained in techniques for handling difficult patrons and they must understand that, despite the fact that they are getting paid very little or nothing at all, they are there to provide a service.

Coping Strategy 2: Help Students to Help Themselves and Encourage Peer Tutoring

Care is taken at the WJC library to mirror the services offered on the Main Campus. This is necessary to ensure that university resources are equally available to all students. This means, for example, that all electronic resources, including virtual reference services and subscription databases, are accessible to users in both locations simultaneously. Cataloging and other technical services are done centrally at the main library at Mona. The WJC library services offered include: circulation of prescribed and recommended readings, orientation tours, bibliographic instruction, Internet access and training, reference assistance, online public access catalog, databases, e-books, electronic journals, and virtual reference. For a small fee the WJC library offers the following reprographic services: photocopying, printing, laminating, spiral binding, and scanning. Student assistants have been invaluable in assisting with reprographic services because as assistants they learn the technology and the resources, but as students, they experience needing to use the services, too. They understand firsthand what it's like to lose their money at the photocopier or when they have trouble opening an e-book, which makes them empathetic to other patrons in the same situation. Rely upon your students for this reason: they know instinctively how to handle their peers' frustrations and emotions.

Peer tutoring has proven to be extremely valuable in helping to reach a larger number of students. This tutoring assists them to function independently in the use of electronic library resources. Hernon and Whitman[3] speak to the fact that some customers prefer to help themselves and "may not request or require assistance preferring to find information on their own or with help from their peers." However, the quality of the self-service experience needs to be taken into account and both preliminary training and troubleshooting services should be made available to mitigate patron problems. Training is of paramount importance for student assistants because they are the library's peer tutors. If the assistants know the ins and outs of the service, they can help solve patrons' problems before they arise.

OTHER SELF-HELP TECHNIQUES TO AVOID PROBLEMS

- Lecturers at WJC have been encouraged to utilize as many e-books and electronic sources as often as possible so that students can access more course information remotely rather than be forced to come into the library to compete for heavily used print textbooks.
- Book drops that are cleared several times daily are provided away from the library to facilitate students in the ease of return of materials borrowed. Book drops are cleared at regular intervals, which is preferable to having students crowd the circulation desk to return items to the library staff.
- Self-issue systems such as that provided for by the UWI library's integrated system software also represent useful self-help customer service. Students are able to loan, renew, and return items independently.

- Photocopies can be done by patrons themselves using prepurchased vendor cards. These are among the time-saving devices that come in handy for solo librarians. Also helpful is software that allows students to prepay and manage their own print accounts. At the UWI library self-copies cost less than those done by library staff.
- Online database training and OPAC tutorial accessible via the library's web pages are provided as another self-help service to patrons.

Students have the habit of coming into the library to ask if a book is available. They are then gently reminded or shown that the library's OPAC is available on the Internet and that circulation information regarding how many copies of a book are owned by the library is displayed there. Before visiting the library in person, patrons are encouraged to ascertain whether an item is on the shelf or already borrowed. If out on loan, the expected due date is shown. Information such as fines owed can also be checked on the OPAC so that students come into the library with this information. Students are blocked from borrowing if fines exceed an established limit. When students are taught how to help themselves, they require less help from the solo librarian. However, each of these self-help methods is also a breeding ground for disgruntled patrons who still expect library staff to do everything for them and who demand waivers for fines they've accrued. Gently helping these patrons and firm yet sympathetic advice will turn these sorts of problem patrons into better, more self-sufficient patrons in the future.

Coping Strategy 3: Utilize Client Feedback Systems

It is important to acknowledge all feedback received, whether written or verbal. Complaints should be treated as valuable feedback. Often these point to areas that need improvement or clarification. This means taking all problems reported and suggestions given seriously. The worst response from the library is to ignore or make excuses and have an attitude that says, "We have always done this and will not change." Be dynamic. Be flexible. Continuous improvement will keep the library and parent institution on the cutting edge. If a requested service is not provided, serious consideration should be given to exploring the viability of the suggestion. Oftentimes what a patron says in anger can be found in the unspoken thoughts of many more patrons who are too shy to come forward with complaints or questions.

At the WJC library, both online feedback as well as a suggestion box are utilized. A specially designed form is placed beside the suggestion box and the library's response is written beneath each comment or suggestion. The form is then displayed on the library's notice board. Care is taken to protect the identity of the person providing feedback. Where optional contact details are provided by the patron, they will also receive a personal response via the contact provided. It is useful to maintain a database of suggestions and responses along with action(s) taken as concerns/suggestions may be repeated by other patrons at a later date. Follow-up is critical. We have to do what we have promised. I have found that it is better to under-promise and over-deliver than to promise more than can be reasonably accomplished in good time.

DEALING WITH PROBLEM PATRONS IN PERSON

Some students display impatience, both with perceived institutional shortcomings and with the behavior of other students. Such militant students can prove to be useful allies to the solo librarian. For example, students who abuse library resources and choose to pay fines rather than return library materials on time, especially at critical junctures such as when assignments are due and exams imminent, have been known to earn the ire not only of library staff but especially of their offended peers as well. Such assertive students will confront their colleagues where possible and will also storm the library to report on selfish practices and insist that something be done about it forthwith. Peers who confront peers works more effectively than overdue reminders generated from the library. Students are very quick to learn that the library protects the privacy of patrons and will not give out names of people who have checked books out, but students who need certain texts are often correct that a classmate is the selfish culprit. Classroom announcements and intermediary professors are most helpful during these times, both to the students and to the library, which, most of all, wants items to be accounted for.

Coping Strategy 4: Face Problem Patrons and Plug Information or Resource Gaps

I recently had the experience of a student coming into the library and complaining long and hard, sustained and loudly that she would not pay her outstanding fees until an outstanding grade was posted. She was fully incensed as she needed to check her examination results online and e-mail an assignment but the computers in the nearby computer lab were functioning slowly and she needed to hurry. Unfortunately, the first library computer she attempted to use returned a network error and she "lost it."

TIPS FOR DEALING WITH ANGRY PATRONS

- Firstly, dealing with angry patrons such as the girl mentioned above involves staying calm oneself and allowing the patron to vent without interruption. To interrupt may cause them to start all over again or harden their stance.
- Secondly, empathy is important. The patron is upset, emotions are involved, a solution is needed. To be indifferent, offer an excuse, or shift the blame will not ameliorate the situation.
- Acknowledging the problem, apologizing, and taking full responsibility for assisting the client in finding a solution is the most useful response. While it is true that both the causes and solutions may be outside of the scope of the library, my personal maxim is that the patron at the end of the interaction should leave feeling helped.
- Become an ally by committing to help the patron find a solution in the shortest possible time. It is OK to refer to someone else who may be better able to assist, but be sure to pass on the necessary information regarding the nature of the problem, and not force or allow the patron to have to tell his or her story again as this may reignite anger.

In the case of our angry student mentioned above, I was able to listen and empathize and acknowledge that she had a problem and that I understood why she would be so angry. After a few unsuccessful attempts at helping her to log on to a couple library computers (I suspected that she had forgotten her password and needed to have it reset), I allowed her to use the staff computer at the reference desk where I was seated and already logged on. Thankfully, that computer was not one affected by the temporary network problem on which the systems personnel were already working remotely. Thankfully also, the library was not very busy at that time. However, I had to keep answering her in softer tones for a while before she eventually lowered her voice. In the case where the library is crowded or the librarian is busy assisting other customers, it may be tempting to drop everything to try and placate an angry patron who noisily interrupts. However, it is useful to maintain a first-come-first-served policy. Importantly, all clients should be acknowledged even if one is only able to stop briefly and ask if they are able to wait or return at a more convenient time.

- Do something unexpected. Before the patron described above left, I was able to point out some alternate resources that would help with her assignment. A textbook she wanted was also already out on loan, thus adding to her frustrations. By the time she left the library, she was mostly pacified, with her anger shifting somewhat to the state of tertiary education worldwide. The day following the outburst, she returned to the library to return material borrowed on overnight loan. This time she was calm and courteous and prepared to display reasonable behavior.

ABUSIVE CUSTOMERS

Despite our best efforts, some students may display abusive antisocial behavior that borders on or is threatening. Some persons disagree with the maxim that the customer is always right, and it is a fact that, in libraries, we sometimes have to deal with the customer who has done wrong. Library services are "free" for the most part but only on a trust basis; the library trusts patrons to return materials when they are due. Patrons who ignore this trust accepted the possibility of incurred costs when they entered into the agreement regarding the loaning of an item. Limits have to be maintained with abusive patrons who disregard or conveniently forget about the agreement. The librarian has to remain respectful, as customers may not always be right but they are customers and are entitled to service. However, sanctions may have to be applied when the desired effect is not met. See table 11.1 for more ideas on handling patron problems.

Table 11.1. Other Patron Problems and Useful Solutions

Reported Problem	Solutions Tried	Comments
Access and technology issues such as inability to sign onto computers, slow connections, or pages timing out before loading	Scan computers regularly and use up-to-date virus protection programs on machines. Report problems in a timely manner to the Information Technology Department. Follow up until there is a resolution.	
Copyright issues such as patrons wanting to copy more than the allowed portion of a work as prescribed by photocopy license.	Use of copyright forms to be filled in and signed by patrons. Display posters and other relevant information regarding copyright license.	Useful especially with a rush of persons wanting to copy during class breaks. Some may have to be asked to return to collect requests.
Dealing with patron requests from outside the established clientele.	Accommodate as possible. Follow institutional policy. Make appointment to return if librarian is busy.	
Students requesting help with assignments such as checking references against citation styles.	Make appointment to return if librarian is busy.	
More space needed. Library seats all taken.	Laptop loans for student to work away from library have helped with space problems.	
Need to use library facilities for longer periods during exam times.	For two weeks vary library opening hours to cover critical periods. Collect statistics on library usage to support increased expenditure for additional student help where necessary.	

Conclusion

Anticipating and preventing patron challenges will save the solo librarian's time and allow for improved customer service. The maxim "attitude is everything" is very important when dealing with patrons. While the attitude of some patrons may be less than desirable, the solo librarian cannot match them in this regard. Professionalism, coupled with a genuine desire to have a positive outcome at the end of the interaction, is an important service response.

The Registry of UWI, Mona has made the University's Customer Service Charter[4] available to all staff. This describes UWI's emphasis on "the provision of an excellent teaching, learning and research environment, a vibrant student body and a highly motivated staff." It itemizes patterns of expected behavior in such areas as responsiveness, communication (oral and nonverbal), and attitudes. Institutional support for ensuring excellent customer service practices will assist the efforts of the solo librarian in dealing with patron problems and problem patrons and should be sought and encouraged.

Notes

1. Peter Hernon and John R. Whitman, *Delivering Satisfaction and Service Quality* (Chicago: ALA, 2001), 22.

2. Cheryl Kean and Faith McKoy-Johnson, "Patron Aggression in the Academic Library," *New Library World* 110 no. 7/8 (2009): 375.

3. Hernon and Whitman, *Delivering Satisfaction and Service Quality*, 2.

4. Registry, University of the West Indies, "Customer Service Charter and Standards for the University of the West Indies, Mona," 2008.

Part IV

PROFESSIONAL DEVELOPMENT

CHAPTER 12

Continuing Professional Development

Eva Hornung

Continuing professional development (CPD) is one of the buzzwords of our time. Many professions are implementing voluntary or mandatory schemes, which offer official recognition of CPD undertaken. The field of Library and Information Science (LIS) is no different. Larger libraries often actively encourage their staff to participate in professional development and even dedicate some of their resources toward it. As a one-person librarian (OPL), however, you might feel that you are missing out on some of these opportunities. So what can you do? Here are some tips that I gathered through a study on OPLs and CPD that I am currently undertaking, but also some general advice on what worked for me as a solo librarian. You might come up with some more ideas yourself, but perhaps some of these suggestions are new and stimulating for you.

What Is CPD?

There are probably as many different opinions on what constitutes CPD as there are self-styled CPD "gurus" out there. And it is all very confusing. It basically comprises all activities, be they formal (which usually refers to an organized event which carries some official recognition, such as a certificate of attendance), nonformal (organized, but no official acknowledgment), or informal (everything else) that helps you with your development. They usually take place within a professional context, but can also relate to personal learning. Essentially, "continuing professional development is a process of lifelong learning in practice."[1]

Basically everything you do counts toward CPD. Not many other professions are as exposed to it as librarians are, so it should not become a burden to any of us. Accountability, however, dictates that we need to take an organized approach to show that we can keep up with other professions. We all can think of training courses we would like to attend, so this article will give you some pointers toward what else is out there. How much you can participate in all of this, however, depends on your personal circumstances. In particular your line manager, who most likely is not an LIS professional, will determine the parameters in which you can operate.

How to Make a Case to Your (Indifferent) Management

Well, if your management is only indifferent, you could be one of the lucky ones. When I interviewed solo librarians for my study, I was told about situations where people were downright hostile toward the idea of their OPL pursuing CPD during their working hours! But that is on the extreme side of things. Usually managers are receptive to CPD that is linked to the organizational goals, so make good use of that fact. It may be training offered in-house, people shadowing, learning on the job, working on a committee, or courses relating to the subject area you are working in.

One piece of advice I received is to keep a record of achievements and put together a portfolio. Often we do great things but forget about them as soon as they are accomplished. I have a box under my desk where I throw in certificates of attendance, print-outs of e-mails from happy customers, a copy of a report the library was involved in, a new brochure I developed, and so on. Consider writing a personal development plan to keep track of where you are and where you want to go by reflecting on what you have learned so far. Where are the gaps? How can you measure what you have learned? What are the short-term and long-term goals? This exercise allows you then to argue for support from management. Outline how certain CPD activities could improve your performance and therefore save the organization money in the long term. Your portfolio will help you make a case. For ideas on what it could look like, check out CILIP's website (see "Resources").

How to Keep Up with the Information Explosion

A. WITH THE SUBJECT AREA YOUR ORGANIZATION IS IN

The first port of call for many OPLs with regard to everyday queries is probably the Internet. Job experience is a vital part of a solo librarian's CPD. The good news is that a lot of CPD can be done for free and without spending any extra time on it. A word of warning: a lot of the information posted online is not peer-reviewed, so take it with a pinch of salt. This is only a flavor. Of course there are many more websites and services.

Good resources include:

- YouTube for videos that show you how to do something
- SlideShare for PowerPoint presentations and documents
- Wikipedia for a specific term, topic, or person
- BUBL for Internet resources in academic subject areas

If you are more interested in finding published articles, try the Directory of Open Access Journals for most subject areas. It gives you full access to free periodicals, all of which incorporate some sort of quality control.

Many organizations as well as universities offer online courses for information professionals. Check the professional association in your state or country to see what they offer. You might be able to get a discount if you are a member.

B. WITH PROFESSIONAL MATTERS

Other than on-the-job learning, there are a couple of other avenues you could follow. If you have not already done so, consider joining an LIS professional association. This is money well invested. They not only provide training courses and conferences, but also publications and often access to databases, such as Library and Information Science Abstracts (LISA). And they are great for moral support and networking. Apart from gaining LIS-specific knowledge, you also get career advice and hear about vacancies, policy developments, and international news.

Things you could do:

- Join a professional association.
  - o Volunteer to serve on a committee.
  - o Read their magazines and e-bulletins.
  - o Try to make it to at least one conference or seminar a year.
  - o Check out the regional branches and special interest groups.
  - o Subscribe to their mailing list for updates on what is happening in the world of LIS.
- Join your local public library.
  - o Everything you read is CPD and they often have LIS books!
  - o Take advantage of a great opportunity to network with colleagues in a different library. Perhaps you could work together on a project.
  - o You might get ideas for your own library, e.g., on successful displays.
- Check out local providers who offer adult education classes.
- Visit other libraries for exchanging ideas and shadowing colleagues.
- Start up your own group of like-minded OPLs in your area.
- Go back to college.
  - o You might be interested in a part-time or online degree to further your academic qualifications: for a list of LIS universities worldwide, see the resource section at the end of the chapter.

How to Keep Up-to-Date in a Sustainable Way

In our profession there is a need to keep a constant overview, not only of our field but also of the subject area of our expertise. Unfortunately, spending time away from the library is not really feasible for most OPLs and presents a huge barrier. Here are some things you can do to keep up-to-date from the comfort of your own armchair (and desktop).

Subscribe for free to:

1. RSS feeds: Many websites and blogs sport this little orange symbol. When you click on it you will see a website full of HTML code. Copy the address line with a right click of your mouse, scroll down to "copy," and insert it into your RSS reader. There are many different readers

out there (see "Resources"). I use Google Reader and find it very easy to navigate.

2. Journal e-alerts: Many print and electronic serials publish their table of contents for free. This helps you keep up with the latest research and practical developments in LIS and other subject areas. If you do not know what you should be reading, log onto the online catalog of a university that runs an LIS department and scroll through the titles that they hold. You might also be able to negotiate access to the full text of these periodicals—the alumni association of your own alma mater might also have special arrangements for former students.

3. E-mailing lists: Read about and participate in the discussions in the field. Also, there are probably many lists in your respective subject area (e.g., health sciences, finance, and law). You can browse JISCMAIL (see below) for ideas. You not only get news, but can also post queries to thousands of experts. This can range from getting help with a specific piece of information you need to more general feedback on a new project you are planning. Being part of a networked community of practitioners helps give you perspective during tough times, which is a great way of keeping your sanity!

4. Search alerts: Many search engines allow you to set up alerts. You can define the kind of information you are interested in by saving keywords and therefore target all relevant information being published.

Different Learning Styles, Different Ways of Doing CPD

All of the recommendations above are quite broad without taking into account your own specific circumstances. Some might not suit you at all because you are naturally drawn to one method only. This leads us to questions of when and how you learn. Are you the type who thinks things out before they react? Or someone who needs a new challenge all the time? Do you prefer evenings or mornings for learning activities? Do you get more out of formal training sessions or are you happier when trying out something by yourself?

Peter Honey and Alan Mumford[2] identified different ways of learning for different types of learners:

- Activists are people who enjoy new experiences and are open-mined, but are easily bored when it comes to implementation. They enjoy working with others and use brainstorming techniques.
- Reflectors, on the other hand, like to consider a problem from different angles before acting. They thoroughly collect and analyze data and tend to take a back seat in discussions. They have the bigger picture in mind.
- Theorists are stimulated by rational and logical thinking. They love complex and challenging problems where they can analyze, probe, and develop theories. They are not comfortable with ambiguity.
- Pragmatists need a connection between their job and the learning activity. They are attracted to new techniques and applications once they are of a practical nature. Long-winded discussions are not for them.

Each type responds to distinct ways of doing CPD. According to Honey and Mumford[3] activists might seek out new opportunities where they have to think on their feet to solve a problem and where they can bounce ideas off other people. Chairing meetings and role-playing exercises are some examples. In contrast, the reflector would prefer a more structured learning experience where they are not put under pressure. Observing others, watching a film, or compiling research reports suits them. A theorist will also opt for clear guidelines and structured situations, but are more drawn toward question-and-answer sessions or tutorials where they are intellectually challenged by other people. The pragmatist on the other hand wants to be shown how to do things by and get feedback from an expert. Models and techniques must be based on real life and include examples.

People usually display traits of several of these categories, but there is often a strong tendency toward one or two of them. If you are unsure about which type you are and would like to test yourself, check out Honey and Mumford's books (see "Resources"). Depending on what type of learner you are, here are some thoughts on what might work for you, keeping in mind that your personal preferences and work-related factors need to be considered. Sometimes we need to think outside the box and surprise ourselves!

You could branch out by writing for publication, either in the field or outside. Many LIS journals, for example, regularly announce call for papers. If the prospect of writing a full paper frightens you, why not start with a book review or conference report? It would give you a flavor of what is involved and the feedback you get from the editors will help you fine-tune your skills.

Along the same line would be presenting at a conference. Have you undertaken a project that you are particularly proud of? Most OPLs could talk forever about their libraries, so just put it on paper. A poster session might suit you better. The professional associations are again a good source of information on upcoming conferences and seminars. Involvement with in-house presentations and organizational reports could prepare you before you advance to a more international audience. Furthermore, no matter what area your organization is operating in, chances are that there are trade fairs or exhibitions that you could attend either as a visitor or as a presenter.

Like it or not, OPLs are not only librarians, but also teachers and trainers of other staff, volunteers, or work experience students. Whether we give our customer one-to-one tuition or group sessions in information literacy, there are plenty of CPD opportunities. They could take the shape of a formal presentation or a more informal, hands-on get-together. Both ways are valid and you might switch between them depending on the occasion. Ironically, most of us are CPD providers to other people, but we tend to neglect our own needs.

Attending and actively participating in meetings is another good example of practical CPD. You learn about the internal workings of your organization and can acquire new competencies, such as preparing agendas, writing minutes, and chairing a group of people. Your listening and debating skills will also improve! Other committees you belong to, whether they are part of a club you belong to or a professional association, will provide you with further chances.

At some stage in your career, your work experience will become a valuable resource to others. Being a mentor to other LIS professionals or other members of staff is yet another CPD method. If you cannot participate in face-to-face meetings with your mentee, use online communication channels, such as e-mail or a discussion group. This is particularly effective when you need to overcome distance. You also do not need to close the library for that.

If you are more adventurous, consider a job exchange or visiting libraries in other countries. Why not combine that with a holiday abroad? A lot of professional associations run exchange programs and sometimes they even help with the costs involved. In some schemes you will have to write a report upon your return or accept a professional from another part of the world to be a guest at your library in return.

In conclusion, it can be said that there are plenty of opportunities for CPD for OPLs. You do not need a lot of money or time to pursue it, just an open, curious mind. Events that are happening outside your workplace offer scope for additional CPD. You might be a member of a book club or attend readings in the evening. Or maybe you like writing a personal journal and could extend that to a professional diary reflecting on your work? Learning new languages or new software programs in your spare time could lead to new work practices. They will definitely extend your horizon. Your hobbies are part of your personal development and your lifelong learning journey.

As an OPL, you are best positioned to plan and evaluate your own CPD demands. There are no other LIS professionals in the vicinity whom you could benchmark yourself against, which can be both a challenge and an advantage. Your management will have to trust your judgment, so there is an obligation on you to follow best practice. Having a professional development plan, which outlines current work practices, critically assesses areas for improvement, and offers strategies for getting there, is a first step. It will show your organization that you are a professional who is committed to CPD and it might even influence your prospects of a financial reward if you are partaking in an appraisal system.

Should there be no demand by your employer to engage in CPD, do it for yourself and for the good of your information service. It will make your life easier when you are performing your everyday duties. Perhaps more importantly, it will also give you an edge should you apply for another job. The topic of CPD nearly always comes up at interviews, so make sure you can demonstrate that you have been an active participant in professional development. Hopefully this article will help you identify some means of CPD that you can pursue without too much effort. A library is the best possible environment for learning, which makes working in one all the more valuable. By helping other people we are exposed to new concepts and information on a daily basis, so learning should come naturally to us. After all, as they say, it is impossible to "not learn"!

Resources

FOR WRITING YOUR PORTFOLIO

Chartered Institute of Library and Information Professionals (CILIP): www.cilip
.org.uk/jobs-careers/qualifications/cilip-qualifications/chartership/pages/charter
shipforms.aspx.

FURTHER READING

Brine, Alan. *Continuing Professional Development: A Guide for Information Profes-sionals*. Oxford: Chandos Publishing, 2005.
Bryant, Sue Lacey. *Personal Professional Development and the Solo Librarian*. Lon-don: Library Association Publishing, Library Training Guides, 1995.
Honey, Peter, and Alan Mumford. *The Manual of Learning Styles*, 3rd edition. Maidenhead: Peter Honey, 1992.
———. *Using Your Learning Styles*, 3rd edition. Maidenhead: Peter Honey, 1995.
Siess, Judith. *The Visible Librarian: Asserting Your Value through Marketing and Advocacy*. Chicago: ALA Editions, 2003.
———. *The New OPL Sourcebook: A Guide for Solo and Small Libraries*. Medford, N.J.: Information Today, 2006.

EXAMPLES OF FREE RSS READERS

Feedreader: www.feedreader.com/
Google Reader: www.google.com/reader
RssReader: www.rssreader.com/

DIRECTORIES

Directory of Open Access Journals: www.doaj.org/
JISCMAIL (UK based): www.jiscmail.ac.uk/

INTERNET RESOURCES

BUBL: www.bubl.ac.uk/
SlideShare: www.slideshare.net

Wikipedia: www.wikipedia.org
YouTube: www.youtube.com

LIS SCHOOLS WORLDWIDE

Tom Wilson's World List: informationr.net/wl/

Notes

1. Cathy Peck, Martha McCall, Belinda MacLaren, and Tai Rotem, "Continuing Medical Education and Continuing Professional Development: International Comparisons," *British Medical Journal* 320 (2000): 432.

2. Peter Honey and Alan Mumford, *The Manual of Learning Styles*, 3rd edition (Maidenhead: Peter Honey, 1992), 5–6.

3. Peter Honey and Alan Mumford, *Using Your Learning Styles*, 3rd edition (Maidenhead: Peter Honey, 1995), 9–13.

CHAPTER 13

Professional Growth for the Solo Librarian

Kimberly Mitchell

Professional growth: for no other type of information professional is this activity more vital than for the solo librarian. Your day is filled with everything from strategic planning to shelving. You are everything from captain of the ship to navigator to crew. And who sometimes doesn't feel like a galley slave when clearing out paper jams from the photocopier? With so many roles to fill, professional growth is vital to your library, your career path, and even your mental health.

Despite all this, for no other type of information professional is professional growth so elusive and difficult to pursue. It may feel like you can barely keep up with the urgent, let alone set aside time for continuing education, networking, or professional reading. In addition to lack of time, there is the isolation associated with being a solo librarian. Opportunities for informal learning and the exchange of ideas that daily contact with colleagues engenders are not at your fingertips.

The solo librarian is firmly in the captain's seat when it comes to keeping current with the profession. Unless your particular career path requires CE credits and other activities for certification, professional growth involves self-directed and self-motivated learning. Opportunities are difficult to seize, whether for time, budgeting, or staffing issues. In an era of cutbacks, when many libraries are being closed, how do you justify the cost and time associated with professional growth opportunities? And when you must prove daily your value to your organization, how do you justify leaving the helm to attend events?

Fortunately, new methods of learning and networking abound. This chapter will explore these opportunities, as well as discuss how to pursue traditional professional development options when you are alone at the helm. Whether you are just out of graduate school or a seasoned professional, some of this material will be new—and some of this material certainly will be familiar to you. As careers, tools, and people change, it is worth revisiting professional growth opportunities that perhaps were previously dismissed.

Learn

Continuing education doesn't just mean taking a workshop at a professional conference anymore. Thanks to breakthroughs in information technology and social media, formal and informal learning now takes place in many forms and venues. Today, your professional horizons can expand without ever leaving your desk.

FROM A DISTANCE

Learning is a kind of natural food for the mind.

—Cicero

Designed for students who are not physically on site with the instructor, distance education takes place over the Internet. Its hallmarks are convenience and adaptability, making it an increasingly popular and accepted form of learning in today's wired world. Many students obtain their degrees entirely online, including the master's in library science, and continuing education opportunities range from semester-long full-credit courses to two-hour training sessions. A survey of a popular graduate school's CE catalog reveals classes in archives, career management, school librarianship, information organization, library management, search techniques, and information literacy. Class lengths range from four-week courses to half-day workshops. With such rich variety, you can find just about anything to accommodate your interest and schedule.

MIX AN APPLET, COOKIES, MOODLE, AND STIR

Sound like a recipe for disaster? Lots of jargon is thrown about when the topic is distance education. With so many new tools for teaching and learning—and the possibilities ever expanding—it may seem the vocabulary associated with online learning requires its own tutorial. Don't be intimidated. Familiarity with neither the terminology nor technology is a requirement to take a class. Online learning tools are easy to access and use, and sometimes as familiar as e-mail.

Let's Talk Distance Ed.

Many courses are taught within an online learning management system (LMS) called Moodle, which is freely accessible on the Internet. An LMS is a collection of integrated tools that allow you to participate in online distance education. For a distance learning vocabulary crib sheet, see the eLearner's Glossary at www.elearners.com/guide/faq-glossary/glossary/.

Distance education occurs in one of two environments—synchronous or asynchronous—or in a blend of the two.

WE'RE ALL IN THIS TOGETHER

In synchronous distance education the teaching happens in real time via two-way communication. Synchronous formats include conference calls, videoconferencing (think Skype), live streaming video, and instant message or online chat. The live participation builds a sense of community and encourages the exchange of ideas. Strictly synchronous education usually comes in the form of web-based training—short workshops and training sessions that last only a few hours.

TIME TO REFLECT

In asynchronous distance learning participants are not necessarily online at the same time. Asynchronous CE is highly flexible, allowing you to log in and do the work when most convenient for you. Because real-time participation is not expected, asynchronous distance education supports a more reflective learning style and is accommodating of busy schedules. Examples of asynchronous learning tools include on-demand streaming, listservs and discussion forums, personal blogs, and podcasts.

Many online CE classes and workshops blend the synchronous and asynchronous styles, incorporating features of each and supporting varying learning styles. In a blended course, for instance, the student will do an online reading assignment, attend a live streaming lecture, post reflections about the reading on a personal blog, then participate in a real-time chat with other students about the ideas presented in the lecture.

Which style is right for you? Determine what you want to learn and how much time you have to devote. A half-day synchronous workshop is a good fit if you wish to update established skills or would like an introduction to an emerging trend in the field. If you wish to study a larger topic or acquire a skill set entirely new to you, the deeper, more reflective learning of a longer course with asynchronous elements may better meet your needs.

HOW TO FIND DISTANCE EDUCATION OPPORTUNITIES

- Many graduate schools of library and information science offer affordable, convenient online courses and workshops.
- Check with your professional library associations, library consortia, or other local library groups.
- Be alert to free or nominal-cost training and education opportunities from product vendors.

Create Your Own Wiki

A wiki is a communal spot on the web where people contribute and share content around a particular topic. With a wiki, you can build a network of colleagues and share ideas in an informal setting. Can't find a wiki that meets your needs? Start your own using Google Sites, a free service that allows you to create your own wiki in minutes.

INTRA-ORGANIZATION OPPORTUNITIES

Human resource departments are interested in keeping their employees' knowledge and skills current. Check with your organization's department to see if they offer general workshops. You might be able to enhance your computer skills or refine your public speaking techniques.

Human resources departments also offer workshops specific to the field in which you are working. If you work at a hospital library, for instance, you will likely have a medical terminology course available to you. If you are in a school library, you might be able to take workshops in child psychology or education. No matter what the topic, acquiring additional knowledge about the field you serve will enhance your searching skills and help you better know your constituency.

Nonprofits are sometimes awarded funds from major philanthropies, such as the Hearst Foundation, for employees to pursue continuing education. If you work for a nonprofit organization, check with your human resources department to see if there is a separate endowed budget for these scholarship opportunities.

RESOURCES

- Library webinars: neflin2.blogspot.com/. This site lists free webinars with library-related content. Note that events sponsored by local library cooperatives are not listed here.
- Simmons Graduate School of Library and Information Science continuing education catalog: www.simmons.edu/gslis/careers/continuing-education/workshops/.
- University of Wisconsin–Madison School of Library and Information Studies continuing education catalog: www.slis.wisc.edu/continueed.htm
- Library wikis: librarywikis.pbworks.com/w/page/17064483/Collaboration-between-Libraries. Directory of library-related wikis.
- Podcasts for librarians: www.jenkinslaw.org/researchlinks/index.php?rl=307. Directory of library-related podcasts. Also check iTunes University.

Connect

When you are genuinely interested in one thing, it will always lead to something else.

—Eleanor Roosevelt

Learning isn't confined to formal classes and workshops. Lifelong learning depends on the many informal learning opportunities that we encounter every day. Interacting with colleagues can be a fun and enriching way to keep current on your knowledge and skills.

Networking can take place in person or online. Traditional networking happens face to face, at events like conferences and workshops, but social media now makes networking on your computer easy and fun.

TWITTER

You might be surprised by who is sending out those short, timely messages known as tweets: *Library Journal*, the New York Public Library, and Google Books to name a few. If sending out tweets isn't your style, don't worry—you don't need to tweet to be on Twitter. Think of this service as your very own P.O. box to receive daily dispatches from colleagues and well-known personalities like Margaret Atwood.

Setting up a Twitter account is as easy as providing an e-mail address, choosing a user name, and selecting some people to follow. Their tweets will automatically populate your Twitter page and you can scroll down to view.

People on Twitter make use of the hashtag to label the topic of their tweet. Hashtags have the "hash" or "pound" symbol (#) preceding the tag. For example, #libraries. The hashtag is hyperlinked, bringing you to other recent tweets using that same tag. It you do decide to start tweeting, don't forget to add your own meta-data, so others can easily locate your tweet by topic.

Twitter Tips

Don't know who to follow? Get started by browsing the Books section. Search for people you know and professional associations you are involved in. Look for the "Follow Me" icon on websites or blogs you visit. Or search the online directory, Just Tweet It, for librarians or people in the field you serve. You'll be surprised how quickly your list will grow.

FACEBOOK

Many librarians and libraries are now on Facebook and use it to network. The social media outlet is an easy way to build and maintain relationships with colleagues you meet at workshops, conferences, and other professional gatherings. If you feel uncomfortable sharing those New Year's Eve photos with your colleagues, create a separate list of these Facebook friends and limit their access to your content by refining your privacy settings.

BLOGS AND LISTSERVS

Reading and commenting on blogs written by librarians or others who write on a topic of interest is a good way to keep up on your knowledge and build contacts. If you don't already have blogs that you regularly follow, find some using Google Blog Search. Many librarians blog these days.

Keeping up on websites and blogs of interest can be overwhelming, which is why many people choose not to use these tools. If this is a barrier to you, consider setting up an RSS reader and have the information come to you. RSS readers are free and aggregate new content from your chosen sites on one personalized page. Popular RSS readers are Google Reader, NewzCrawler, and Feed Demon. Be your own information curator, and don't be afraid to weed. It will be easier to absorb the content you are interested in if you eliminate what isn't useful.

Joining in or even lurking on professional listservs is another easy way to keep up with the profession and the issues of the day. If you can't keep up with a barrage of e-mails delivered to your inbox, subscribe to a digest version. Print it out for your lunch or commute time. Or, if you have a mobile device, such as a smartphone or iPad, read the digest online when you have a spare few minutes.

CONFERENCES

Conferences are the flagship traditional professional growth event. They are one-stop shopping for networking, continuing education, and other learning opportunities, such as lectures, poster presentations, and panels.

However, it is not always feasible for the solo librarian to attend a conference. Issues of costs and coverage may make attendance prohibitive. A good way to build a case for conference attendance is to make an appearance on a panel or present a poster at the event. Your participation generates good PR for your institution and may make your attendance worth the investment for your organization. Look for announcements for these opportunities on professional listservs or the event's website. Just be sure to secure your official participation well in advance of the event date in order to receive your organization's buy-in.

If there are simply no resources in your budget for conference attendance, there may be a scholarship or grant to support you. Watch for opportunities from your professional association, a vendor, or even the event itself. These funding opportunities are often reserved for newer members of the profession, first-time attendees, or those who are presenting a poster or paper.

Sometimes you just can't make the case for leaving the building. The good news is that many conferences are going virtual. Harnessing the same synchronous technologies used in distance learning, these conferences are becoming more popular as travel budgets decrease. Virtual conference announcements appear in listservs and professional journals or through your professional association.

If you cannot attend a national conference, look for nearby events sponsored by local chapters of national associations. Or look for regional consortium events. Joining the planning committee for these events is another opportunity to connect with colleagues and ensures that the event is one you can actually attend!

RESOURCES

- Library-related conferences: library2.usask.ca/~dworacze/CONF.HTM. A running list of library conferences, including date and location, with events listed several years out.
- Just Tweet It—librarians: justtweetit.com/education/librarians/. A directory of librarians on Twitter.
- Top RSS readers: email.about.com/od/rssreaderswin/tp/top_rss _windows.htm.
- CataList: www.lsoft.com/catalist.html. A catalog of professional listservs.

Write

The Possible's slow fuse is lit / By the Imagination.

—Emily Dickinson

Writing is an excellent way to learn new things while serving your profession at the same time. There are many venues for your writing, from refereed professional journals to self-publishing on the Internet.

PROFESSIONAL JOURNALS

Publishing in professional journals doesn't always mean reporting the results of scholarly research. If you don't have time, interest, or expertise for the experimental, outcomes-based research you read in professional publications, take heart. Journals are always in need of columnists and reviewers. A column piece might be an opinion essay, a report of an event you attended, or a book review. If you like to read, look in to becoming a regular book reviewer for a journal. These are great ways to break into publishing, get your name out there, and forge new professional connections. *Writing and Publishing: The Librarian's Handbook* explores these and many more opportunities for professional writing.

BLOGS

The self-imposed deadline in blogging is an excellent motivator to explore new things. Setting up a blog is easy and free with services like Blogger, Wordpress, or Blogspot. Just be sure to include a disclaimer that your expressed opinions do not necessarily reflect those of your employer. What might you write about? Start a running list of topics that interest you—new trends in the field, a strongly held opinion, a personal reflection about the profession. Or arrange to interview a colleague. By keeping your list current, you'll never be short on ideas. Be sure to set a writing schedule and stick to it. Blogs that attract regular readership publish new content several times a week. Visit some established blogs to get a sense of the tone and content you might want to use for your own writing.

Whether you garner a readership of five hundred, fifty, or even five people, remember that the main point of your blog is to give yourself a venue to learn and grow.

EDITORIAL BOARDS

If you like to edit and are familiar with research methods, serving on editorial boards is another way to learn more about your profession and establish contacts. An editorial board term limit may run for two to three years, and your commitment may be to give feedback on several papers per year. Your feedback will include notes on content and style. Editorial board members are also asked to encourage writers to submit articles to the journal, which presents you with more opportunities to make contacts and keep up on the latest trends in librarianship.

RESOURCES

- A Library Writer's Blog: librarywriting.blogspot.com/. A resource to help identify publishing and presenting opportunities in library and information science.
- Academic Writing Library Blog: academicwritinglibrarian.blogspot .com/. Publicizes calls for papers and posters.
- Carol Smallwood, ed., *Writing and Publishing: The Librarian's Handbook* (Chicago: American Library Association, 2010).

Mentor

I think I have learned that the best way to lift one's self up is to help someone else.

—Booker T. Washington

The mentoring process pairs a beginning librarian with a more experienced librarian. Whether you are a mentor or mentee, the relationship is a learning one. For the new librarian, working with a more established professional gives you a much needed sounding board, especially when you are a solo librarian without the benefit of daily face-to-face contact with colleagues. For the seasoned professional, providing guidance to a new member of the profession can open new ways of thinking. Interacting with a mentee might also lend new insight into emerging trends.

The American Library Association's divisions and round tables sponsor mentoring relationships. Special library associations, such as the American Association of Law Libraries and the Medical Library Association, also arrange mentoring relationships.

Another way to mentor is to host an intern. If you have a library and information science department or school in your area, check to see if they need to place students for experiential education. Teaching one on one will invigorate you personally and professionally—and it never hurts to have the extra help!

Another form of mentoring is peer mentoring, which pairs professionals who possess about the same experience in a relationship of mutual encouragement and support. Peer mentors might check in with each other once a week to share triumphs and troubles and to keep each other on track. Peer mentoring is now moving to the virtual sphere, making it a perfect outlet for the solo librarian, for whom face-to-face meetings are not always possible. Here, the relationship takes place mostly over the phone or through e-mail or videoconferencing. Peer mentoring relationships are more informal than traditional mentoring. If you wish to start peer mentoring, reach out to colleagues individually, rather than relying on your professional organization. Invite participants through a listserv announcement.

RESOURCES

- ALA-Wide Mentoring and Recruiting Efforts: www.ala.org/ala/aboutala/offices/hrdr/abouthrdr/hrdrliaisoncomm/otld/ALA_Mentoring_and_Recruitment_Efforts.cfm.

Plan and Document

Inaction saps the vigor of the mind.

—Leonardo da Vinci

While the resume or CV is the traditional record of your accomplishments, other methods of documenting your learning are useful tools for planning and tracking your professional growth. Start by initiating and maintaining a learning log to keep track of what you are learning, especially those informal educational opportunities that might not make it to the resume. The learning log is a diary of sorts, documenting the date and time of your learning, what you learned, and how you might apply your new knowledge. The learning log then can be expanded into a formal learning plan, in which you identify your learning needs and outline specific actions, including time frames and anticipated outcomes, to fill those gaps.

The beauty of maintaining a learning log and plan is that you can easily transfer the information you document to a professional portfolio that can be presented to colleagues or your administration. The professional portfolio identifies your achievements and strengths, helps you spot gaps, and demonstrates competence.

Present your portfolio to your administration at annual review time. If you can tie past continuing education, networking, or conferences with specific outcomes for your organization, this makes the case for future opportunities. Be sure to keep this documentation handy for updating your resume or CV when you are searching for a new job.

Enjoy Yourself

I never did a day's work in my life. It was all fun.

—Thomas Edison

The isolation and demands of being a solo librarian make development and growth vital for your mental health both on and off the job. It is easy to fall into inertia, stagnation, and performing responsibilities by rote—a dangerous path that eventually leads to burnout. A commitment of even ten minutes a day will set you on a path toward growth and discovery.

The professional development possibilities outlined here are just a few of the many you can choose from, and innovations in learning and networking will present still further opportunities. Don't feel you need to do it all. Pursue what is enjoyable to you. Follow the spark of your passion. The energy you invest will be returned to you in an enriched life, both personally and professionally.

General Resources

- Beyond the Job Blog: www.beyondthejob.org/. Articles, job-hunting advice, professional development opportunities, and other news and ideas on how to further your library career.
- Library Professional Development Blog: libprofdev.wordpress.com/. Resource for professional development opportunities.

Part V

INTERNET-BASED IDEAS FOR LIBRARIANSHIP

CHAPTER 14

Double Your Staff With Instructional Videos

Claudia J. Dold

Do you ever wish there were two of you in the library, one to take care of the routine questions so the other one could get on with the more challenging work? The two staff librarians in my special library faced that same problem when our research institute started several undergraduate and graduate academic programs. One day, we were serving research faculty and staff; the next day we had hundreds of undergraduate, graduate, and postdoctoral students. We saw a dramatic increase in the demand for basic instruction and reference. Since adding staff was not a possibility, working smarter was our only option. Further, with the library open twelve hours a day, each of us was "solo" for half of our shift. In this chapter, I speak from experience when I explain why instructional videos are good tools for librarians. I describe specific examples of videos I have created and offer advice on how you too can create successful videos.

The Video Solution

Why was video our solution to the personnel shortage? First, a well-constructed video offers answers to the kinds of questions we all face: repetitive, basic questions on services, resource use, and common subject-specific topics. Since the library videos provide a solid orientation to a resource or service, both faculty members and students benefit from them. When patrons take the time and initiative to view the videos, I see less of that "overwhelmed" behavior and more genuine intellectual curiosity and purpose-driven research when they come to the library for help. Consequently, I spend more of my time working on the "critical thinking" aspect of their research instead of teaching the "how to." For example, I can work with the patron on constructing complex search strategies rather than offering basic instruction on how to perform an author or title search.

Second, a video is available for the user around the clock, seven days a week. In that respect, a video is better than face-to-face service because it offers instruction in select, targeted services that exceed the library's normal hours of operation. Students appreciate knowing there is help available when they need it, even if the library is closed.

Third, patrons can watch a video as often as needed. Video offers patrons just-in-time instruction, when and where they want it. While a patron may be reluctant or embarrassed to ask for remedial instruction for a second or third time, the video is a ready resource to refresh or improve one's skills.

Fourth, video is not that difficult a media to master, especially if you have a particular purpose in mind. With forethought and planning, even your first video can look good and serve your needs. There are a number of video-production software packages available for both Macs and PCs. Camtasia by TechSmith (www.techsmith.com/camtasia.asp) is my software of choice. It comes with friendly and helpful tutorials to get the new user started, and it has advanced features for experienced videographers.

Finally, a review of the recent literature[1] offers insight into current video applications for teaching purposes. The overwhelming and consistent message is that today's students and young professionals are comfortable with video, they prefer video as a communication device for learning new procedures, and they learn efficiently when they see as well as hear the instructional messages. For more information, I recommend the articles referenced at the end of the chapter.

Video Products in My Library

In collaboration with the other librarian in my special library, I created a number of different types of videos based upon the spectrum of patron knowledge of, and demand for, library resources. Conceptualizing our patron information needs as types of questions, my colleague and I envisioned several specific series of videos to address these questions. The first series focused on orienting the patron to the library and teaching basic skill sets. These skills included how to find the library, how to contact us, how to look up our hours of operation, how to open an inter-library loan account, how to search for materials within the university library system, and how to find serials in the stacks. One of the most successful videos, based upon number of views, addresses how to narrow a topic effectively when writing a research paper. We also created a video that describes the focus of our library, which serves persons interested in mental health services research and policy. User feedback pointed at the value of thinking about what the patron really needs to know and how to present it, especially for general library information.

I planned a second series of videos with my fellow librarian and the heads of two academic departments. We designed this fifteen-part video series specifically to teach graduate students the necessary skills to research, organize, and write their theses for their programs of study. Feedback from faculty and students has provided valuable insight into how each group uses the videos, as well as ideas for expansion in future series.

Working with the director of one of the graduate clinical internship programs, I used his narration to create a video that describes the program requirements and directs students to specific web links and essential documents. It is posted on the departmental website where it serves as a publicity piece for the program and as ready-access for students. Feedback from students to the clinical director indicates broad approval of the conversational tone on a procedure that students often find stressful. The program director is pleased to have a means of getting his message out, consistently and in its entirety, to all interested students, and to have more time for working with students on clinical issues.

In addition, I have had requests to capture lectures, to create course material for use as course supplements, and to record short testimonials used in the college promotion campaign. My video skill set has even shown its value in my own professional development. We use a virtual poster session that I created for a national conference to promote our library. It is accessible through YouTube at www.youtube.com/watch?v=TZy2pwTBSLU.

Thinking about Your First Video: Know Your Audience

My audience is comprised of university students, staff, and faculty who take advantage of their instructional technology-enabled world. They view video on their phones, in the classroom, and on course management software. We, as librarians, are also an audience. We listen to all types of questions and requests. So when my colleague and I started talking about a creative solution for our own problems, we immediately thought of using video to answer the usual questions—who, what, when, where, and how. We then categorized the types of questions into topics that would easily convert to video.

Video-creation programs are readily available and they are affordable. With no previous video experience and that unbounded exuberance that comes from a really good idea, my colleague and I wrote our first script. Then I imagined visuals to complement the text. Storyboarding is the process of selecting images and other content that will accompany your text in order to illustrate and clarify your message. Since some learners are visually oriented, the right images may be essential to conveying a concept to your viewers. Armed with a digital camera, I took photos that I thought would enhance my video. I also drew diagrams and scanned them into a digital format that the program can use. It is easy to bring Clip Art into a video, and there are Internet sources that permit the use of photographs without copyright restrictions or fees.

In my experience, an audience is more willing to endure poor image quality than poor sound. While Camtasia allows for sound recording and editing, I prefer to record the audio component, edit it, and then import it as a sound file into the video-creation software. I use Audacity, a free online program for sound files, to edit my narration (audacity.sourceforge .net/). While the program is intuitive for simple edits, Audacity also has an online manual that includes advanced features.

The better the original voice recording, the better the final product. Not only do you have less editing to do when you start with a clean recording, but you end up with an overall product that has a consistent vocal cadence, pitch, and resonance. If you misspeak during the recording, just catch your breath and begin reading your script again at that last segment that didn't come out well the first time. Editing out misspoken units is far easier than trying to apply sound patches later.

Sometimes there is no better way to learn than by watching someone else. Camtasia permits video capture of on-screen segments, so the viewer may watch the mouse-directed arrow make clicks and choices that lead to the desired end. Capturing a sequence of steps in the video is a valuable tool when demonstrating the use of a database or a computer technique.

Viewers may watch the video and hear the narration as often as necessary to learn the procedure. A bulleted list recapitulates the steps and gives users a quick review.

To aid our students with hearing impairments, all of my videos are closed-captioned. In Camtasia, I import the reading script as a text file and then parse it into captions that synchronize with the audio track. Be sure to edit the text so it faithfully represents the recorded audio before performing the captioning tasks. I also provide a link to the text file. Patrons use the text as a guide to the video content and as quick access to referenced URLs. Since the text mirrors the content of the captions, there is little additional work to providing the text as a .pdf independently from the video.

Creating Your Script

Before writing, take the time to think through the purpose and the primary learning goals of your video, especially if you are creating a series of videos. For example, if the student needs to know how to use your interlibrary loan (ILL) system, introduce the process of registering as a user in the ILL system before you actually use the ILL feature in the video. While this advice may seem intuitive, planning the sequence of concepts and learning modules will save time and effort when you move on to scripting individual videos. Most of my videos run between eight and fifteen minutes. If the information exceeds this amount of time, it may also exceed your viewer's attention span. Consider breaking your topic down into smaller units, and then organizing them into videos that stay within a manageable time range. While you may be an expert on your topic, anyone who is trying to learn new procedures can be overwhelmed after a few minutes of unfamiliar material.

Pay attention to the speed and volume of your speech. I still catch myself speaking at one volume at the beginning of a recording session, only to find I have trailed off after the first few paragraphs. Ideally, your patron will set the volume for the video once and then focus on your content. Try to record at an appropriate and consistent volume since increasing the volume electronically using the program software may introduce background noise and distortion. Check the quality of your recording after a few sentences to alert you to any buzz or static that occurs when the microphone is too close to your mouth. Also, pay attention to the level of difficulty of the language you use. Your video may present new terms and concepts to the viewers. Speak clearly, simply, and slowly to give them time to catch the content of your message and relate it to the overall theme.

Tone of voice is important. Regard your video as a way to make a patron feel welcome, even before he or she sets foot on campus. One viewer commented on her relief to hear a friendly voice in the video. Levity works well too, in moderation. I look for an opportunity to inject a humorous photo or comment just once in each video to relieve the dulling effects of information overload. Think of creating a video as an opportunity to design a teaching segment. The video that addresses a defined problem and delivers a clear solution serves both you and your patron.

Formatting Your Video: Style of Presentation

At this point, your video has moved from the idea phase to a sequence of images, diagrams, bulleted pages, and video clips with narration and captions. Your work will look polished if you pick an appropriate color theme for the video and use it regularly. Consistency is even more important if you plan a series of videos. While some variation may make the work less monotonous, a standardized typeface, color theme, and style of presentation will enhance the professional appearance of your work.

LEGIBILITY AND COLOR SCHEMES

Everything needs a certain amount of contrast, space, and size in order to be readable. The eye travels across a computer screen in a specific way, just as it does with print. Wacky color schemes can distract viewers. Dark blue type on a brown background may remind you of a jazz lounge, but it will not make your viewers happy if their eyes cross trying to make sense of the image or the text. Instead, choose colors that are appropriate for your target audience, that reflect your institution, and that convey the kind of feeling you want your users to experience. Colors create impact, so choose wisely. Too low a contrast will not stand out to your users while too high a contrast will be difficult to read. Invest some time talking with graphic designers, do your own research, and examine videos that work for you.

TITLE PAGE AND CREDITS FORMAT

To provide consistency, I have developed a basic format for the title page and the closing page. The closing page covers the credits and important acknowledgments. I use the same image and font for the opening page, and the closing page resembles all my other closing pages. While these pages are specific to each video, they provide a sense of unity and connection within the video series and a professional branding feature for my library and my university. If your library is part of a larger organization, be sure to use the official logo approved for products created by your organization. In addition, credit any photos that are not your own work, and always obtain written permission from a subject if you are going to use the image of that individual in your work.

FILE FORMAT

Rendering is the process of creating the final video from all of the elements you have assembled for the project. Rendering is similar to taking a photograph. First, you populate your composition by putting the items you want in the picture. When you are satisfied with the arrangement, you commit the composition to film. Rendering commits your video creation to a final product, in a particular format. Choosing a video format for your rendered product may require some research into how your viewers watch your videos. Camtasia has recommended settings for various purposes (e.g., posting on a web page or viewing on a mobile device). You may also render your video in several formats and let the users choose their preferred file format.

FILE STORAGE

Video files are large, so having enough space on your server is another important consideration. Saving your collection of images in a central file is always a good idea since you may want to use them on another occasion.

Camtasia offers you the choice of copying all images used in a project to the project file. I recommend this procedure. Once you render the video, you may move the final video product with its supporting images and elements to any site. When you want to update your video, all the elements and images are on hand.

Storage should also address backups of your file. As a rule, always make at least two copies each of your raw material, the not-yet-rendered video project, and the final rendered video. Terabyte external drives are a good investment, but they can go bad and they will take all your files with them. Back up your files on servers that are updated regularly. Review your videos at least once a year for changes to keep your work relevant because the look of the library home page may change and web addresses change all the time. That review also gives you a chance to re-render your work in new formats as needed and back up the video folder. In my experience, back-up locations change as the university reorganizes its storage capacity, as equipment changes, and as better naming conventions present themselves. If you think of your video as your valuable assistant, then keeping your files updated becomes second nature.

FILE-NAMING CONVENTIONS

Devote some thought as to how you are going to name your files so you can find them later. Plan your naming convention and storage needs as part of your initial project planning. A simple naming convention, such as S1-Video04-TestsAndMeasures.flv, will keep series, videos, and content neatly organized. Consider having a working directory and a live directory. In the working directory, you may keep all the pieces and iterations of the videos. The working directory is also your test bed. In the live directory, keep only the rendered copy. Using the same name for the working copy and the rendered copy will allow you to associate the two files quickly. That association is especially important when you want to update or revise a video because the same name (but different file extension) will point you to the corresponding project file.

Reaching Your Audience

Fast forward to when your video is ready. To start collecting the rewards of your investment, patrons have to use your product. They have to know where to look to find your video. Our solution at the FMHI Research Library has been to post the videos on the library home page in a prominent position. We also promote the videos among faculty and staff via regular e-mail updates during the year. Our professors consider the library videos as core course content and post links to them on the university's course management system. Get the word out about what you are doing. Write about your experiences. Talk with other librarians or teaching faculty who are also creating video when you are at conferences.

GETTING FEEDBACK

Listen to the feedback you receive, consider the comments, and then look for ways to implement the ones that are valuable to you and your audience. To justify your investment in time and money to create the videos, survey your users. Camtasia allows you to embed a survey using their software, or you may opt to use Doodle, Survey Monkey, or a host of other web-based survey tools. Since participation is voluntary, you cannot know how many people benefited from your work and did not respond. Alternately, you could use Google's Analytics to keep track of how many times certain links were clicked on the web page. Sometimes number of "hits" is a good usage statistic. However, by surveying, you will receive valuable comments, suggestions, criticism, and perhaps that most rewarding feedback of all, a compliment!

Conclusion

Video is a contemporary medium that users understand well. Producing a video is within every librarian's skill set. Video software is affordable, whether it is open source or a commercial product. By focusing on your patrons' particular needs for information, you can use video to deliver clear instruction in an efficient manner. Video has a real advantage over face-to-face library instruction. As the creator, you control the distractions that otherwise interfere with good communication. So start with a good idea, script it, and pull together the images and screen captures that will highlight the "how-to" aspects of the instruction. Put a smile in your voice and project yourself. Your video will cheerfully repeat the same information and the same instructions, always in the same sequence, by day and by night. You could not hire a better employee.

Note

1. James L. Collins, Catherine P. Cook-Cottone, Judith Schick Robinson, and Roberta R. Sullivan, "Technology and New Directions in Professional Development: Applications of Digital Video, Peer Review, and Self-Reflection," *Journal of Educational Technology Systems* 33, no. 2 (2004): 131–46; Stacy K. Dymond and Johnell Bentz, "Using Digital Videos to Enhance Teacher Preparation," *Teacher Education and Special Education* 29, no. 2 (2006): 98–112; Julie Gainsburg, "Creating Effective Video to Promote Student-Centered Teaching," *Teacher Education Quarterly* 36, no. 2 (2009): 163–78.

CHAPTER 15

The New Coconino Community College Library

A LIBRARIAN, COLLABORATIVE LIBRARY SERVICES, AND AN ONLINE LIBRARY

Estelle Pope

One Librarian and an Online Library

Imagine walking into a new job as the librarian for a community college and seeing all the books in boxes filling up a cubicle. You are told there is no integrated library system, that the physical library space is now part of the Student Center, and that the nearby four-year college library has created a web page for you with links to all the online databases and library services. The library is now primarily online, you need to purge most of the physical books, and you will be the only staff in the library at the college. In the summer of 2010, this was what my first few weeks entailed. At the end of the first semester, I have a better understanding of where the library is headed. Some days, I feel like a pioneer out here in the Wild West, trying to create some order out of chaos, applying my knowledge of library principles to ensure our students and faculty receive the best service and resources for their studies. My conception of library has changed in this position, where books aren't the hallmarks but the links; connections and new collaborations represent the college library.

Shortly before I started working at CCC the library transitioned from a small physical library to one that is primarily online. Being the librarian in this new library model has been a great and challenging experience. I write here about my experiences and observations thus far as a solo librarian with an online library. In this chapter I hope to give you a glimpse of my experience thus far, make some observations about being a solo librarian with an online library, and share some hopes for the future.

Defining an Online Library

I was nervous about a shift to an online library when I started, and still feel very aware that an online library needs clear definition to be a good service for students and faculty. From the start I have had the benefit of a newly formalized partnership with Northern Arizona University's (NAU) Cline Library, an academic library at a four-year college less than ten minutes from our campus. For all physical library needs, the students and faculty at CCC have access to most of the Cline Library collections and services, which is a much larger set of research materials than CCC alone could ever provide. This collaboration with NAU is an example of educational institutions working together to save resources and to promote cross-connections for students and faculty, and is a wonderful addition to the library offerings for CCC.

I am aware that in spite of this collaboration, we no longer have a true physical library on the CCC campus and that I am the only face of the library. As a result, I spend a lot of time reaching out to faculty and students and piloting new ways of marketing library service. I feel fortunate to be assisted in my role as CCC librarian by NAU, but more so by an ever-present online library. Creating an online library is also nothing new for libraries as services and resources are increasingly provided online. The new idea for me is that I need the online library to complement, substitute, and enhance what I am able to do as one person. A lot of defining the online library is in marketing resources to the faculty and students who will need them. I hope through my efforts that the CCC community will accept the online library as a tool and a space for their learning and research and will accept me as its ambassador.

Elements of the Online Library

WEBSITE

The library website is critical in the success of an online library. Technically every library that has a website has an online library. Part of the transformation from just a website to an online library is in the presentation and design. To start, simply calling the website the online library can aid in the transformation. An online library consists of whatever your library users need the most. You can guess at several of them, including collection information, contacts, hours, links to important resources, and technology support. The needs will evolve over time, and flexibility is key in the ongoing development of the online library. Assessment of services and resources and communication with users is important. Techniques I have used include brief surveys for students at the conclusion of classroom instruction, consultations with faculty about teaching needs, and online surveys from the website and through communications with faculty and students. Additionally, I conduct collection analysis based on faculty and curriculum needs and usage statistics for our online resources to determine future purchases or cancellations.

Online Library Elements

- Link to online databases, preferably with a search box
- Reference services: chat, text, phone, e-mail
- Link to library catalog, ILL and request services
- Tech support information, librarian contact information
- Documentation of technology, tools, databases, citation help
- Tutorials and handouts given in the classroom
- News and updates, in the form of newsletters, blogs, or critical announcements

SEAMLESS ACCESS

Where possible, simplifying the user experience will help in making the online library a success. This means using the same user log-ins for online library resources and services as other log-ins used in your community, such as a student ID or e-mail log-in. Embedding library resources and services in the other online spaces that students and faculty are using, such as course management tools and college portals, will help to encourage use of library resources and make them easy to access. Use of federated search tools provided by your database vendors to make the initial searches cover a broad range of topics makes it simpler and easier for new library users to get started and begin accessing needed content. Suggestions for subject-specific access to the online databases can be made on the website through web pages for the academic programs and subjects at your college.

COLLABORATION WITH YOUR INFORMATION TECHNOLOGY (IT) DEPARTMENT

Working closely with your IT department is critical in building your online library. Help the IT staff to understand what you contribute to the institution and how IT can support you. Even if you have limited technological expertise, if you can describe what it is that you want the online library to do, IT staff should be able to determine which tools could achieve your goals.

At CCC, IT has been essential in creating the online library. IT administrators helped in the creation of the online library and facilitated the use of our campus log-in as the log-in method for online databases. Help desk staff field questions related to the library log-in and help troubleshoot with students. Web developers train and suggest tools for the creation of links to online resources, videos, and blogs. Partnerships depend on good relationships, and so it is important to me to get to know the IT staff, to respect their talents and their roles in the college, and to communicate openly. My goal is to provide excellent services and resources to students and faculty and to make staff shine through our work.

ATTENTION TO PROBLEMS

Along the lines of good collaboration, it is important to keep IT and other departments informed of any problems. This can be the hardest aspect of the collaboration because it requires honesty and persistence, especially when problems impede your library service. Because my library is primarily online in focus, I rely on IT and technology functioning heavily. We had one problem the first semester that revealed a significant database issue requiring the work of several IT staff to resolve. If I hadn't spoken up and been honest and inquisitive about the nature of this problem that several students were reporting, we might have had more significant failure and alienated students from using our online library.

Physical Aspects

A DEPARTMENT OF ONE

The hardest part of being a solo librarian thus far is being a "department of one." It is hard managing your time, goals, and tasks all by yourself. It is hard having others misunderstand what you do and underestimate your needs, services, and resources. You are, as a solo librarian, the library director thinking about the library's vision, future, and budget. You are the stacks manager and circulation department, managing the books and media, making sure items get returned and are safely stored. You are the instruction librarian and systems librarian, plus many more roles, all by yourself, and it can be quite overwhelming to wear all these hats and manage your time in each of these roles. On bad days, you wonder if one person can really do all these things and do them well.

The precedence of our online library at CCC over a physical library is a challenge. Logistically it makes sense to me to be mostly an online library. Because I don't sit at my desk all day long, I can't oversee a physical collection, manage book circulation, shelve materials, and expect to provide any instruction or work with faculty and IT, and I don't have any staff to help me. One question I struggle in answering to faculty and students is whether there is a library at our college. Technically yes, we have a small library in the traditional sense. We have a book collection of approximately 1,500 titles and a video collection of approximately 1,000 titles. We have a college archives and a room where all these materials are housed. Faculty can check out materials or place them on course reserve, but because we don't have an integrated library system, this information is all managed in Microsoft SharePoint and requires some trust that faculty will be honest about what they have taken from the library. Because I am not always in the library space, faculty sign out the materials themselves on the honor system. There is no library as place anymore, though, and sometimes I think this is the main cause of student and faculty confusion. Without shelves or study space the library is just another website.

THE INVISIBLE LIBRARIAN

I feel invisible as the librarian, since I don't have a brick-and-mortar space where students come to hang out and study and faculty come to gather materials. To address this feeling of invisibility, and the need to make sure our CCC community understands that they do have a library, I am piloting new ways of being present on campus. I am holding "out of office" hours around campus with my laptop and a sign that says "Ask Your Librarian" a few times a week at high-traffic times of day. I am also doing the same in the faculty lounge a few times a week, sitting at a table in the area where faculty congregate. My hope is that by being more visible, even if people don't ask me questions about the library or get some research help, they see me and know that I am here. Another strategy I'm using is traditional marketing through signs and bookmarks. I created limited edition "art" bookmarks with our new CCC library slogan—"Take your library with you"—and the web address of the online library. I posted "Ask Your Librarian" signs around campus that list all the ways to contact library services. Since we share services with Northern Arizona University, we have near 24/7 reference via chat, text, phone, or e-mail.

A SMART COLLABORATION

One aspect of my position that is unique is that our library has entered into an Intergovernmental Agreement with NAU to provide joint library services. This is largely the reason that I am able to focus my attention on the online library, while not needing to provide more traditional physical library services and materials. Through the partnership, NAU's Cline Library is our college's "physical" library. Our students, faculty, and staff can borrow books and media; can use computers, laptops, and study rooms; and can request document delivery and inter-library loan from Cline Library. In addition, library staff members from various departments provide assistance. The electronic resources librarian negotiates some of my online database licenses and helps in the management of these licenses. IT helps in linking to our online resources through a proxy server and managing data loads of our patron information in their integrated library system. The public services staff provide an "Ask a Librarian" service that is available to our campus, utilizing chat, texting, e-mail, phone, and in-person reference assistance when needed. Public services staff can also be hired if I need help in providing classroom instruction. The Archives and Special Collections staff have consulted on our college archives and include me in regional meetings on archives.

One of the associate university librarians serves as my main point of contact for all issues, and we meet on an ongoing basis to discuss matters related to the library and to my own professional development. A group of library, academic, and information technology staff from both institutions meet regularly to discuss issues and plan for further adjustments to the collaboration. I report to the Dean of Arts and Sciences at my college, which has been a great way for me to connect with faculty and have the dean understand the more subtle aspects of library resources and services. The dean attended all of my orientation sessions at the Cline Library when I first began my position and is learning the "library speak" so that she can better support me in my role at the college. When I need help from other librarians who know the "library speak," I am lucky to have my colleagues at Cline Library.

Redefining "Library"

THE BOOK STEREOTYPE

Outside of the library world people are familiar with only a small portion of library services and resources, even in an academic environment. At CCC we purged approximately 75 percent of the physical collection because of the move to a smaller space and staff reduction to just one librarian. Faculty are perplexed by the changes, and my guess is they, like me, feel uneasy with no books around. The online library is a way to provide vast amounts of information to students and faculty for their academic work, but is hard to explain and showcase in a physical way. The administration decided to make this transition and is eager to see the physical library collection minimized, while faculty appear somewhat undecided about the transition and continue to request physical course reserves and check out videos for use in their classes. Providing access and handouts on how to get to the online library will be enough information for some faculty, but most would probably benefit from an instruction session like the ones done for students. Getting faculty attention will continue to be a challenge given heavy course loads and commitments. Everyone needs assistance in adjusting to the online library and in seeing what is available. A next step for this solo librarian is to start providing faculty with customized information about what is available in their discipline or to address specific topics in their courses.

THE FUN OF IT

Being a department of one is gratifying in ways that you can't experience as a librarian in a large library. I will notice that students ask me to show them the citation tools in the databases repeatedly, and then I can decide to create an online tutorial on using the citation tools in the databases for the library website based on this immediate feedback. I analyze all the statistical information that I then pass on to my supervisor and administrators at the college. I can review the statistics available from vendors to determine the best information to measure the library's impact and plan for all future changes to our resources. I make all the signs, posters, and bookmarks and thus have creative control over the designs. I decide the direction of instruction and how to convey information to students and make all the faculty connections. I teach all the classes and am the face that students see. Part of the reason I entered the academic library field is that I like doing a little bit of everything and enjoy a little of most fields in higher education. In the role of a solo librarian, I get the chance to do and enjoy a little bit of most aspects of the academic world. And I have learned a tremendous amount about the overall functions of most of the departments in our college. This, I hope, will enable me to better communicate the role of library resources and services across the college and help others to understand and advocate for what I do.

A VISION OF THE FUTURE

The future of this online library has already begun, and I feel being a solo librarian is helping me to explore new ideas and learn as I go in ways I'd never be able to do in a larger library. Some services I'm building would not be "cutting edge" in larger institutions, but for a small community college are great innovations. Being a library of one allows me to implement services and online library features and test to see if they meet our student needs, without much effort or investment. Some areas I am exploring include video tutorials available to students and faculty on the library website and in their online course pages. Also I am creating customized resource pages for classes based on the subject areas, literary works, and topics covered in a class. I am looking for ways to partner with other departments on grants and digital projects.

Since I am new to this position, and this is the first year of the new model of service, I feel very in the moment about what I am doing. There is much to do right now to keep services available and to build the online library. In some ways I feel like a pioneer, and not just because I am in the western part of the United States. I struggle to find models that fit what I am doing, and I am lucky to have a supervisor and a college president who trust my training, judgment, and ability to make decisions that support the library. I think the combination of supportive supervision, access to needed resources, and the ability to work both independently and collaboratively is aiding in my enjoyment of this work and the hopeful success of the online library. I feel encouraged that the online library will have far-reaching benefits for our students, based on the early input of faculty and students. I hope that sharing my own struggles, challenges, and accomplishments in this role will help other pioneers working as solo librarians in their efforts to provide excellent library service.

CHAPTER 16

No Budget? No Problem!

Eileen Boswell

As a librarian flying solo, you may find that the pressure to innovate and keep your users happy is aggravated by a lack of funding to support the creative projects you've always wanted to try. These are tough times, and many libraries are facing budget shortfalls or cuts across the board. Luckily there are a lot of free tools to enhance your library, many of which were developed by librarians like you who needed a way to enhance their library services free of charge.

This chapter includes information on the following free tools:

- Social bookmarking
- Google suite
- Instructional videos from Common Craft
- Wiki software

The tools and tips in this chapter are great whether you have a budget or not, whether you are alone or not, and no matter what type of library you run—from a small public library to a large specialized collection. Learning about these tools will improve your library's operations, and you may also find tools your users could apply to their own work. You will learn how to create a quick and easy Ready Reference catalog using social bookmarking through Delicious, how to use Google sites for an easy site interface or wiki, and how to find great free instructional videos through Common Craft and YouTube. You will also learn how to integrate these tools as you build your free library so the combination is customized to your users' needs. Keeping your users in mind throughout this chapter will help you choose the tools that are best for your situation so you can "right size" your library.

A word of caution: be careful not to think that free tools will be a panacea to all your library problems or challenges. It would be unwise to adopt a free tool just because it is free or because you think "everyone is doing it." It is, however, easier to experiment when funding is not an issue. Remember, too, that free does not always mean fast. A lot of the tools described in this chapter will require time for you to experiment. As you are exploring them, document what you have learned, think about how best to implement each tool for maximum user satisfaction, and then use periodic and strategic evaluation methods to gather feedback from your users.

Social Bookmarking

Social bookmarking tools such as Digg, Reddit, StumbleUpon, Instapaper, and Delicious offer ways of organizing your own web traffic as well as getting recommendations from others. Each tool is a little bit different, but they all share some common features. A bookmark is a way to keep track of a site that you find useful, and when you decide to bookmark a site, you can add tags made up of keywords that describe the site. Bookmarking has both an organizational purpose (keeping track of sites you may wish to return to) and a social purpose (recommending sites to others). The various social bookmarking tools available for free have different features that make them more or less ideal for the social and organizational functions that a library might have.

With each bookmarking service you can expect to create an account by choosing a username and password and providing your e-mail address, and some level of security is involved with each type of account. Reddit requires that you complete a CAPTCHA (Completely Automated Public Turing Test to Tell Computers and Humans Apart) each time you share a bookmark with others, and you are allowed only a limited number of recommendations in any given time period. StumbleUpon lets you store and share unlimited bookmarks, but each time you share you have to indicate whether the link you are recommending is something that is "appropriate for work." There are ways to use each tool to connect and share with people in your network, whether through e-mail or separate inboxes that reside in the tool itself.

Other social features include "liking" a link by giving it points or a written recommendation through a comments feature, or voting on a link to determine its placement in a "Suggested Links" list. StumbleUpon and some other services will show you who else has "liked" or recommended a particular resource. Besides the various social features, each tool has different levels of compatibility with mobile devices. If you use a Kindle, you may consider using Instapaper as a bookmarking tool since it has an application whereby all your chosen bookmarks for each day can be transferred to a Kindle and you can read those tagged resources later, offline. If your library checks out Kindles, you can synchronize your bookmarks for your patrons on each Kindle. Synchronizing across media and devices is a fast and easy way for solo librarians to accomplish a lot of work in little time.

The tags you use to describe a site can be a combination of keywords you create, choices from a drop-down menu, or suggested tags based on what others have used to describe the site. Your choice of tags will vary depending on whether you are using your bookmarks primarily for yourself or for other people. If your primary goal is organizational, rather than social, the tags need only have meaning to you, whereas if you want other people to use your list of tags, you should choose keywords that make sense in your library's particular context. In most cases tags can be alphanumeric, but two-word tags with spaces may be problematic.

> *Tip:* Your choice of tags will vary based on whether you are using your bookmarks primarily for social or organizational purposes.

Delicious (www.delicious.com) is an excellent social bookmarking service. Anything that has a URL can be tagged through Delicious, and you create the terms for your tags. You can use Delicious tags to apply comprehensive metadata to a website or document, or you can just apply a few quick-reference tags that will help you organize your list of websites. The advantage of Delicious over other bookmarking tools is that each set of your tags corresponds to a URL you can share (once you adjust your settings) so that your lists of bookmarks can be public. You can also adjust your settings so that your new bookmarks are sent out to others via Twitter or through an RSS feed.

If your library uses an existing controlled vocabulary, or an established set of subject headings such as Library of Congress Subject Headings, your tags should correspond to that terminology. Additional tags can be used for non-subject-related metadata, such as the format of the resource (e.g., HTML, PDF, PPT). Another idea is to have a "Ready Reference" tag and have the list of these (which will reside at www.delicious.com/[Your User Name]/ReadyReference once you set it up) displayed in a prominent place on your library's home page or intranet portal. Your bookmarks will offer your users a slice of the Internet that you have already vetted and organized. Use this especially for things that Google may not be indexing or organizing for you, like local history (for public libraries) or specialized documents (for special libraries). Think about the combinations of tags you would like to make available so that your users can quickly find the resources they want. A resource with more than one tag applied will show up in a list of all the bookmarks with that set of tags. For example, a special librarian supporting a research project on welfare may have tags that configure to enable the list delicious.com/[YourUserName]/FoodStamps+Legal+Video, which could take a staff member directly to a specific type of resource needed.

Public librarians working alone might use Delicious to tag local history documents that already exist online, but which may not be easily findable with a commercial search engine. Special librarians may want to create small, specialized collections and then make them available to staff. You can also start a community cataloging project to have people tag resources in your catalog (or new ones that they suggest) with their own terms or a set of terms you suggest. This will get some initial bookmarking done for you and give you ideas for new tags. It has the added benefit of involving users in a new system so they can help train others when you go live, and it introduces them to a new way of organizing their own resources.

SUGGESTED TAGS TO START A LIBRARY CATALOG IN DELICIOUS

- "ReadyReference"
- "FAQs"
- "Legislation"
- "Local_Interest"
- "MediaCoverage"
- Specialized terminology for collections specific to your library

- Administrative tags to organize your own work, such as "ToBeCataloged" and "TimePermitting"
- Format tags such as "HTML," "PDF," "PPT," "image," "video," or "podcast"

One of the main reasons to use Delicious to organize your lists of recommended websites is that it makes retrieving your favorite sites very easy. You can search within your tags by typing the name of any tag in the search box while you are in your main list of bookmarks. You can also search for tags within tags, similar to sorting data in Excel by multiple criteria in a strategic order.

Once you have several tags created, experiment with the various view options. You can see an alphabetical list of your top two hundred tags, all tags alphabetically, or a tag cloud that displays each tag in a font size that correlates to how many sites you tagged with that keyword. To really get the most out of Delicious, follow the instructions to download and install a toolbar (sometimes called "bookmarklets") in your browser. The bookmarking toolbar will have one button that enables you to tag a site directly and another button that takes you to your list of bookmarks.

Google Suite

The Google suite of tools (www.google.com/options) offers more than just e-mail and search functions. Having a Google account gives you simultaneous access to mail, shared documents, weblogs and analytics, news alerts, a well-organized blog reader, easily editable websites that can function as wikis, and even YouTube, which is now owned by Google. However, you or your organization may be leery of relying on Google's free tools for a large portion of your work or of having Google collect data on your search patterns. It is best to check with your supervisor to find out if these concerns exist before starting a Google account for official business.

Gmail is a way to get a free e-mail address and account (as opposed to a program such as Outlook, which does not provide you with an address or with electronic storage space for e-mail). Even if you have an e-mail address at your library, you may want to use Gmail to set up additional general purpose accounts, such as "GlenCountyReference@gmail.com." This may be an easier option than having your IT department (if you have one) add additional e-mail addresses to suit your library's needs. Adjust the options for "Forwarding" in the "Settings" tab of Gmail to have messages from these various accounts all forwarded to an address that you check regularly.

Once you have a Gmail account you have access to shared document features via Google Docs. This service provides basic word processing and spreadsheet functions, similar to Microsoft Office, but without as many complex features. Using a Google Doc makes collaboration easy because you can "share" each document you create by simply adding someone's e-mail address. The system then sends an invitation to that person to view and edit your document. This function is semi-private in that only users whose e-mail addresses you have selected can access your documents, and you decide the appropriate level of editing privileges for each person. For an easy survey tool, try the "Forms" option within Google Docs, which allows you to format and share a survey, the results of which automatically accumulate in a spreadsheet that resides in your Google account. This is a simpler and less expensive (i.e., free) alternative to Survey Monkey, which requires a minimum monthly payment to maintain an account.

Tip: Google Docs offers a "forms" option for surveys, which is a free alternative to Survey Monkey.

Your Google account will also offer the option of creating multiple "Sites," which are essentially wikis integrated with your other Google services. Google Sites allow you to set up and edit basic web pages through a user-friendly text editor. While editing, you will also have the option of viewing and editing the HTML code behind the main content region of each page. You can apply style templates and themes offered by Google and edit the sidebar setup to customize the navigation of your site. You can also attach files to any page of your site, although storage space is limited.

Another option for an easy website through Google is to use Blogger software. Blogger will not allow you to attach documents to your pages the way you can with Google Sites, but it makes available several "widgets" with pre-installed code that can make your site a lively and interactive place for your library users to visit. Use the "Posts" area for long-form content or announcements while your sidebar widgets can offer survey tools, short content collections in bulleted link lists, an archive of your blog posts, and more.

WIDGETS AVAILABLE FOR CUSTOMIZING SITES IN
BLOGGER

* Blog stats
* Followers list
* Search box
* Slideshow of photos from your blog
* Survey tools
* Blog archive
* Text lists
* Link lists

Google has made creating your library's own website very easy with Sites
and Blogger and is an excellent option for librarians who are their own
webmaster.

Instructional Videos

You may be surprised to learn that of the more than two billion videos
hosted on YouTube's servers, many are of an educational nature and
would likely meet a librarian's high
standards for instructional resources.
You can view YouTube videos for
free, although some videos will be accompanied by ads. You can also find
the code for most videos right below
the viewing screen so you can embed
videos in pages of your blog, Google site, or other HTML-based pages.
Evaluate these resources as you would any other additions to your library
collection, and catalog them by tagging them in Delicious or adding their
URLs to another cataloging system you use.

> Tip: Look below a YouTube
> video display for the "embed"
> code to add it to your site's
> HTML code.

When you find a video that appears to be part of a series (e.g., searching "Insulation" will display several series of home improvement videos),
click the username for that video to find out if it is associated with a subscription or "channel." Many government agencies are now hosting their
own YouTube channels. For example, the Department of Transportation
offers a series of videos that many transportation librarians subscribe to.

One advantage of these subscriptions is that they are generally made accessible to users with disabilities before they are posted, so you can rely on an accompanying transcript or captions for each video.

YouTube's interface is available in over thirty languages, with videos posted from all over the world. If you have a Google account, use it to sign in the next time you use YouTube. One of the first subscriptions you should add to your account is the Common Craft collection posted by Lee Lefever. (Search the username "leelefever," as one word, to find this feed.) These are free versions of instructional videos that you can purchase in a higher-quality version from www.commoncraft.com for more formal, professional use. Common Craft explains complex topics "in plain English," and their videos are typically under four minutes each. Making the Common Craft series available offers your library users concise explanations of technology tools such as wikis, RSS feeds, and Google Docs, in addition to videos that explain topics as diverse as compact fluorescent light bulbs, the stock market, and even zombies. Besides searching for good subscriptions through the YouTube interface, start looking for the YouTube logo on sites where you tend to find good resources so you can start building a rich set of subscriptions for your library.

Wikis

Wikis are a great tool for starting a simple website to use for collaborative projects or for your organization's intranet. The word *wiki* comes from the Hawaiian for "fast." Platforms such as MediaWiki, Wetpaint Central, and PBWorks offer you free tools to create a simple website that, as with Google Sites, allows you to determine the access and editing privileges of each person you invite to collaborate. You can also use a wiki to organize internal activities, shared documents, and event calendars. One librarian at the Department of State has started what she calls an "A to Z list" of department information that employees need for accounting procedures, timesheet policies, federal holiday information, and other useful tips. If you're new on the job, consider starting a "Getting Started" page for new employees and use it to document what you yourself are learning about company policies and norms. This will be a great way to introduce library services to other new employees in the future, and they will see how resourceful you are.

Wikipedia is a community-created encyclopedia that uses MediaWiki software. While some librarians prefer peer-reviewed or more formally published reference tools, many have come to see Wikipedia as a valuable free resource. Entries in Wikipedia can be created by anyone with a username and password, and the editing history of each page is made available adjacent to the entry in a separate tab. Additionally, you can view any associated discussions that accompany the editing history to see when and why editors made the changes they did and how other readers have reacted. Wikipedia entries display warnings when citations are incomplete or questionable, when editors have not adhered to the Wikipedia style guide, or when readers have suggested that a particular topic's entry should be split into two articles. If you have not spent very much time with Wikipedia, a fun way to discover it is to set your Internet browser's home screen to en.wikipedia.org/wiki/Special:Randompage. This will deliver a different article to you each time you start a new browsing session and will show you the breadth of what Wikipedia has to offer.

> *Tip*: Set your library computers' home screens to en.wikipedia.org/wiki/Special:Randompage and users will see a different article each time they visit.

Conclusion

Now that you know about these free tools, it's time to begin experimenting with them. Start small, try one at a time, and get feedback from your library users as you implement new tools that affect them. Many of the tools mentioned in this chapter have Twitter feeds and blogs so you can follow them and learn about current problems and solutions, as well as new features. If a user asks you a question about one of these new tools, document it so you can create a list of frequently asked questions, which you can use for training later on. Ask your most active users for testimonials so you can justify the new tools to your manager if necessary. Use these testimonials when promoting upcoming trainings. Also, ask your users what free tools they use and which ones are their favorites. You will discover a wealth of ideas in your patrons.

Part VI

ADMINISTRATIVE TASKS

CHAPTER 17

From Solo Librarian to Super Librarian

Jenny Ryun Foster

Running a library on your own is like donning the role of Supergirl, but without the cape and suit. With some creative enthusiasm and a good old-fashioned roll-up-your-sleeves-and-get-dirty mentality, you can fly through the skies, boosted by your own success on a job well done. This essay is a practical, on-the-job description of a blended library—a special library within a private university devoted to graduate study in psychology and the behavioral sciences—open seven days a week with one full-time professional librarian.

Identify Goals and Prioritize: What Comes First, the Plan or the Process?

The many departments of a larger academic library are compressed into micro-departments in a solo library. The solo librarian is the administrative, acquisition, cataloging, circulation, reference, inter-library loan, and electronic services librarian all wrapped up in one. Add formal instruction, community building, publicity, and accreditation committee duties and that could leave the solo librarian overwhelmed and paralyzed—a state similar to the energy-sapping effects of kryptonite.

The most important part of running a solo library is identifying job priorities. This often comes straight out of the job experience, as the solo librarian is busy with day-to-day job duties as soon as she unlocks and walks through the front door. With some thoughtful planning, the solo librarian can become proactive instead of reactive—this is done through creating a strategic plan.

Strategic planning can be a formal or informal process, but the crux of this process is to understand what the priorities are for the library, based on the solo librarian's experience and the library's relationship with the parent institution. This library mission is tied closely to the institutional mission: supporting students matriculating through the institution's academic programs, as well as the faculty who are experts in their field. Additionally, the institution's mission of providing training opportunities for students to work with diverse, marginalized, and underserved populations directly reflects on the materials that the library should provide.

Keep in mind that in a solo library, one can "plan," but one will most likely be planning at the same time one is answering the phone, looking up a journal article for a faculty member (who needs it for a class that started five minutes ago), and fixing the copier, which is spilling toner all over the floor. Therefore, strategic planning for a solo librarian should be a mix of thoughtful, behind-the-scenes design and flying by the seat of one's pants.

SWOT ANALYSIS

A general SWOT (strengths, weaknesses, opportunities, and threats) analysis can help with brainstorming ideas. If the solo librarian happens to be unjamming the library printer while completing the SWOT, she may only get through the "S" and "W" at first, which is still effective. Identifying library strengths and weaknesses will define the core library goals—strengths must be preserved and weaknesses improved upon to meet the needs of library stakeholders. Again, in terms of this chapter, stakeholders in the library are the faculty, students, and staff of the private university.

Whatever comes out of this brainstorming session must have a practical aspect and must answer these questions:

- Can it be accomplished?
- How is it accomplished and in what time frame?
- How is it known that it has been accomplished successfully?

For example, one of the biggest weaknesses identified in a solo library would be that the collection or budget is too small. Even large, multimillion-dollar libraries have difficulty securing additional funding. This fact does not mitigate the need that the smaller library has, but it is a larger context within which solo librarians often struggle. Therefore, the solo librarian must transform the budget statement into something that is doable; in other words, if the collection budget is "X" dollars, what can be purchased? Answering the next question helps the librarian tap into the community and garner support, as well as identify stakeholders if they haven't already been identified. Who are the items being bought for? Is it required/supportive of the courses offered in the programs? Sample theoretical and practical applications from the strategic process are identified in table 17.1.

Opportunities and threats, the latter two letters of the SWOT acronym, focus on external factors to the library such as opportunities in the community that can propel the library forward or challenges in the environment that "threaten" library success. Challenges can be overcome and, consequently, will improve the library and perhaps the institution as a whole. In the same vein as strengths and weaknesses, once the Os and the Ts are identified, they would need to be operationalized. The solo librarian must figure out how to take advantage of potential opportunities and overcome challenges identified by this analysis.

Often, the O and the T might interrelate—a threat could actually be an opportunity to further library achievement. Securing accreditation is a great example of this O and T relationship. Without accreditation, schools have difficulty remaining open, which is a sure threat to the library and the institution at large.

Accrediting bodies require colleges and universities not only to provide quality education, but also to have the ability to assess or prove that students actually learn what they're supposed to be learning. The library can participate in this process by providing instruction and circulation data, assessing student usage and satisfaction, and assessing library performance. In this case, the opportunity and the threat could be listed in the same table. See table 17.2.

ARTICULATING LIBRARY GOALS

The strategic planning process enables the solo librarian to establish goals and objectives for the library. Answering questions that result from the SWOT analysis will transform library priorities. These priorities may have

Table 17.1. Strengths/Weaknesses

	Strengths
Theoretical: General impressions, usually easily identified.	Practical: How is this known? How can this be preserved or improved upon?
Faculty/students value the library and its service.	Circulation, database usage, interlibrary loan statistics. Complete a user satisfaction survey on different aspects of the library, broken down by program/stakeholder, on an annual basis. Publicize new titles, database resources, and new services as available.
Library staff is helpful.	Based on user satisfaction survey results. Compare data on a year-to-year basis. Analyze trends—focus on areas of improvement, support areas of strength. Join listservs or community groups to keep abreast of new ideas/services that may be helpful to stakeholders. Conduct library instructional seminars for new students; offer "guest" library instructional seminars in courses with new students and/or continuing students pertaining to special research topics. If all else fails, smile.

Weaknesses

Theoretical	Practical: Make it doable.
My budget is too small.	What can be purchased with limited funds?
	Can the library enter into a group purchase with other libraries in the larger community for electronic resources?
	Does the library qualify for educational/training discounts?
	Is interlibrary loan an option?
Not enough professional staff.	Can work-study students be hired? If so, what are potential job duties: circulation, weekend coverage, etc.?
	Can data prove that additional professional staff is needed/necessary?
	How can a case be made for more staff? If not this year, maybe next year, if/when more programs are added?
Collection development is lacking.	What courses are being taught? What are the course descriptions?
	If there is a subject specialty in the collection, who are the major publishers?
	Is there a faculty committee that can help inform collection choices?
	Can a library committee be formed to help plan for purchases?

Table 17.2. Opportunity/Threat

Theoretical	Practical
Accreditation for the school/program is pending or up for review.	How can the library assist in accreditation? What are accreditation requirements as related to library support? How can library data be used for accreditation purposes? How can library performance be assessed as useful or successful? Can the library design a self-study assessment tool? Once a library self-study has been designed, how can it be implemented? Can results be folded into the institution's accreditation self-study plan?

been intuitive or taken for granted at first, but now the proactive librarian will turn them into actionable, quantifiable, descriptive objectives. For example, conferring with stakeholders who are experts in their subject area, acquiring up-to-date materials, cataloging them so that people can locate them in the online catalog, and circulating new materials to the people who want them are all intuitively part of completing one's day on the job, but they're also part of a larger goal of the library, which is quality service. The solo librarian is both running the library in a logistical sense and ensuring access and usage of library resources by the community—all functions relating to and identified in the strategic plan.

The planning process also helps define the library in the context of the overall institution. It articulates and answers questions such as: What is the role of the library? Is it purely supportive in meeting stakeholder needs? Or is the library a part of the steering committee of the institution as well? This particular library impacted accreditation—data from library usage and assessment were also used for general and special program accreditation. Because of this, the library's role expanded beyond the front door and the book drop, beyond the physical boundaries and into the planning process of the institution itself.

ADVOCATING FOR LIBRARY RESOURCES

Finally, the strategic planning process and outcomes can give the solo librarian valuable tools to advocate for much needed resources. To tell an administrator, "I need more resources for X collection," or "I need new computers," may not have the same impact as "Our records indicate that library circulation is up 25 percent, but 10 percent of resources have been damaged and another 10 percent of the titles have been superseded." Statements such as "Student and faculty satisfaction with our computers has shown a 45 percent decrease" may lead to further collection funding and new computers.

Based on library data and institutional size, the solo librarian may even think of advocating for another professional position in the future, especially if it can be justified by library usage and data. Perhaps some day, the solo librarian can make a credible case for being solo no more.

From Priorities to the Front Lines

When that front door opens and a student walks in disputing an overdue fine, along with twenty e-mailed reference questions waiting in the library inbox and the phone call that a link isn't working on the website . . . this is probably not the time when the solo librarian is thinking, "Good thing I have my strategic plan in place." However, a good strategic plan is like an umbrella that provides shelter and support to all the duties covered by it, or like a flashlight guiding the practitioner down a path with curves and turns in the middle of the night. Planning is especially important when conflicting job responsibilities arise, as it can help the librarian make choices that might or might not be intuitive and provide justification as to why such choices are made.

Job tasks will most likely align themselves in a lock-step position to the core library functions. Because these tasks are ongoing, they would easily have been identified and organized in the strategic plan: resources need to be cataloged, the website needs to be updated (or created in the first place), students are asking questions, faculty need assistance with resources available for their classes.

A typical day can begin with general, library-centric tasks, but special projects may arise, and then the solo librarian may wonder where to start. Luckily, Supergirl is not the only one with connections to superhero relations; the solo librarian may have others within the community to assist.

COMMUNITY BUILDING

By reaching out to school administration, faculty, and students, the solo librarian has many superheroes at his or her service. To put it generally, faculty are subject experts in their fields; students are, if not experts, then quite vocal, about the services they require; and the administration are considered experts in defining institutional policies. Depending on the situation at hand, the solo librarian can and should consult his or her respective superhero when needed, but it's also up to the solo librarian to use judgment as to when to consult and when to personally take the reins and make decisions.

INSTITUTIONAL DECISIONS VERSUS SOLO LIBRARIAN DECISIONS

Security issues would most likely be referred to the governing administration. Who is in charge when there's an emergency? How and when do library users access the space—is there a security guard? Are there security cameras? If so, can they be installed in the library and/or circulation area? Is there a panic button system? Most likely, health and injury emergencies in the workplace are, thankfully, not left up entirely to the solo librarian, so it's best to be advised of the institution's disaster/emergency preparedness plan. At the same time, larger institutions may not take into consideration the special requirements of a library during emergency situations, so it is up to the solo librarian to have the library's needs included in any disaster response plan.

On the other hand, the solo librarian can make decisions on setting library hours by balancing available resources with what's actually possible. Is it necessary to be open seven days a week, as well as in the evening? In an academic library, with weekend courses, most definitely yes. A higher education institution will have federal work-study students available; in a one-person library, a pool of student staff is a necessity. To maximize the hours without burning out the librarian and student staff, perhaps the library cannot be open all day and all night every day, but only when courses are in session or compromising half days on Sundays. To further balance student staff burnout, during intercession breaks library hours can be shortened; students can choose between taking a much-needed rest or earning extra money and working longer hours.

STAFFING THE SOLO LIBRARY

Staffing in general is a challenge and a balancing act. For a library such as in this chapter, a dedicated student staff is a must. Not only can students assist with day-to-day activities, but they are invested stakeholders of the library and of the school itself. They also have the ability to provide valuable publicity about library services and resources to students who otherwise might not know about them. In this day and age, how many students give up on looking for a resource if it's not found online? Student work-study staff are ambassadors to their peers and provide firsthand knowledge of library services such as extended inter-library loan.

ADDING NEW PROGRAMS

Similar decision-making issues come up with expanding subject areas in the library. If new programs are added to the curriculum of the school, it goes without saying that new materials and resources also need to be added. How does the solo librarian prioritize? First, by advocating seed monies for a new collection—usually included in the start-up cost of a new program; second, by consultation with subject area specialists (faculty) and good old-fashioned research into the publishers of the field. Definitely do not underestimate the power of other librarians; research schools with similar programs and contact their librarians and/or peek into their library holdings for ideas.

NUTS AND BOLTS OF RUNNING THE SOLO LIBRARY

Other front-line decisions impacting a solo library concern the nuts and bolts of running the library itself. Is there a budget for an online public access system (OPAC)? If so, what kind of software/hardware package would be appropriate for the collection? Would one package provide multiple functions, such as cataloging, serials, circulation, and reporting, as well as a user interface for the public? Or would a simple, web-based product be a better option? Some solo libraries can manage on non-MARC records, but others can't function without them. Ultimately, the solo librarian is the one who would make that choice for the particular library.

The sample library in this chapter was connected to other similar libraries across the country, in a national university setting. This system provided the ability to connect all library collections into one OPAC and share the cost with one contract. While the physical distance between the different libraries made sharing of materials difficult and time consuming, some inter-library loan, especially with respect to journal articles, was available at a minimal cost.

Other cost-sharing initiatives included access to electronic resources. It made sense for the solo libraries under the same parent institution to enter into database contracts to cut overall costs. Not only were group purchases often cheaper than individual agreements, but the invoicing could be weighted based on student body count at the respective library sites. For an independent solo library, institutional cost-sharing options may not be available, but local agreements may exist. The local library association invited libraries to participate in group database purchases, but this library declined to participate since an internal option was available.

CARING FOR THE SOLO LIBRARIAN

Professional development, when it can be fitted in among cataloging books and updating the library website, is also paramount to running a library alone. Seeking opportunities to network with similar librarians with similar collections provides the solo librarian with a community to learn from and brainstorm with. While a parent institution may hesitate to send a solo librarian to national meetings and events, participation in web forums and presentations as well as subscribing to pertinent listservs are a cost-effective way to keep current and abreast of new developments in the field. Often, a solo librarian can feel isolated and it is paramount that the librarian communicates with peers—this will affirm the solo librarian's position and provide a sounding board to share ideas and even create positive, lifelong professional relationships.

Conclusion

While this chapter focuses on a library in a higher education setting, planning and actualizing library priorities and goals can be translated to other institutions. The basics of running a solo library are a balancing act of strategic planning and successfully completing the tasks at hand. Those very tasks are what drive the strategic planning process, as they help the librarian understand what the priorities are; hence the question: what comes first, the plan or the process? By keeping the priorities and goals of the library in sight, the solo librarian can manage the library without becoming overwhelmed by competing job responsibilities and secure success for the library and for its stakeholders.

The solo librarian is a superhero in his or her own right—it takes guts, creativity, and sometimes extraordinary patience and a sense of humor to be successful in running a library alone. A mix of planning and on-the-job flexibility will ensure that the solo librarian is poised for achievement and, at the very least, able to navigate the many landscapes of library management and service.

CHAPTER 18

Oh, Those Dreaded Annual Reports

Virginia L. Eldridge

Does the phrase "annual report" conjure up endless hours of tedium and give you chills of dread? An annual report need not be a chore, and it need not be particularly time consuming. Defined as a yearly accounting of the library's activities and usage, an annual report can be brief or extensive. Often a mere handful of pages will do, depending on your organization's needs and the report's intended use.

Annual Reports as Opportunities

You're a solo librarian, so why add to an already overwhelming workload? Your organization may require an annual report, of course. Even if it doesn't, you should consider submitting one. Think of it as your chance to shine! You know the value of the library, but does your organization? Do your sponsors? Either way, an annual report enables you to confirm the library's importance, and it offers the ideal venue for showing how you have increased productivity, saved the organization money, been of service to community groups, and any number of other contributions. After completing the report, you might be as surprised as your boss at how much you have accomplished over the past year. You can also easily transform your annual report into an inexpensive and very useful public relations tool, helping the wider community appreciate your significance and contributions.[1] And don't forget—if you decide to change jobs, your annual reports provide the ideal foundation for an updated resume.

Timing Is Everything

An annual report usually runs along the fiscal year calendar but can be published during any twelve-month period. When to publish an annual report depends on whether your organization requires one and your purpose in providing it. If the organization does not have a specific annual report deadline and you intend to use the report data during budget hearings, using the fiscal year may be your best choice. If you want to use the annual report as a public relations tool and you can choose the report's submission date, you may prefer the calendar year (or some other schedule) so you can create the report during your slow period. Often such slow periods come near the end of the calendar year for special (e.g., law, medical) libraries and in the early spring for public libraries. And consider this: if your supervisor already requires monthly or weekly reports, you can easily bring those together into an impressive end-of-year version.

What if you hired on in the middle of a fiscal year or reporting cycle? Just do your best to recover needed statistics from earlier in the year. Check your files—both print and electronic—for anything your predecessor might have left behind. Search carefully. Often the information you seek is available but buried in seemingly endless and overwhelming numbers of files. And don't be afraid to contact your predecessor for additional information. If all that fails, construct a solid report on what you do know and date the document accordingly.

The All-Important Audience

Who will see this annual report? Is it for your boss alone, or will it perhaps be published on the library/organization website? Will the report be shared with the library's stakeholders? Carefully consider your intended audience before starting. That audience will certainly influence the report's content. Information that goes to your supervisor might not be appropriate for an entire organization, much less for the general public. And your intended audience should also influence the report's language. Library jargon will make sense to those with a library background, including perhaps a supervisor, the library board, and the library system office. But try to avoid such technical terminology when addressing those without a library background. Normally the annual report's audience would at least include your immediate supervisor and perhaps others in the organization. But also show your report to those in charge of budget decisions. It can't hurt, and it just might lead to a larger budget for your library next year—maybe including a raise for you!

You might want to produce two versions of your annual report, one designed for internal use and another for public relations. Distribute the latter with a cover letter to friends of the library, local fundraisers, library associations, and websites. Consider sending out press releases with particularly interesting information drawn from your annual report. Publishers and editors might just decide to do an article about your library. But be sure to check with your supervisor before going public.

Getting Started

After you determine your audience, begin the process of preparation. Start by studying previous annual reports, including your predecessor's and others. You can consult internet articles and samples[2] as well as examples provided at the end of this chapter. Courses on writing annual reports are also available (see "Resources"), but tend to be geared toward producing slick, multicolored products for a company's stockholders or for nonprofits seeking grants. Find out what your boss would like to see. Every organization is unique so report contents vary. A law firm library and a county library, for example, may require different styles, information, and statistics. Be sure to tailor the report to suit your purposes. A good place to begin is with an outline, selecting from the items listed below in the "What to Include" section.

With outline in hand, start gathering your raw data, notes, and statistics. Libraries have historically collected information on visitor numbers, the number and type of reference questions asked and answered, and library cards issued. If figures are compiled on a regular basis, you have quick, easy, and almost foolproof access to numbers on short notice. Even so, if your fiscal year runs July 1 to June 30, do not begin drafting your annual report on June 29! Plan ahead. Most library management systems have ready-made reports that produce collection and circulation data. Supplement these. Note and date everything you can think of and edit later. Be creative and thorough. Gather data on who comes in, how many telephone reference calls you receive, the number of computer users, and tours given, just to name a few. Compile this data in a spreadsheet or manually on a paper chart. Keep a file folder handy to store thank you cards, for example, and flyers advertising library events. Collecting information throughout the year will greatly simplify the writing process. As soon as you submit your annual report, start collecting information for next year's report.

Making the Report Your Own

Not every annual report will cover everything listed below and some librarians may want to include things not on this list. Others may feel uncomfortable providing personal information, such as degree qualifications or photos of library activities that include easily identifiable patrons. For security reasons, libraries should be careful about including photos in reports to be made public. Often parents are thrilled to see their child's picture in a newspaper or annual report, but some are leery of publicity. Concerns about children's exposure to sex offenders are not uncommon, and patrons may prefer a low profile for other personal reasons. Ask the subject (or parent/legal guardian) for permission first. Such caveats aside, the annual report should reflect your library, its accomplishments, and its needs.

Consider beginning your report with an introduction, the library's mission statement, and a brief summary of the year's accomplishments. Follow with a detailed report of the year's events, covering such areas as:

- Technology/equipment (inventory, purchases, and upgrades)
- Space planning (additions and remodeling)
- Grants (those applied for, those received, and how they were used)
- Library hosted events (such as Summer Reading Club or National Library Week)
- "Green" efforts (wasteful library spending reduced, recycling projects)
- Preservation or conservation
- Collaborative efforts with other libraries
- Library volunteers (don't forget to report on these important folks—numbers and hours worked, friends group events, monies raised)
- Publicity (including newsletters and newspaper articles)

Be sure to include what you personally did over the last year. Include continuing education classes completed, conferences attended, papers presented, and your professional organization memberships. Did you receive any awards or other forms of recognition? How about the time you volunteered and other community outreach efforts? Remember, this is your opportunity to stand out—don't be shy!

A large part of your report will be statistics. Make the numbers interesting by varying how you present them. Charts, lists, and narrative discussions—each plays a part. Consider all or some of the following:

- The library collection (number of volumes, CDs, DVDs, serials)
- Number of registered borrowers
- Number of books/materials ordered
- Circulation numbers
- Annual visitors chart (by week or month)
- Number of web page visitors
- Database access
- Number of reference queries (note interesting or funny questions)
- Inter-library loans (ordered or fulfilled)
- Financial report (how your budget was spent)
- Statistics showing growth (compare current vs. last year or ten years ago, for example)
- Return on Investment report (demonstrating how much money the library saves by not buying multiple copies of books, videos, Internet subscriptions, and so on). For examples, see douglascountylibraries.org/AboutUs/LibraryValue, www.wyla.org/roi/ and http://nnlm.gov/mcr/evaluation/roi.html.

After presenting the past year's accomplishments, take the time to list your goals for the upcoming year. Discuss the resources (both financial and human) needed to meet these goals. This not only showcases your plans, but it can help get your boss and others excited about the future.

Are there some things you might want to leave out? Yes. You don't have to report on absolutely everything. A certain county librarian might not want to report how she got in trouble with the county commissioners for ordering lollipops for the children. (That will be our little secret.)

Final Decisions

With the content established—text, charts, photos—you must decide how to present your report. Print format, though most common, might not be the best delivery method. For example, someone running a film library may discover that video reports get a better response than paper ones. Not a problem. These days quality amateur video is easily and inexpensively created. Such a presentation could be readily placed on a website instead of (or in addition to) the written version.

Plain paper with black ink is the least expensive choice regardless of the chosen duplication method; however, if you are including photos you may opt for the more expensive color ink. A limited number of reports to be circulated locally may be printed in-house, but distribution of larger quantities may best be done with full-color, slick brochures from a professional printer. An annual report can be presented on a single sheet of paper, a bi- or tri-fold brochure, a multipage booklet, or in a newspaper format. It can be organized chronologically, topically, by library/non-library duties, or any numbers of other ways. Determining how best to organize your information will depend on what you choose to share, what you decide to emphasize, and your intended audience. Studying samples will give you some ideas. Font styles also help you impart your various messages and deserve some thought. Varying fonts and font sizes helps differentiate section headings from actual information, making it easier for the casual reader. But beware—too many font changes can be confusing and unprofessional. Does your library have its own logo or "brand"? If so, include it on your annual report, other promotional materials, and your letterhead. If your library doesn't have a logo but the parent organization does, use their logo to help tie the library to the larger entity.

Conclusion

Don't dread the thought of writing an annual report. See it as an opportunity instead. Identify your audience and write for them, highlighting your accomplishments. Try to complete an annual report—even if it is only one page. As Diane McKenzie said in her Library Grits Blog on June 27, 2009: "Cannot afford time to write an annual report? My feeling is that you can't afford not to."[3]

Resources

FOR FURTHER READING

Holcomb, Jean M. "The Annual Report: An Overlooked Opportunity to Tell the Library's Story." *AALL Spectrum Magazine* (June 2003): 10–12.
Roth, Robert. *The Writer's Guide to Annual Reports.* Charleston, S.C.: BookSurge Publishing, 2009.
Taylor, Carolyn. *Writing the Nonprofit Annual Report.* San Francisco: Wiley, 2001.
———. *Publishing the Nonprofit Annual Report: Tips, Traps, and Tricks of the Trade*, 1st ed. San Francisco: Jossey-Bass, 2008.

E-COURSES

www.nonprofitmarketingguide.com/annualreports.htm (accessed October 30, 2010).
www.nonprofitmarketingguide.com/resources/live-webinars/ (accessed October 30, 2010).

EXAMPLES OF ANNUAL REPORTS

Carol and Madison Library System, Arkansas: www.carrollmadisonlibraries.org/media/document/annualreport/2008_Annual_Report.pdf.
Clark County Law Library, Washington: www.co.clark.wa.us/law-library/documents/Annual%20report%202004.pdf (accessed October 30, 2010).
Jones Library, Massachusetts: www.joneslibrary.org/report/index.html (accessed October 30, 2010).
New York Public: annualreports.nypl.org/2009/ (accessed October 30, 2010).
Oakland Public Library, California: www.oaklandlibrary.org/Annual_Report.pdf (accessed October 30, 2010).
Oklahoma State University: www.library.okstate.edu/annualreport/index.htm (accessed October 30, 2010).
Palestine Public Library, Texas: www.palestinelibrary.org/Librar%20Report.pdf.
Riverside County Law Library, California: www.lawlibrary.co.riverside.ca.us/RCLLAnnualReport0708.pdf (accessed October 30, 2010).

HELPFUL WEBSITES

"About.com:Nonprofit   Charitable   Orgs":   nonprofit.about.com/od/ nonprofitpromotion/a/annualreps.htm (accessed October 30, 2010).

Diane McKenzie, "Importance of Creating an Annual Report," Library Grits Blog: librarygrits.blogspot.com/2009_06_01_archive.html (accessed October 30, 2010).

Forbes.com: www.forbes.com/2004/07/12/cx_ml_0712reports.html (accessed October 30, 2010).

"How to Complete the Public Library Annual Report by TSLAC": www.tsl.state .tx.us/ld/librarydevelopments/?p=2729 (accessed October 30, 2010).

Nonprofit Marketing Guide.com: www.nonprofitmarketingguide.com/resources/ book/how-to-write-nonprofit-annual-report/ (accessed October 30, 2010).

"State of Iowa, Annual Report Template for School Libraries": www.statelibrary ofiowa.org/ld/school-librarians/reqandsupp/anrpt/view (accessed October 30, 2010).

ANNUAL REPORT MODELS

Annual Report August 31, 2001[4]

Mediaville County Library, Mediaville County, TX
Telephone: (555) 555-5555
Email: Mediavillelib@xyz.com
Librarian: Jane Bowen-Smith, M.L.S.
Library Hours: Wednesday 10–8
Tuesday, Thursday, Friday 10–5
Saturday 9–2
Closed Sunday and Monday

The Mediaville County Library's mission is to provide a variety of educational and recreational resources to the residents of Mediaville County. To accomplish this mission during the 2000–2001 fiscal year, the library loaned 50,000 items to 3,240 registered cardholders, gave twenty-four library tours to students of the Mediaville Independent School District and two library tours to the New Beginnings Literacy Program, answered 5,168 reference questions, and presented a weekly story time to 123 preschool children.

The most unusual reference question was "How many stomachs does a cow have?" while the most popular reference question was "Did George Washington really cut down a cherry tree and tell his father he did it?"

Our goals for the 2000–2001 fiscal year included expanding our Summer Reading Program to include teens, rejuvenating the Mediaville County Library Friends of the Library organization, and increasing the number of volunteers to eight volunteers with three additional continuing education sessions.

FRIENDS OF THE LIBRARY

The Mediaville County Library's Friends organization worked with local businesses to provide backpacks and paperback books for Summer Reading Club prizes. They also provided the funds for two feature movie rentals and helped with the cost of craft supplies for several children's and young adult craft programs offered throughout the year. The Friends' biannual Book Sale raised $1,546.25. Another book sale, planned for November 10, 2001, will be held in the library's meeting room. Details will be available after October 15. Please mark your calendars and check out the book sale. Monies will be used for next year's library activities and Summer Reading Club expenses.

SUMMER READING CLUB

This year's Summer Reading Club had 1,500 registered participants between the ages of five and seventeen. The theme, *Top the Jokeboy—READ*, a spin-off of last spring's *BatKid* movie, was the State Library's adopted program with all plans and handouts coming from our regional system and the State Library. Prizes were donated by local businesses and the library's Friends organization. The Summer Reading Club kicked off on May 20 with a showing of the movie *BatKid* and activities included two additional movie nights, a low-rider show for the teens, and the ending party on August 10, which included the awards for the best jokes submitted by each of four age groups. Younger children attended three special pajama story times and everyone was invited to create and submit their own jokes for the August 10 Party-In-The-Park.

VOLUNTEERS

A giant thanks to our nine volunteers: Jayne Smith, Robin Brown, Jason Jones, Lacey Wayne, Dwayne Roberts, Debbie Roberts, Bill Green, Beth Sager, and George Holten. Everyone assisted with the daily tasks necessary to smooth library operation and enabled the library to remain open when I was unable to be in the building. Volunteers contributed a total of one thousand service hours and attended a total of two hundred hours of continuing education for the year. Thank you all. We could not have had the successful year we had without your dedication, caring, and interest.

ADULT ACTIVITIES

Our monthly book discussion series had another successful year. Attended by an average of ten participants including two teens, the books included one Graham Green and a Danielle Steel title. We also provided the site for a joint community concert series sponsored by the Library Board and the Chamber of Commerce. The four performances were well attended and we hope to continue the tradition at some future time.

YOUNG ADULTS

In addition to the Summer Reading Club's low-rider show and the feature movies, local teens, ages twelve to eighteen, enjoyed a well-attended Halloween monster-fest and a Holiday Craft Workshop.

CHILDREN

One hundred twenty-three preschool children attended a weekly story time from September 2000 to April 2001. Two sessions were available in order to accommodate both preschool schedules and individual parents bringing their own children. Older children attended a variety of craft workshops and special holiday pajama story hours and had an opportunity to write and present their own puppet show. The puppet show was exceptionally well received by both parents and children as evidenced by requests to offer this program again.

GOALS FOR 2001–2002

Establish a small literacy collection to support the New Beginnings Literacy Program and increase the number of library visits from this organization from two to six.

Continue expanding the Mediaville County Library Friends of the Library organization in both membership and activities.

Increase the volunteer recruitment and training by another four volunteers and an additional continuing education program by working with our regional library system office.

Develop a formal donation policy.

SUMMARY

Overall, the Mediaville County Library had a busy year with much help from the Library Board, library volunteers, and the Friends of the Library. Library programs during this past year were well received and we have received requests to repeat several of them including the concert series, Summer Reading Club, and low-rider show. Areas in need of work include developing a small adult literacy collection, improving library marketing to residents of all ages, and developing a formal donation policy.

I thank you and the Library's Board of Trustees for allowing me the privilege of serving as your library director.

Jane Bowen-Smith

Copies Delivered to Library Board of Trustees:

Jan White (555) 556-1234 (District 1) Carol Stern (555) 646-8000 (District 4)

Dan Smith (555) 554-2356 (District 2) Clem Nile (555) 746-5000 (District 5)

Tracey Boudin (555) 555-6894 (District 3) Kim Night (555) 551-2500 (District 6)

Notes

1. "Marketing the Small Library," Kansas State Library, 2002, www.sksways .org/KSL/development/marketing_the_smalllibrary.pdf.

2. Cindy Chick: www.llrx.com/extras/annual.htm; and Kristin A. Cheney: www.aallnet.org/products/pub_llj_v97n03/2005-28.pdf.

3. Diane McKenzie, "Importance of Creating an Annual Report," Library Grits Blog, Saturday, June 27, 2009.

4. Created by Laurie Selwyn, 2010.

CHAPTER 19

Security Tips for the Solo Librarian

Jonathan Frater

"Todd:" A Study in Library Vandalism

We have a vandal in our library. Lacking any real information about him, I've been calling him "Todd." I've never met him (her?) but I know his work well enough: older, worn books that have turned up in various stages of destruction. Todd has a distinct modus operandi. He takes a nonfiction paperback book, and tears huge gaps in the center pages while leaving the cover intact. Nine times out of ten, it's a student browsing the stacks who reports these wrecked tomes to me or another librarian. (Todd has nailed thirty-six volumes as of this writing.) I would love to catch him in the act and deal with him personally. Unfortunately, being responsible for forty thousand print volumes and nearly twice as many electronic titles, plus several hundred students each day means there's a real limit on what I can do. Or is there?

Common Library Security Issues

Books disappear from the shelves. Theft is the most common reason, and we've seen it many times in our daily work without necessarily calling it that. Patrons (and sometimes staff) borrow books or video tapes or DVDs and CDs and don't return them. Most often this is simple neglect on the borrower's part. Sometimes patrons are motivated by political or religious beliefs to rob the public of a particular title that deals with an objectionable subject.[1] Vandalism is rather less common and generally involves damage to library property: cut computer cables, damaged volumes, abused furniture. Regardless of the cause, the loss to your facility is real.[2]

Crimes against individuals in libraries are rare, but they have been known to happen. Inappropriate patron behavior such as trespassing or viewing porn is something all librarians will have to deal with from time to time. Securing your workplace's network will help with online issues. Basic safety precautions and common sense should deter all but the most determined individuals.[3] Should they make an appearance, calling for help remains an option.

Library Security Policy

Everything begins with developing a functional, well-planned library security policy. This is a must, both to create a solid plan for protecting your staff, collection, and property, and for legal redress should it come to that. Breaches of library security rarely come to legal action but if they do, you want to be able to show a police officer or a judge that you acted appropriately within the structure of your operating policy.

Each library has its own needs and structure, but there are three areas of concern that your library security policy must deal with:

1. Which actions or events constitute a violation of the library staff or property
2. A list of general security procedures
3. Formal disciplinary procedures, both for staff and patrons

This list is clearly not exhaustive. Additional areas of application you might also consider policies for include rules of patron behavior, specific security procedures for library departments (if your library is large enough for this), information technology equipment security procedures, and so on.

FLOOR PLAN

If you don't have a floor plan of your library, draw one. It's simple and there are a number of good books on the subject of drafting if you're really ambitious about it. Use a pencil and a sheet of square graph paper and make the scale manageable (one square should equal five or ten feet). Identify walls, doors and what direction they swing open, stairwells, elevator shafts, and windows. Then place your stacks, shelves, and furniture. When you're done you'll have a perspective on your workplace that you might not have had previously, which leads me to my next point, line of sight.

LINES OF SIGHT

All points within structures have lines of sight (LOS). An LOS is essentially a direct visual line from you to any given point in the library. Anywhere your eyes can't reach is called a "blind spot." The trick is to arrange your workplace such that you create as many lines of sight and as few blind spots as possible. When someone is able to hang out in an area where he can't be detected, he's more likely to harm your library's property. I'm not talking about secure situations such as closed stacks, back room offices, or other sections of the facility that are nominally inaccessible to patron traffic. I mean the library proper: reading room, banks of computers, periodical racks, where patrons are likely to be most of the time. Additionally, think about where you work and what you do on a daily basis that might be altered for the sake of visibility. A change as simple as raising your chair a few inches can enable you to see over monitors that might be blocking your vision, for example.

The layout of your work space is obviously unique, but knowing it well makes the difference between being distracted by watching for vandals and the damage they do and being able to concentrate on your job. One obvious if extreme solution to this is to rearrange your library's layout. Few librarians will do this; it's just too strenuous. Rearranging furniture, however, is much easier.

ROAMING LIBRARIAN

Another solution to blind spots is to set a schedule where you get out from behind the desk and walk around the place. When security guards do this it's called "walking the floor" and its purpose is to keep at least one set of eyes on the area that's being patrolled at all times. Clearly, if you're all alone, complete coverage won't be possible. But it does let patrons know that you're on the job, and that you're around. The best schedule for this might be at random, between daily chores or whenever you feel the need to stretch your legs, for example. A routine, predictable schedule is almost as good, but it needs to be regular enough for you to be visible to the patrons and frequent enough that the patrons don't forget you're there.

SPOT CHECKS

Whenever you pass the stacks, pull out a book and leaf through it. Page through the books as you reshelve them. Straighten the newspaper and magazine racks. This only takes a few moments and gives you an idea of the general quality of the volumes on the shelf. Damage to a spine is often a clear indicator of a problem. So are gaps between pages (this is how I picked up on Todd's doings).

MIRRORS

Go to your local supermarket, or most other retail stores, even (perhaps especially) your local bookstore. What do you see mounted in the corners of the store near the ceiling? Large round mirrors. These simple but effective devices are designed to deter shoplifters by letting them know that store employees are watching and can see them literally from around the corner. You never really know who's watching. Besides which they really do work.

GATES AND RFID TAGS

A more ambitious project is to install RFID security tags on your books and a matching gate reader at the entrance to your library to alert you when a book is being removed. There is also a matter of software installation in your circulation computer. The problem with this solution is the relatively high expense and difficulty of installation. Also, if it breaks, you'll have to ask the company who installed the gates to have a repairman take a look at it if they can't talk you through the procedure on the phone. A worse problem is the daunting prospect of manually affixing several thousand security tags on your print volumes by hand one at a time. One final reality is that gates can be circumvented by simply ripping a cover or page out of the book.

SECURITY CAMERAS

Cameras present an even more potentially expensive proposition than RFID tagging but one which, if properly done, incurs less hassle for you personally. The problems in this choice are technical rather than labor-related, but a great deal depends on the quality of the equipment and the quality of the service involved. Two words: hire professionals. A cheaper, simpler alternative is to mount fake camera housings, which involve flashing LED lights, at several locations in your library. Oftentimes, the perception of a secure location is enough to prompt a move to an easier target. With a bit of luck, these should deter all but the most determined assailants.

Any solution you adopt must meet your particular needs and abilities. Remember, you can always learn a new skill or ask for increased funding, but you can never be in two places at the same time or become an expert in a strange new procedure overnight. Ask for advice from librarians in situations similar to yours. Most importantly, ask for references from any security company you are thinking of hiring.

The Law Is on Your Side, But . . .

Things get ugly. When they do, call for backup. With that said, remember this: you are a librarian. That means you are in charge of maintaining the collection, the facilities, and the equipment. Feel free to correct someone who is obviously violating the rules set forth in your library security policy. Loud noises, misuse of equipment, damaging a volume, and so forth are things within your responsibilities. Never confront someone who is clearly out of control. Fights, loud and obnoxious patrons who resist all requests to settle down, and any threatening moves at all are grounds for calling for help. Types of help include:

1. Helpful patrons: You run the library alone but you are rarely alone in the building for long. You may have some especially supportive patrons

who are willing to keep an eye out for disruptive activity and inform you of it. (You never know until you ask.)

2. Security: Large buildings, especially office buildings, often have their own security people on hand, generally employed by the real estate entity that owns the property. You should get to know all of them by name and assignment (i.e., by which floors they can be found on and when) and the names of their managers or supervisors. Memorize the phone extension where they may be contacted if a potentially danger-ous situation develops. You should at least know the names of the team assigned to your floor; you'll be amazed how quickly they learn who you are just by greeting them in the morning and wishing them a good night.

3. Police: You want to develop a positive relationship with your local po-lice. Even college campuses often have their own police departments; it couldn't hurt to ask if one or two of them could include the library as part of a regular patrol. Perhaps a nonemergency phone number is available for a librarian to use in order to avoid straining the 911 switchboard. My point is: calling the cops is always an option. But be warned. If you call them to settle a loud and destructive argument be-tween two or more patrons, that's one thing. If you call them because there's a man in a bathrobe feeding pigeons on the sidewalk outside the library, well, that's something else. 911 is for emergencies only.

Train Your Staff

Before I became a librarian, I worked in a number of different occupa-tions; arguably the worst one was pushing software at a retail chain store in Manhattan. Retail, however, is an excellent environment to learn secu-rity strategy: shoplifters are generally the industry's worst, most persistent problem. Several times a year, the corporate headquarters sent their chief of security to give us some basic training on what to look for and how to spot the problem individuals before they had the chance to do their thing.

The training boiled down to this: watch everything all the time. Be aware of what goes on around you. Know your customers—shoplifters are often your best customers, it turns out, buying a ten dollar item and steal-ing a fifty dollar item—and know when someone has entered the premises and when they leave. Keep an eye on people who are constantly looking over their shoulder at you or always turn their back on you when you walk by. If someone is sitting at the computer and is trying to angle his body so that you can't see the display, be aware of it. If someone is physically trying to move the furniture to shield him- or herself from your view, make a note of it. Listen for sounds your library is not known to make on its own: moving furniture, breaking glass, pounding on wood or metal, for example. Know the difference between the sounds of a friendly argument and a fistfight. Always be willing to ask if help is needed. And roam. Often. Nothing deters your average troublemaker like the attention of the staff.

Secure Your Equipment and Electronics

Information technology (IT) permeates all aspects of teaching, researching, outreach, communication, and the business and facilities function of the library. It also happens to be a huge security leak for those knowledgeable and unscrupulous enough to take advantage of it. The days of simply not clicking on any e-mail with an executable file attached to it are over (though that danger still exists—don't click). Bigger security problems will emerge from outdated software—specifically, script languages like Java and Adobe Products (Flash, Shockwave, Reader, Acrobat). These open doors can allow malicious code to enter; all you need do is visit the wrong website. The fix is simple: whenever your PC flashes a symbol declaring that "an update is available" click on it. This will limit your computer's vulnerability through those particular infection vectors. Following that your biggest worries will likely be viruses, adware, and so-called script kiddie amateur hackers. Luckily, these are relatively simple problems (broadband network security is an example of a relatively complex problem), requiring a bit of investment in intruder-control software.

An anti-virus application is essential. We use McAfee Anti-Virus at MCNY, but others are available: Norton Anti-Virus and Kaspersky Anti-Virus are both well-known, capable options. Whichever you choose, update it frequently.

To prevent spyware, we have Super Anti-Spyware installed on our computers. This is a free application that can be downloaded at www .superantispyware.com. Others include adblockplus.com, www.ubuntu .com, and noscript.net.

Script kiddies is a term used at many police departments to describe kids—children, some of them—who think breaking into computers is cool, but don't have a sufficient understanding of them to make it happen. Their solution is to log on to "haxor" sites and download "warez," meaning scripted applications to do the dirty work for them. They run scripts, enjoy some success, and then get caught. Your best defense versus the script kiddies is to keep your operation simple: use a unique password for each PC on your network. Set your e-mail reader to list messages instead of automatically viewing them. Disable pop-up windows on your web browsers. Many companies offer website blocking applications to ensure that inappropriate websites (aka porn sites) are not viewed in the library. But be aware that these are not foolproof or particularly good at determining contextual nuance. Software that blocks porn may also block information on sexually transmitted disease, breast cancer, and contraception.

Never install any application on your computer if you don't understand what it is, where it came from, or how it works.

DETERMINE YOUR OBJECTIVES

Your library security policy should spell out how your electronic resources are not to be used. What is not on the list should be generally permissible, with the understanding that this list needs to be re-evaluated every so often. You can save time and effort by going to your favorite search engine and seeing what other IT departments consider good policy (I find that searching by institution name yields better results than looking for general terms like "Internet security" does). Obviously, you can't plan for every possibility, but make sure the rules you choose to include are clearly defined.

ENFORCE YOUR OBJECTIVES

Don't make rules you can't enforce. You can make sure that a rule against using cell phones, eating, and drinking in the computer lab is enforced through personal effort. Denying someone access to your collection based on his or her clothing selection, however, would be inconvenient for everyone. Assign responsibilities. Decide what actions and knowledge you are personally capable of assuming on a day-to-day basis. Supervising electronic resources is time consuming, and at many large libraries, demands a full-time employee. Assign your ISP everything else. Always keep building your skills. The world literally runs on computers these days—librarians who keep their IT skills current will be better able to manage their facilities than those who don't.

KNOW HOW MUCH SECURITY YOU CAN AFFORD

You have a budget; we all do. Most ISPs provide a minimal level of security for their clients, even the solo librarians. This should include basic amenities such as a firewall, IP recognition of databases, subscription usernames and password protection, and so on in their monthly subscription fee. Your budget needs to handle the fee payment schedule—it's very easy to purchase more security than you can afford in a single year.

DETERMINE WHO WILL ENFORCE YOUR SECURITY

You as the facility manager are responsible for knowing how your security system functions, what might go wrong with it, what does go wrong with it most often (keep a daily or weekly maintenance log), how to troubleshoot these common problems, and who to call when you diagnose a problem you can't handle. Anything more complex, such as PC breakdowns, RFID gate malfunctions, software glitches, and programming faults, should be handled by your ISP. Another thing you will be responsible for by default is informing your patrons when some piece of equipment is unavailable and giving them a realistic idea of when it might be returned to their use. A hard and fast rule is: if the ISP tells you that the problem will be fixed in an hour, tell the patrons it'll be several hours. If the ISP tells you several hours, it means tomorrow. If they say it will take days, tell the patrons that you don't know, but your ISP is working to fix it as quickly as they can. The Internet is a vast, incredibly complicated machine, and like all complicated machines, it sometimes breaks, disrupting your service. Don't shout at your ISP sales rep when this happens; call their tech support department to ensure that they do know about the problem, then call every day or so for an update. Knowing their customers are watching them sometimes does wonders for service.

Conclusion

As a final word, remember not to get lost in the details. You are a librarian; the library and your patrons are your greatest concerns. It's easy to worry incessantly about what might go wrong; concentrate on documenting what has gone wrong and then implementing policies and plans to fix it or to ensure that it does not happen again. It's a learning process; a bit of trial and error is involved. Even though you might lose some volumes, some patrons, or some services, just remember to never lose your head.

Notes

1. E. C. Abbott, "People Who Steal Books," *Canadian Medical Association Journal* 165 (2001): 12–13.

2. J. W. Griffith, "Library Thefts: A Problem That Won't Go Away," *American Libraries* 9, no. 4 (1978): 224–27.

3. John T. Kirkpatrick, "Explaining Crime and Disorder in Libraries," *Library Trends* (Summer 1984): 13–28.

CHAPTER 20

Supervision Made Simple
RUNNING A SCHOOL LIBRARY ALONE

Rebecca Marcum Parker

Expectations are higher, budgets are tighter, and, as librarians, we want to ensure the safety and academic growth of our students. Excellent library floor plans, furniture arrangements, and student procedures will help you to provide a rigorous, well-supervised school library environment. Creating world citizens and lifelong learners in a safe environment for all is crucial.

Library Floor Plan and Furniture Arrangements

This year, I was excited to find that I would be in a different school building! I love challenges and looked forward to forging new relationships with students and staff. When I entered my new library, I was thrilled by the inviting yellow walls and it was smaller than my previous library—an easier room to supervise. I was concerned, though, because of the placement of the circulation desk, the tall bookcases, the odd furniture arrangement—the computers were in two different areas, the reference collection spanned four different spots, and two small bookcases were away from the walls, creating a barrier. Since I run a busy program with students using computers, searching for books, reading, and writing—often all at once—I needed to rearrange to create a barrier-free (or with as few barriers as possible), easy-to-supervise library. I see my library program as a full, varied program much like an orchestra. As the conductor of an effective library environment I rely on a carefully created floor plan, clear expectations, and procedures for anything students need to know how to do.

A well-organized and thought-through library floor plan including a good furniture arrangement is a must for a librarian working solo. These ideas will help you develop an organized, easy-to-monitor library:

- Start your plan by deciding where your story area/carpet and the circulation desk will be placed. Also choose an area where you will most likely stand when talking with classes who sit at tables. Try to have these spots as close to each other as possible.
- From this, create four specific zones in your library so that like items or furniture used for the same purpose are in one area. Have all student computers in one area, your tables for class use in another area, an area for your story area/carpet spot, and an area for shelving. In a rectangular-shaped room, I like to arrange the areas from lowest to highest; I place the circulation desk in the middle of one of the long walls, and, from the vantage point behind the circulation desk, I place the story area/carpet on my left with the back of my story reading chair against the wall, the table area in front of me, and the shelving to the right.
- If possible, use bookcases that are three shelves or about forty-two inches high. It is much easier to supervise students using shorter bookcases. It will be easier for you to see student activity and for students to ask for help.
- If you must use taller bookcases (this is what I have), invest in convex or dome security mirrors. Place the end of the bookcase that is furthest from where you usually stand or sit against the wall, and have students enter and exit an aisle only from the end closest to you. The area between a bookcase and the wall is very difficult to supervise; keep students from being in or using that area. If you can put a barrier at the end of the bookcases, that could make a great storage area.
- If you have an area of shelving that is more difficult to see than other areas, make this the area for your professional collection.
- If you have a spot that is hard to monitor, place a couple of tables there and designate that as an area for staff and adults to use as a tutoring area for one-on-one services or for working with a small group.
- Finally, find a spot that you can easily see from most areas but that is not that visible to students in the main table area; place a small table or two there for students who need to work alone without distractions.

After you have made the necessary decisions, test your plan. Sit in your story reading chair, sit and stand behind the circulation desk, and test out the spot you plan to use when talking with classes seated at the tables. Does your plan make sense? Can you see as many areas as possible from each point? Ask other school librarians to come test your floor plan and give suggestions. After tweaking, try it with trusted students and ask for their ideas and concerns. Make any needed changes.

Library Expectations and Procedures

Once your library is arranged, prepare the students for using the library effectively by having clear expectations/matrix plus procedures for class visits, class checkout, individual visits and checkout, and using computers. If you expect a student to know a procedure, post it, teach it, and re-teach it when necessary. I include my expectations in my library book checkout contract that both students and parents sign; on the back of the contract are my district's computer and Internet usage form and permission slip that students and parents sign. By signing this slip, students know that they are accountable for expectations and procedures, and issues can be solved easily by having students take responsibility and ownership for their behavior. It also helps save time in the future when problems occur, which is crucial for a solo librarian. I hand this out and review it during my first two library lessons of the year. This is my library contract:

2010–2011 PHILLIPS LIBRARY CONTRACT

In the library I am *responsible*; this means I will:

- take care of all library materials,
- return any library books I find (even if it's not mine),
- only use library books checked out to me, and
- let my parent/guardian know if I have an overdue or lost book.

In the library I am *safe*; this means I will:

- keep all chair legs on the floor, and
- make good behavior choices.

In the library I am *respectful*; this means I will:

- listen carefully so I can follow the directions,
- treat others how I want to be treated, and
- use a right-sized indoor voice.

In the library I am *a learner*; this means I will:

- ask questions when I don't understand—my responsibility as learner.

I understand what is expected: I accept the consequences of my actions.
Student signature _____
I will help my child in keeping this contract, ask my child about any overdue books, and help pay for any lost books.
Parent/Guardian name (print) _____
E-mail address _____
Cell number (home, if no cell): _____
Work number _____
Parent/Guardian signature _____

Make it possible for students to function independently—they enjoy being self-directed, and then many activities and students can be supervised by a single librarian. I see each class once a week, and I teach my expectations at the beginning of each year and revisit them after winter break, when students have been out of the academic environment for a couple of weeks.

So that teachers know about the availability of the library and other library information, I e-mail this welcome letter to teachers and staff at the beginning of the year:

WELCOME TO PHILLIPS LIBRARY!

Is your class/small group working on a project? Will you miss your checkout time for the week? Is a student finished reading their library book or do they need help? I love having a full schedule, and we are fortunate to have library time available for educational purposes as well as a reward time for students.

If you want to bring your entire class to the library, plan a time and a lesson with me in advance; we will cooperatively teach the lesson.

If you are sending small groups or individuals to the library, you do not need to notify me in advance. Please send them with a written pass including (1) student's name, (2) date and time, (3) purpose for the visit, and (4) your signature. Individuals and small groups can come anytime I am in the library; if I have a class they might need to work independently.

I have duty every day from 7:00–7:30 a.m., 10:00–10:30 a.m., and at the end of the day. I am available at all other times.

Library services: Many services and types of assistance are available, including unorthodox requests. I am here to help you! Periodically, I will send out forms requesting information about your lessons/units of study so that I can mold library lessons; you may fill them out individually or as a grade level (state documentation of collaboration).

Have extra students/class with you? If you have extra students (part or all of another class) and they don't have another assigned support during your students' library support time, feel free to bring the extra students/class.

Library budget ordering: Please e-mail me a list of books/materials you'd like for me to order for the library. A great library book/materials collection includes input from everyone! Lists can be turned in anytime; I order throughout the year, and any list turned into me by November 1 will definitely be ordered for this year. All requests need to be in writing (state documentation).

When I am teaching classes in the library:

- If you need to pull a student, quietly get them and catch my eye.
- Please e-mail non-urgent notes to me. During library instruction, phone calls go to voice mail. Instruction is my top priority. I want students to be successful, and interruptions can trigger misbehavior.
- Thank you for honoring scheduled times. I have an atomic clock in the library in case you aren't certain of the time.

Also:

- I fill material requests within twenty-four hours of the request; please submit it in writing (state documentation). E-mail works best. Exceptions can be made for subs or emergencies.

- I must check out all materials on the KCMSD circulation system, except videos, before the materials leave the library.
- I am happy to search Kansas City Public Library's or Mid Continent Public Library's catalogs for materials. I can place them on hold, too, if you want to give me your card # and pin.
- Messages sent to the library with students need to be written (students forget).
- *Please* share suggestions, ideas, feedback, and so on regarding anything library. I am always looking for new ideas!

Thank you and I look forward to assisting you in having a terrific year!
Rebecca Parker, Librarian

Phillips Library Expectations Matrix

I form my expectations and procedures to mesh well with building expectations and procedures; students can more easily absorb expectations and procedures if they aren't a completely new concept. Use the same wording and language. These library expectations fit my school's matrix format:

Be responsible!
- Take care of library materials.
- Return any library books you find.
- Only use library books checked out to you.
- Let your parents know if you have an overdue or lost book.

Be safe!
- Keep all chair legs on the floor.
- Make good behavior choices.

Be respectful!
- Listen carefully so you can follow the directions.
- Treat others how you want to be treated.
- Use a right-sized indoor voice.

Be a learner!
- Ask questions when you don't understand—it's a learner's responsibility.

Phillips Library Procedures: Class Visit/Checkout

My class visit and check-out procedure makes it possible for students to work independently, so that I can occasionally help a student who is making an individual library visit.

- Place your library book on the circulation desk and go to assigned seat quickly and quietly.
- Look at Mrs. Parker so she knows you are ready to start.
- Mrs. Parker will give the assignment/reading plus any necessary materials.
- Begin working on your assignment/reading.
- Mrs. Parker calls a first group of students for checkout and gives shelf markers. When called, go to the stacks and find a book. Students who can't check out should work/read quietly.
- While students look for a book, Mrs. Parker talks to new students and answers questions.
- When a student has both a book and a shelf marker in hand, he returns to his seat and reads quietly.
- The next group is called and Mrs. Parker calls students from the first group to the circulation desk to check out.
- When the second group is finished, Mrs. Parker checks their books out to them.
- Read or work quietly until you leave or we move to a different activity.

Post learning goals and depth of knowledge information so that students, as well as visitors, can review what you expect as they work independently. Seat students by varying levels of ability so that a stronger student can help a struggling student while you are supervising or helping others.

My district and school use Positive Behavior Support methods, and I have a club for students who consistently follow the matrixes in every area at school. They receive a badge to wear daily and receive special privileges, such as checking out an extra book and reading/working on the carpet with a pillow or a beanbag, if they choose. I ask these students to help monitor blind spots and assist during checkout since I have the taller bookcases in my library and I check out books to one group when another group is selecting books. Being asked to monitor others is a big selling point in persuading students to make excellent choices so that they can be in the group, too. You also might consider using a self-checkout system, or allowing an older student to check out books so you can monitor the stacks.

Phillips Library Procedures: Individual Visit

In addition to the procedures, I let teachers know that students sent to the library while I have a class need to be able to work mostly independently; they need to have excellent behavior and work habits. Some teachers will send a student assistant to help a student who has excellent behavior but some academic challenges.

- Student comes to library and goes directly to Mrs. Parker with a pass signed by their classroom teacher listing the student's name, reason for visit, date, and time. Student signs in at circulation desk.
- Student discusses needs with Mrs. Parker. Mrs. Parker must have your Internet form checked off in order for you to use a computer.
- If checking out a book, get a shelf marker and look.
  or
- If using a computer, go to assigned computer.
  or
- If coming to read, find spot and enjoy yourself.
- See Mrs. Parker when you are to leave, and get a signed return pass.

The student sign-in sheet at the circulation desk is a must; mine asks for their name, the date, the time, the purpose of their visit, and their teacher's name. By requiring students to sign in, you have a complete record of who is in the library in case of a fire or tornado; take the list and your seating chart (if you also have a class in the library) with you when you evacuate so you can be sure all students you are accountable for are safe. Also, if anyone has questions at another time regarding a student being in the library on a certain date at a particular time, you can easily check for their name. Finally, the student sign-in sheet is excellent documentation of library use; it can be used to give library use data to your administrators, district leaders, and your state education department. A simple sign-in sheet is a very easy way for a solo librarian to accomplish a variety of important objectives simultaneously.

Student Computer Use Procedures

Computers drive instruction, provide information, and are important for creating documents. Many students don't have computers or Internet access at home, so it's important that students have ample opportunities to use library computers. Students can come use computers when you have a class receiving instruction in the library if you create, post, and teach procedures. These are my student computer procedures:

- Turn in parent-signed Internet form.
- See Mrs. Parker; she will assign you a computer.
- Sign in at your computer, and put clipboard back in its spot.
- Log on using your district user name and password.
- Computers can be used for educational purposes only. No music, no movies, no violence, no noneducational games.
- Save documents on your network drive.
- Stay on task; respect others.
- If you need help and no classes are in the library, respectfully call Mrs. Parker over. If she is teaching a class, wait until class is working independently or they leave.
- Print only with permission. You need to take notes instead of printing information, unless your teacher talks to me in advance.
- When you are finished, clean area, collect your belongings, and log off your computer.
- Let Mrs. Parker know you are finished.

Create a Successful Library Environment

Once your expectations and procedures are in place, be consistent so that students know that they must be followed. If individuals or small groups using the library do not follow an expectation or procedure, ask once for them to tell you the reason why you are forced to speak with them; put the responsibility of naming the issue on the student(s). Ask the student to tell you how they are going to solve the issue. Allow them to stay if the problem is not repeated. If it is repeated, even if the student is under a tight deadline, fill out their pass and send them back to class; this can be a valuable lesson and will show students that the expectations and procedures are important and must be followed in order for all to be able to learn in the library.

Students will learn valuable lessons that will help them for life if you teach and model respectful library behavior. If necessary, have students role-play asking another to work more quietly, move to allow them to pass, and so on, and use class time to have a student-directed discussion about different learning styles and the need to respect others' learning and work time.

With expanded expectations and tighter budgets that don't always allow for additional help, librarians working solo need to provide multiple learning opportunities and ensure the safety of students. Excellent library floor plans, furniture arrangements, and student procedures will create a rigorous, accountable, well-supervised school library program. Be the conductor of a library orchestra of well-prepared students working effectively to reach their learning goals.

Part VII

ASSESSING, WEEDING, AND MOVING COLLECTIONS

CHAPTER 21

Placing One Foot in Front of the Other

LEARNING HOW TO ASSESS
THE COLLECTION

Stephanie Renne

Organizing and assessing an entire library or archival collection on your own can be a daunting task. At the onset, there is an overwhelming amount of materials and it is challenging to know where to begin when faced with partially labeled boxes, papers, or multimedia items that are situated in complete disarray. As an independent professional, one must be confident in his or her training and utilize available resources of the field, such as professional associations and library or archival literature, to determine how to begin. Each library and archival collection is unique and must be treated as such, demanding an analytical approach that requires in-depth research specific to your situation, institution, and materials. This article offers suggestions to independent librarians and archivists on how to get started organizing your collection when you don't know where to start. The organizational process requires you to investigate the collection, share your expertise, take action, process and prioritize, and establish an identity. Ultimately, you must rely on your training, intuition, and experience, and take the process in stride, one step at a time.

Investigate the Collection

Initially, you must familiarize yourself with the collection and investigate its materials and their content. You must analyze the context within which your library or archive exists to better understand the needs of your collection. Consider your relationship with the larger institution or community

229

and the resources available to your library or archive by asking questions such as:

- What is your budget?
- What donors are involved?
- Do you have any existing deeds of gift?
- Do you own the rights to all of your materials?
- How does the library or archive contribute to the education/scholarship of your larger institution or community? Why is it important?
- How does your institution contribute to your library or archive?
- How are you connected to your institution?
- Who makes budgetary decisions for your collection?
- From where do you receive funding?
- Who is interested in your collection?
- Who are you primarily serving?

Once you have determined the budgetary, user, and institutional constraints surrounding the collection, you will be able to understand the parameters within which you will be working. Research into the provenance of your materials and the history of your institution can illuminate an incredible amount of information about your collection. By uncovering background information about your collection and the situation of your library or archive, you will better understand its content and can highlight the meaning, value, and uniqueness of your materials. This research is important as it can provide increased interest in your institution and its collections, which can open the door for future funding, program support, or collaboration. Following a contextual analysis of the situation within which your collection exists, it is imperative that you familiarize yourself to the individual items in your collection before you can consider organizing its contents. These collection assessments should consider the following:

- Budgetary constraints, donors, funding
- User needs, management, institutional relationships
- Material inventory (formats, languages, subject, provenance if known)
- Equipment inventory (serial and model numbers, services needed)
- Collection measurements (linear or cubic feet, boxes required)
- Space assessment (lighting, shelving, climate, disaster protection)

- Services required (preservation, computer, web, and audiovisual)
- Identity (mission, policies, and provenance)

You should conduct an equipment inventory and a material inventory and take collection measurements to determine how to optimize space within your library or archive. An equipment inventory lists each piece of equipment owned, with its serial and model numbers noted, and maintenance services that are required. A material inventory lists each format owned, languages used, and subject matter considered. Collection measurements are taken in linear feet for those materials that will be stored directly on shelves and in cubic feet for those materials that are stored in archival boxes. These initial assessments of the collection should also include a consideration of the space and condition within which the collection is stored, as well as the required services needed to maintain your collection.

- Does the space provide proper lighting and ventilation?
- Is there climate control?
- Is the collection stored on steel cantilever shelving?
- Is the collection protected from fire, earthquake, and flood disasters?
- Are the materials stored in a secure location?
- What actions must be taken to bring the collection up to current and expected standards for a working library or archive?
- What services will be needed to maintain your equipment and materials?
- What services does your larger institution provide?

It is better to have limited information about your collection than having none at all, and inventory lists will provide you with a quick reference to and assessment of your materials that will be helpful when making detailed decisions for collection organization and preservation.

Share Your Expertise

After you have taken initial measurements and assessments to familiarize yourself with the collection, it is important to share your expertise with your home institution by providing a summary of your collection and its contribution to the larger community. As an independent librarian or archivist, you serve as the main advocate for your collection and must highlight its value in order to receive institutional support. Your position is one of service to the collection and the institution, and you must consider how to optimize its use and preserve its value for the surrounding community. It is important to share your expertise by contributing project proposals, collection updates, and recommendations for material use. These reports should highlight current library and archival standards expected and appropriate actions required for the ideal care of your collection. They can range in topic from proper shelving needs to costs of processing supplies to space requirements and constraints to moving your collection and constructing a new facility. These analyses will also help you with grant writing, project proposals, and funding requests as needed in the future. The condition of any collection is in the control of its librarian or archivist and requires an individual who will advocate for the importance of providing its funding, preservation, and use. You serve as a consultant and a gateway to the materials within your library or archive, and your expertise and contribution determines the level of care provided for your collection. Without your advocacy, the library or archive will not survive.

Take Action

Now that you have prepared lists and determined the situation of your collection, it is time to take action to secure funding, create project plans, determine proper storage for your materials, and connect to other institutions of a similar nature for support. Through project proposals and expert recommendations, you will be able to negotiate for funding to support your collection. It is best to start within your institution, exploring available endowment and donor funds as well as applicable grants. You can also apply for outside funding with various institutions and nonprofit organizations considering the subject matter and/or contribution of your collection, such as the National Film Preservation Foundation (NFPF) or the National Endowment for the Humanities (NEH). Once funding has been secured, you will need to create project plans and timelines for completion. If no funding is immediately available, it is still important to plan for the future by considering all the needs of your collection, whether you can currently support them or not. A project plan should consider current standards for collection storage and preservation, proposing steps that need to be taken to achieve these ideals.

Before you can begin to organize the materials within your collection, you will need to establish if the collection is being stored properly. By providing proper storage for your collection, you will better preserve its materials so they may last in perpetuity. It may be necessary to move the collection, purchase shelving or archival quality boxes, establish climate control and lighting limitations, and plan for disaster protection. Each collection will have distinct needs and priorities for storage and preservation. When considering storage options, issues of climate, lighting, shelving, disaster protection, and security must be addressed to adhere to current standards and practice. These concerns should be documented in your primary collection assessments and will help to determine the storage priorities that your collection demands. This evaluation should include a listing of all of the formats that constitute your collection, the linear and cubic footage of your collection, the archival boxes required to store your collection, and the labels and barcodes needed to identify your materials. Once you have determined the proper storage requirements for your collection, you must measure your collection so that the materials can be organized in a way that will optimize their space and use. Assuming that your collection is composed of multimedia materials of various formats, you will have to determine which materials can be separated into subcollections by format or subject matter, transferred to boxes, and prioritized for organization. Vendor and contractor relationships will need to be created as project needs are determined and proposals are approved. Included below is a list of some national vendors that are widely used, can be found online, and will help you get started researching what resources and services are most appropriate for your budgetary and spatial situation.

- Shelving
  - Compact/Moveable—Spacesaver, MONTEL
  - Cantilever/Fixed—Demco, Gaylord, Highsmith, Bretford, Tennsco
- Supplies
  - Library—Demco, Gaylord, Highsmith
  - Archival—University Products, Hollinger Metal Edge, Archival Methods
- Climate Control
  - Temperature and Humidity (HVAC units)—Sanyo, Lennox, Siemens (ordered from local heating and air conditioning company)

- ◦ Light—dark window shades, filtered lighting (ordered from local electric and window companies)
- Disaster Protection
  - ◦ National Fire Protection Association (fire safety, film handling)
  - ◦ National Institute of Standards and Technology (seismic standards)
  - ◦ Federal Emergency Management Agency (flood and disaster response)

Given that you are working independently, it is important that you also stay in touch with the current standards of practice by referencing articles and resources that are already available to you through the literature of the field. A list of resources is provided at the end of this chapter, serving as an introduction to the relevant literature available to help you with the various facets of collection organization, processing, management, and storage. It is important to familiarize yourself with the research and practices of the rest of the field so that your library or archive will meet the standards expected of your institution. Additionally, you should try to network with other colleagues by attending conferences and workshops, giving lectures, and contributing publications. Participating in professional organizations will keep you up-to-date with the standards and practices within the field and will provide a forum for new ideas and suggestions for collection management and care. Given that you are independently managing your collection, professional organizations offer a platform to connect to other colleagues that understand the nature of library and archival work and can provide real and practical solutions to your issues and concerns. Usually speaking with other librarians and archivists about your collection and building assessment problems leads to new ideas that you had never considered.

Process and Prioritize

In order to further care for your collection beyond initial assessments, it is essential that you determine priorities of collection processing and development. This includes a consideration of preservation, cataloging, display and exhibits, as well as programs, outreach, and research. Before a collection can be fully organized, individual materials must be assessed for preservation, donation, and value. It is your responsibility to survey each item in the collection and determine what materials require preservation or conservation. If you do not have the training in preservation (including digitization and/or restoration), there are a number of outside vendors that provide these types of services. Asking for recommendations from other librarians or archivists in the area that are in charge of similar collections can help you develop a list of local vendors. Many regions share digitized collections; you may be able to weed out material if another institution has the same item available in a digital format. Collaboration between libraries in this manner builds a welcomed, mutually beneficial relationship. Additionally, you should evaluate each item in the collection for its applicability to the subject matter and users at your institution. Materials that do not fit the mission or subject of your institution should be marked for donation and relevant organizations should be identified to whom you can deaccession inappropriate materials. Furthermore, materials that are not of archival or library value or quality should be removed from the collection and recycled or donated to a prison, shelter, or nonprofit organization willing to accept such materials.

Cataloging and processing must be performed according to current library and archival standards, and subcollections that are in high demand should become your first priority. A librarian or archivist just starting out in a new position should check circulation records to identify frequently used items. For cataloging library materials, a standard library OPAC that holds MARC records as applicable to your materials should be used, such as Voyager or Millennium. Find the most appropriate OPAC to your collection, ideally connecting to a regional network for increased circulation of your materials. OCLC Worldcat provides the best forum for collaborative cataloging and should be one of your first resources when copy cataloging your materials. For archival materials, there are many open source programs, such as Archivists' Toolkit, that record scope and content notes, collection summaries, descriptive entries, and finding aids. A timeline should be created for collection processing and item cataloging that suits your situation and rate of production. For seasoned librarians and archivists, a rate of approximately six to eight items per hour is considered to be productive, though this rate may fluctuate depending on your other responsibilities. Given that you are working independently, be sure to take into account the demands of your job that will limit the time you can devote to collection processing and cataloging and be realistic about what you can get done.

In addition to collection organization and preservation, one must consider future projects that will promote the materials and further research in your subjects of interest. Materials can be put on display and exhibits can be advertised to the public to draw interest to your materials, collections, and institution. Outreach programs can be created to work with other departments or institutions both within and outside of your organization to present material from your collection, whether through film screenings, archival exhibits and open houses, music performances, classroom studies, community workshops, instructional sessions, or historical lectures and presentations. These activities are often fun to organize and they are an effective way to bring good press to your library. Oftentimes people who attend these activities have personal interests in the material presented, and they may become a potential source for financial donations to the collection to benefit a particular subject. You can also offer student internships and volunteer opportunities for interested parties and provide a space for researchers to come and utilize the materials within your collection. Once a catalog of records has been created, your collection can be disseminated and used. Materials can be circulated or restricted to in-house use according to their condition and preservation needs.

Establish an Identity

Once your current collection has been assessed, organized, and processed, it comes time for your library or archive to establish an identity for its collection. The identity of a library or archive orients the subject of its collection and determines its future direction. This orientation requires the librarian or archivist to determine appropriate rules of circulation; create a mission statement for the library or archive; improve acquisition and collection development policies; create standardized forms of contract (deeds of gift, equipment loans, volunteer contracts); establish donation and gift policies; perform web development; provide reference services; identify further preservation needs; work to keep current relationships with donors; supervise researchers, interns, and volunteers; and prepare grant proposals for continued support. The more outreach you do, the more your library or archive will be used and a respected reputation will be established. Ultimately, you should consider the importance of your role in providing a public service to the user, getting the most use out of your materials, and preserving our cultural heritage and its resources for the future of research and scholarship. The solo librarian must find a balance between all of these tasks while keeping public service in mind at all times.

Although it can be difficult to know where to start when you are independently organizing a library or archive, realize that there is more than one way to approach processing and storing materials and each situation is unique to your institution and its collection. As an independent professional you must be confident in your training and when in doubt, know that you can rely upon other colleagues, professional organizations, and library and archival literature to provide you with the resources that will get you started. All it takes is the courage to place one foot in front of the other and begin.

Some Helpful Resources

CATALOGING AND PROCESSING

American Library Association. *Anglo-American Cataloging Rules*, 2nd edition (AACR2), 2002 revision: 2005 update. Chicago, Ill.: ALA Editions, 2005.

Bachli, Kelley, Judy Moser, and Pat Vince. *Dublin Core Metadata Elements Best Practices, Version 1.1*. CCDL Metadata Sub-Task Force, 2005. ccdl.libraries .claremont.edu/inside/CCDLmetadata.pdf.

Bowman, J. H. *Essential Cataloging*. London: Facet Publishing, 2003.

Greene, Mark A., and Dennis Meissner. "More Product, Less Process: Revamping Traditional Archival Processing." *American Archivist* 68, no. 2 (2005): 208–63.

Olson, Nancy B. *Cataloging of Audiovisual Materials and Other Special Materials: A Manual Based on AACR2 and MARC 21*, 5th edition. Westport, Conn.: Libraries Unlimited, 2008.

Society of American Archivists. *Describing Archives: A Content Standard (DACS)*. Chicago, Ill.: SAA, 2004.

PRESERVATION

Bailey, Charles W., Jr. *Digital Curation and Preservation Bibliography*. Houston: Digital Scholarship, 2010. digital-scholarship.org/dcpb/dcpb.htm.

Bradley, K., ed. *Guidelines on the Production and Preservation of Digital Audio Objects*. *IASA-TC04*, 2nd edition. International Association of Sound and Audiovisual Archives, 2009. www.iasa-web.org/tc04/audio-preservation.

Casey, Mike, and Bruce Gordon. *Sound Directions: Best Practices for Audio Preservation.* Indiana University, 2007. www.dlib.indiana.edu/projects/sounddirections/bestpractices2007/.

Millar, Laura. *Archives: Principles and Practices.* New York: Neal-Schuman Publishers, Inc., 2010.

National Film Preservation Foundation. *The Film Preservation Guide: The Basics for Archives, Libraries, and Museums.* San Francisco: NFPF, 2004.

STORAGE AND SHELVING

Adelstein, Peter Z. *IPI Media Storage Quick Reference*, 2nd edition. Image Permanence Institute, 2009. www.imagepermanenceinstitute.org.

Moreland, Nancy Graham. *Recommendations for Shelving Inactive Records Storage.* Archives Technical Information Series #65. New York State Archives, 2004. www.archives.nysed.gov/a/records/mr_pub65_accessible.html.

Siems, Earl, and Linda Demmers. *Library Stacks and Shelving.* Libris Design Project, U.S. Institute of Museum and Library Services, 2004. www.librisdesign.org.

Siems, Earl, Linda Demmers, and Edward Dean. *Library Collection Storage.* Libris Design Project, U.S. Institute of Museum and Library Services, 2004. www.librisdesign.org.

COLLECTION DEVELOPMENT AND MANAGEMENT

Crews, Kenneth. *Copyright Law for Librarians and Educators: Creative Strategies and Practical Solutions*, 2nd edition. Chicago, Ill.: ALA, 2006.

Hirtle, Peter B., Emily Hudson, and Andrew T. Kenyon. *Copyright and Cultural Institutions: Guidelines for Digitization for U.S. Libraries, Archives, and Museums.* Ithaca, N.Y.: Cornell University Library, 2009.

Hunter, Gregory S. *Developing and Maintaining Practical Archives: A How-To-Do-It Manual*, 2nd edition. New York: Neal-Schuman Publishers, Inc., 2003.

Stim, Richard. *Getting Permission: How to License and Clear Copyrighted Materials Online and Off*, 4th edition. Berkeley, Calif.: NOLO, 2010.

CHAPTER 22

The Lonely Librarian
A GUIDE TO SOLO WEEDING

Lara Frater

Weeding can be a hard and time-consuming task that often falls by the wayside. How do you make the decision to keep a book or not? How do you handle the often monotonous, time-consuming project of weeding? *CREW: A Weeding Manual for Modern Libraries* states: "If you look at the place of the collection within the library's mission and how a poorly maintained collection negatively impacts the ability to meet that mission, it should become clear that weeding is an important part of the process."[1]

I am the primary person in charge of weeding and collection development. I have done all types of weeding at three different libraries. Although I have worked only in health libraries using Library of Congress or National Library of Medicine shelf systems, this method of weeding can be applied to Dewey as well.

As a solo librarian, it can be difficult to conduct a low-priority task such as weeding when you have reference duty, literature searches, cataloging, and journal maintenance to deal with. I will take you through three different scenarios: (1) minor weeding, usually done during off-peak time to make the collection look neater; (2) priority minor weeding where a small part of the library space is being removed and you have to reduce your collection; and (3) major weeding where your library is moving to a smaller space and it is solely you who decides what stays and what goes.

Create a Process

Before you start any weeding project, set up a process for the most effective way to weed. I suggest including the following three steps. First create a weeding policy. Decide what materials you plan to keep or weed automatically. Decide on a cut-off year, excluding core collection and high usage materials (i.e., do not keep any books published before 2000). A policy is a good thing to refer to when faced with a hard decision on whether to keep something or not. Regularly adhere to the policy. If it turns out not to fit, amend it. Below is a Department of Health and Mental Hygiene's weeding policy from 2007.

WEEDING POLICY GUIDELINES

Weeding the collection makes the library appearance neat and up-to-date and increases circulation.

The following list is a guideline to what materials the library keeps no matter the age:

1. Books on bacteriology and virology
2. Laboratory manuals
3. New York City medical history
4. Medical/health/legal history
5. Proceedings
6. New York City Department of Health documents
7. Videotapes
8. The most recent textbook, guidebook, and handbook on a subject even if the book is not current
9. Biographies of public health figures
10. Serial monographs
11. AIDS/HIV information
12. Vital statistics
13. Books on bioterrorism
14. Statistical methods
15. Forensic medicine
16. Materials owned by less then twenty-five other libraries (except outdated law manuals)

The library follows these weeding guidelines (this list can be superseded by the above list or a staff member):

1. Old electronics books
2. Old computer books
3. Damaged beyond repair books printed before 1990
4. Duplicates for books printed before 1990
5. Outdated law books
6. Any books/reference material that are superseded by a new edition
7. Medical textbooks and procedures before 1990
8. Directories
9. Outdated statistical methods books

Consider this list when deciding where weeded books will go:

1. Books will first be offered to staff by being placed on the free book shelf.
2. Materials left over will be offered to other libraries.
3. Materials left over will be offered to book donation places that pick up.
4. All materials left over will then be discarded.

Secondly, streamline a process for removal. For example, I use this five-step process:

Step 1: Fill up the top shelf of a cart with books (say about twenty) that adhere to your weeding policy.

Step 2: Check the circulation record. If the book has no, low, or no recent circulation, it can be weeded (if you decide to keep it, use the empty bottom shelf of the cart for problem books and ones to keep).

Step 3: If you use OCLC or another kind of bibliographic software, remove the materials from these databases. (Tip: if you use OCLC, use Connexion Client to remove books from the system. It will allow you to withdraw materials in batches.) Before you remove an item, check OCLC to see if the book is owned by multiple libraries and if it can be easily borrowed. If not, you might want to reconsider weeding it. (My library has several one-of-a-kind videos that, while not highly circulated, are historically valuable.)

Step 4: Remove the book from your catalog.

Step 5: Offer the materials up. (More on that later.)

Thirdly, set up a timeline. Give yourself six months or a year to do a project, and then break it into smaller ones. For example, you might consider weeding a shelf or two per week for low priority weeding.

WHAT MATERIALS CAN BE WEEDED AND FOR WHAT REASON?

Your weeding policy should cover which books you need to weed. You definitely want to weed outdated books that can contain faulty information. Be sure to include circulated and reference books as well. Investigate a book's circulation record. If a book has low circulation and/or hasn't circulated in a long time (say three years), it can be weeded.

Reference books may be harder to weed because they often lack circulation records. If you get a yearly reference book (say the *Physician's Desk Reference*), see if it is available online for a similar price. The CREW manual recommends "the automatic deselection of older editions that have been superseded and periodic evaluation by the librarian."[2] Feel free to discard old directories unless they have significance to your library. While a 1966 hospital directory seems good for historical reasons, I doubt you'll get a patron who needs to look at it.

Deciding to keep duplicate books is an issue at the university level where you may need several copies for a course reading assignment. Check the circulation records. Are all copies circulating? If not, you can scale back the amount of copies and keep the amount of average usage. The library doesn't need twenty copies of *A Separate Peace*. A copy can be easily obtained from other libraries or cheaply purchased. I can get a used copy on Amazon.com with shipping for $4, which is not a strain on a student's wallet.

Videos can take up a lot of space and once outdated, they don't circulate as much. VHS formatting is becoming obsolete and even DVDs are slowly being replaced by online videos. However, videos can be hard to weed if they aren't popular titles. For example, our library has a massive historical HIV/AIDS video collection. We have unique videos no other library has. Yet, many of these videos don't circulate, possibly because the format is not as popular. There are a couple tactics to consider in this situation: (1) keep them, (2) see if they can be burned onto a DVD and take up a smaller amount of space, (3) convert them to .avi (Audio Video

Interleaved) files and store them on your network (make sure the copyright allows this), or (4) discard or donate them. The last option is a difficult choice but if no one is watching the film, what is the point of keeping it?

Print journals that you have online coverage for can be discarded. If the online access is unreliable or will cease if you cancel a title, put the print in boxes and then store in a closet. If you have unreliable service, but find you don't go into these boxes after six months to a year, feel free to discard them from the collection. Some older journals may be available free online with an embargo of six months to two years. You may find that some of your journals are online and therefore can be weeded. Journals via Highwire press and Pubmed Central often have free back issues and tend to offer reliable service. Look at titles not used as much. Which ones take up a lot of space? Are they available with ease from other libraries? You might consider weeding them.

If you have vertical files, look at usage. If no one is using them, you might as well donate or toss them. If you want to keep a smaller set, remove printed articles and newspaper clippings (you can always get them again through inter-library loan) and anything online. With microfiche/film, you have condensed media with old technology that most patrons may be reluctant to use. It was very rare in my library to request microfilm even though we have a reader. It's best to keep only materials that no one else has and ones that are used often. For cassette tapes, look to converting them to CDs.

Three Different Scenarios

So you now have a weeding policy and a removal process and are fully prepared to weed. Here are three scenarios for different types of weeding. Before you start, speak to your supervisor and see if you can get a temp worker or a volunteer to help you with the weeding. You will probably have to go it alone but there is no harm in asking for help.

SCENARIO ONE: MINOR WEEDING

The collection is a mess, books are on carts, and journals are out of order and on overflow shelves because they no longer fit. Finding something has become a guessing game. Even though this may be insignificant compared to the patron who really needs your help right now, weeding and neatening a collection will help you in the long run. It will be easier to find things, therefore saving time, and the collection will look a lot nicer. Plus you'll finally have book carts you can use! When I first started my position at the Health Department as technical services librarian, I found a collection of uncataloged materials, books and journals with no space, and a video collection partially cataloged. Even though I was the cataloger, I also had reference duties and new books, videos, and journals to deal with as well. Something like this is time consuming and not a high priority. So the best way to deal with this sort of task is to set aside a little time each day or week for this project. Each week I would go through a shelf or more of books, then decide what I wanted to keep and offer up the rest. The entire project took about two years. After it was finished, books and journals were removed from the carts and shifted. Once everything was complete, the shelves weren't as tight and patrons were able to find materials with more ease.

SCENARIO TWO: PRIORITY MINOR WEEDING

The library was forced to shrink in size to make room for extra office space. This very issue arose in a former position I held where I had to weed four aisles of monographs. The job itself was not difficult but it was time-sensitive and required shifting because not all materials to weed were located in the same area. This scenario required small-scale weeding but had to be finished in a timely manner. Unlike scenario one, this was not a downtime project. Weeding had to be prioritized and in order to meet the deadline, I had to set aside a certain amount of time every day to work on it. When solo librarians find themselves in similar situations, it is best to establish a deadline. Then, estimate by that date how many shelves you need to go through. If you have an immediate deadline, look into getting carts to store the materials so you can weed them at your leisure.

SCENARIO THREE: A MAJOR MOVE TO A SMALLER SPACE

As I am writing this, my library is in the process of moving to a smaller space with about four hundred to five hundred less shelves. While I am not alone, our staff is small and I am the primary weeder. This large-scale weeding is a time-consuming, high-priority task with a deadline. The first thing to do is to figure out how much must be weeded and in what period of time. I counted the shelves of the current library since I didn't have the measurements of our new shelves. Measurements will give you a more accurate picture if you have access to them. I discovered that most standard shelves are about thirty-six inches. Estimate how many shelves (or feet) you need to weed and divide by how many weeks. Break it down to reasonable, weekly goals (remember reasonable, which means perhaps not finishing on time). Leave yourself some extra time because you might run into problems. For this scenario you must prioritize weeding instead of making it a secondary task during your day. Figure out what duties can be put aside while you weed. The best recommendation I can make is to start weeding immediately after you are told about the move. Weeding is time consuming and doing it ASAP will make it easier at the end when time begins to run out.

The following are suggestions of what to do with the leftovers:

- Book sale! If your institution allows it, do it! You will get rid of your leftovers and make money for your library.
- Offer them to staff. Put them on a freebie shelf with big signs. You'll be surprised what is taken. Make up lists of discarded materials and send it around to other staffs and patrons. Let everyone know there are free books available.
- Sell to bookstores if you are allowed. Amazon and Half.com only take a fee if you sell the book. Craig's List may be a good place to sell books in bulk. Better World Books will also give money for certain books and they pay for shipping.
- Offer them on library listservs. If you work in a health library, a great one is backmed.
- Offer them to Better World Books. Even if they aren't willing to buy your books, you can donate most of them. They will pay for the shipping when you donate a minimum of three books.
- See if you can find local charities who can take the books. We donated books that were sent to Africa and China. You'll be surprised how many libraries in developing countries still rely on print and can really use your material.
- Recycle; contact your custodian about what to do to make the materials easy to recycle.

Don't feel guilty . . .

- . . . if you can't finish in time. One person doing a major weeding job is a monumental task. If you are weeding due to a move, and can't finish it in time, you should take everything remaining and finish afterwards.
- . . . if you have to get rid of interesting books that don't circulate. I've come across several of those, but no one is reading them so there is no point in having them. Best to try to find a home where they will be appreciated.
- . . . if you have to throw away materials. I love the environment and hate to see things go to waste, but if no one wants a book or the book is in bad shape, it's okay to toss it. You'll find at the very end of the project, there will be materials that have to be thrown away. Try to recycle it if you can, but if you have to throw it away, don't get upset. You did everything you could to make sure it found a home.
- . . . if someone requests a book you weeded. Some time in the future someone might want a book you weeded. There is no guarantee that every decision about getting rid of a book is the right one. Don't worry about it and order the book through inter-library loan. The CREW manual states: "This situation seldom actually occurs and is certainly less common than a patron asking for a book you decided not to acquire for the library in the first place. A detailed weeding study conducted over a three-year period at Yale University revealed that in two years, only 3.5% of the weeded items were asked for."[3]

What to Do with Materials You Aren't Sure About Keeping

If there aren't a lot of materials in this category, keep them. If the amount of materials is large, you can ask staff and patrons or speak to other librarians who have similar libraries for advice. Look over your guidelines. When you make a decision, no matter what it is, you were right at the time. You probably want to toss the old, uncirculated, and damaged books as a rule. Even if they seem interesting, they won't look attractive in your collection and you may not have the resources to preserve them.

Avoiding Burnout

If you can't weed another book, stop doing it for a day or two. If the project is major, include a few "burnout" days in your timeline. Or consider weeding four days out of the five (i.e., don't weed on Wednesdays). Do not for any reason worry or think about weeding on "burnout" days. You need them to recharge your batteries. Try to take a day off after the weeding project is done, especially if it's a major one such as in scenario three. Make sure you always give yourself a pat on the back for doing this job: "Congratulations, you have undertaken a large project that should have been done by several people!"

Resources

Amazon.com: www.amazonservices.com/content/sell-on-amazon.htm?ld=AZFSSOA
Backmed: www.lists.us.swets.com/mailman/listinfo/backmed
Better World Books: www.betterworldbooks.com/
Directory of Book Donation Programs: www.albany.edu/~dlafonde/Global/
   bookdonation.htm
Half.com: www.half.ebay.com/

Notes

1. Jeanette Larson, "CREW: A Weeding Manual for Modern Libraries," revised and updated by Jeanette Larson (Austin: Texas State Library and Archives Commission, 2008).

2. Larson, "CREW," 33.

3. Larson, "CREW," 76.

CHAPTER 23

Moving a Library

Holly Lakatos

This chapter will provide some practical guidance to help you develop and execute your library move. The key to a successful move is creating a comprehensive plan. Planning should begin as soon as you find out that you will be participating in a library move. As a solo librarian, you must adequately budget your time and resources to ensure that service will not be unnecessarily disrupted and that your new space will function as required.

Budgetary Concerns

Moving costs may represent an enormous financial burden. Some supplies and labor selections will be determined by your budget. If you are moving into a completely new space, you may save by using existing (or secondhand) shelving, cutting your collection size, and doing much of the packing and unpacking yourself. Appropriate volunteers may also save you some labor costs. However, you may need to plan for certain costs including equipment rental, shelving installation, inspections, custodial services, and architectural consultants who can determine if your floor loads, fire systems, and lighting are properly configured and installed.

The library's insurance carrier should also be consulted to determine whether additional coverage is needed for injuries and damage that may occur during the move. You may also consider obtaining a move insurance policy to cover the costs of rare, fragile, or unique items in your collection.

Even if volunteers will constitute most of your labor force, you must still make arrangements to supply adequate water, shelter, first aid, and restroom facilities during the move. Many volunteers will also expect some kind of gift or reward.

Move Team

If your whole organization will be moving, ask to be part of the organizational move team. Frequently, organizations will hire a professional move coordinator who will manage supplies, trucks, and outside labor, and this person will help with the library, too. This person should ideally have experience moving libraries or numbered file rooms (such as medical records). If there is no professional move coordinator, then your organization should appoint a "point" person who has been empowered to make needed decisions and will be available for troubleshooting during the actual move. This person must have enough time and authority to establish deadlines, negotiate contracts with move-related vendors, and work with all stakeholders in your organization to ensure that all move-related activities are completed on time. Even though you may be a helpful librarian, you must not be tempted to take on the role of move coordinator, as you will be busy running the library, in addition to your new tasks related to the library move.

If your organization requires a Request for Proposal (RFP), then details of the move will need to be worked out before bids can be submitted. You will need to describe your collection in terms of linear feet, furniture, equipment, and shelving. You will also need to express the detailed expectations you have of the movers including responsibilities, supplies provided, and timelines. Much of the equipment needed for a successful library move can be rented or bought from your moving company and should be included in any quote or bid.

EQUIPMENT NEEDED (A PARTIAL LIST)

- Adequate book carts, trucks, or movers
- Labels for beginning and end of each cart
- Labels for front and side of each box

- Scaled drawings of new space
- Shrink wrap
- Cardboard boxes or plastic crates
- Dollies
- Floor and wall protectors, including removable tape
- Elevators, ramps, or chutes
- Yardstick or tape measure

Patron Services During the Move

One of the first decisions you will need to make is whether or not you will continue all, some, or no patron services during the move. If you plan to continue service, have contingency plans in place for communication service failures and the inability to access the collection at a specified time.

Begin to advise your patrons of the move as soon as the decision to move has been made, even if you do not have specific dates. For example, if you know you will be moving sometime in the fall, advise patrons: "The library will have a new home this fall. Please enjoy longer loan periods until we've settled in!" or something similar. As the move date approaches, consider sharing more information with patrons on your website or blog, including pictures of move-related activities, checklists of things that you have completed, and fun facts about the move (such as how many yards of bubble wrap were needed to pack that special object).

Change due dates so that patrons are encouraged to return materials to the new space. Provide adequate maps and signage so that everyone will be able to find your new location. If you have an external book drop, also consider replacing it with a temporary sign as a reminder for a few weeks after the move.

If you do not have adequate volunteer staff to retain all services during the move, try to arrange alternate arrangements with other local libraries. For example, if your county law library will be completely closed, arrange for e-mail or telephone assistance from a neighboring county for the duration of the move. Instead of allowing full access to the stacks, have patrons request materials before their visit and page the materials for them within twenty-four hours. Most patrons will be impacted during a complete closure, but having alternate arrangements will mitigate the damage.

Mail and Communications

Compile a list of all vendors, library partners, and community leaders who should be notified of your move. Your phone company will advise you as to whether or not you can retain your current phone numbers, and your Internet provider will advise you if any additional equipment to meet your bandwidth needs should be installed.

Computer servers that are housed at your library will need to be moved with extreme caution. Your computer specialists should be involved in planning the new server room and the location of any computers in the new space. In addition, if your IP addresses will change, you should ask vendors when those new addresses should be added to any IP-authenticated subscription services.

Some communication devices and equipment, such as audio-visual hardware, networked photocopiers, and computer terminals may need to be moved and installed by your existing vendor as part of your service contract.

NOTIFICATION CHECKLIST

Ninety days before the move, notify:
- Patrons
- Community leaders
- Local press
- Telephone/cable/communication vendors

Sixty days before the move, notify:
- Area and partner libraries
- Subscription agents

Thirty days before the move, notify:
- Remaining vendors
- Post office
- Regular delivery services
- Everyone you've previously notified

The New Space

If you are moving into a space that is not owned by your organization, check to see if the landlord has restrictions on the time of day that you can move or install shelving. Also, check to see if there will be adequate parking and loading dock access during your move.

Ideally, you will work with an architect or interior designer to plan your new space. If that is not possible, you will still need to obtain measured drawings of your new space so that you can adequately plan shelving and furniture placement. You may also find software such as Microsoft Visio useful to help you plan spaces to scale. You will need to indicate the new location for each section or column of shelving in your new space. This will help you determine if your collection will fit into the new space, and it will help your movers place materials on the shelves correctly, in order.

When preparing your new space, keep in mind:

- The Americans with Disabilities Act (ADA) requirements
- State and local fire safety regulations
- Emergency egress
- Floor load requirements of shelving and/or microform cabinets
- Anchoring your stacks for seismic activity
- Position of lights in relation to shelving
- Traffic flow through the library

Preparing Your Existing Space

Library moves can prompt two activities that most librarians hate: dusting and weeding. Dusting the collection and cleaning the shelves will help movers avoid respiratory problems while handling your books. Many librarians wait until Move Day to actually dust, but this extra task may slow down your move when you can least afford the time. Weeding your collection in advance will also help your Move Day go faster. The fewer materials you move, the less money you spend on equipment and labor. If you know that your new space will be 10 percent smaller than your current space, aim to weed at least 15 percent of your collection so that you can accommodate room for growth.

After dusting, the next step to prepare your collection is to determine its size in linear feet. The easiest way to do this is to take a yardstick and measure shelf by shelf. Be sure to add extra linear inches to represent materials that are currently checked out or otherwise not on the shelf (.25" for pamphlet, 2" for adult novel, 3" for law book).

If you have too many shelves to do this or are short on time, you can estimate by using your shelf list and sampling the items to determine the average width of each item in your collection and multiplying by the number of items in your collection. You should still obtain a count of how many shelves you currently have, though, to help you determine shelving needs in your new space.

Compress or expand your materials so that they will take up the same amount of shelving space as will be available in the new space. This way, you can move shelves on a one-to-one basis. Mark the beginning and ending of all sections (ranges or columns of shelving) indicating the flow direction. Consider using different colors or symbols for each floor or area that can be matched in the new space. When you have a map of the new space, put a copy of the map at the beginning of each section with the section's new location marked. During the move process, these labels and maps can be taken off the old shelving unit and placed on the book truck and later matched in the new space.

If your library has access to oversized book trucks (also called book movers), consider placing a sheet of colored paper in the last book of each shelf to identify the original shelving scheme. This way, you will be able to load more books on the truck and make each trip more efficient while maintaining organization.

As a safety precaution, you should also verify with your shelving manufacturer that your stacks can be unloaded unevenly without risk of tipping. Otherwise, you will need to install extra tie bars or plan to unload evenly.

Before the move, you will also need to compile a list of all furniture, equipment, and fixtures contained within your library, including dimensions. If these items will not be moving with your library, mark them appropriately or move them into a storage room before the move. Remember to include things like fax machines, photocopiers, and TVs as these may require special outlets in the new space.

NON-BOOKS

Moving materials other than books may require additional planning and equipment. If you are using professional movers, have them look at these materials before bidding, especially if they will require special handling.

Realia and archival materials may require special handling such as climate-controlled trucks or padded boxes. Personnel and other confidential records should be moved in locked or secured boxes and accompanied by a responsible supervisor or guard.

Vertical files should be emptied and the contents placed in boxes. If the cabinet locks, tape the key to the outside of the cabinet or otherwise ensure that the key will be easily accessible during and after the move. The cabinet can then be moved as a piece of furniture. Likewise, microform cabinets should be emptied. The microforms should be placed in trays, then boxed. If you don't have trays, you can make your own by placing inserts in a regular cardboard box to keep the microforms together.

SHELVING

If your move entails moving existing stacks into a different part of the same facility, you may consider using stack movers, which are special dollies that can move fully loaded book stacks. Label each stack and flow direction so that they will be placed in the correct order.

If you are moving into a new space with pre-installed shelving, then mark shelves with labels that match the labels you created for your old space. Verify with your shelving manufacturer that your stacks can be loaded unevenly without risk of tipping. Otherwise, you will need to install extra tie bars or plan to load evenly.

If you will be using existing shelving from your old space, you will need to budget additional time for taking down, moving, and installing the shelving. You will also need to have an appropriately sized staging area that will be able to hold all your book trucks, out of the way, until workers are ready to place them on the shelves in your new space. Before workers begin to unload, place labels on the shelving that match the section numbers in the old space, using your map to help you locate the correct area.

CREATING A MOVE PATH

Fully loaded book trucks are heavy and may cause damage (wheel scuffs, chips, and dents). If needed, line your path with boards to protect floors and use blankets, cardboard, or other heavy-duty materials to protect walls, corners, and elevators. Plan a smooth path for movers where wheels will not encounter resistance over door jams, high-pile carpets, and uneven tiles. Avoid stairs. Instead, build a temporary ramp. Make sure that any elevator you use is capable of safely carrying added weight. If you use professional movers, request that they repair any damage caused during the move.

If your library does not have access to an adequate elevator during the move, you may consider alternate ways of moving books from floor to ground. For example, you may be able to install an external elevator, a scissor lift, or an external chute. These can be rented from construction companies.

Loading and Unloading the Book Trucks

Chances are the people helping you move will have little or no experience moving a library. You should spend some time at the beginning of each shift to explain how your collection is organized and why keeping the books in the correct order is important. You should also go over any safety concerns such as how the bookshelves are to be unloaded (especially if they must be unloaded evenly).

Each book truck needs to be labeled with the following information:

• Book truck number
• New location
• Section number

Instruct workers as to how to properly load the book truck left-to-right, top-to-bottom so that the materials stay in the correct order. Also, show how to label each cart so that the person unloading it will know where to start. Consider preprinting "Start" and "End" labels on each cart. If carts are to be moved out of the building, consider shrink-wrapping each cart so that books will not fall.

If carts are labeled correctly when they are loaded, you will be able to unload with ease. Start by matching the "new location" label to the correct area in the new space. Then, match the "section," and finally, the book truck number. Unload the book truck left-to-right, top-to-bottom so that the materials stay in the correct order.

Safety and Security

Safety should be a priority during the move. All workers must be dressed appropriately (e.g., wearing closed-toe shoes) and cognizant of safety considerations. During each shift change, remind all workers of safety expectations. Demonstrate proper lifting techniques. Have "push" crews assigned to move the heavy book trucks as a team. Provide masks for workers with dust allergies. Point out restrooms and water fountains. Ensure that breaks are taken when needed.

Before the move begins, identify any hazards and mark appropriately. Shelving may become unstable when loading/unloading materials, so make sure that workers are warned and exercise caution. Have first aid kits on hand, and provide walkie-talkies, cell phones, or other communication devices in each area where people are working so that any safety problem can be addressed immediately.

At the end of each move day, the move coordinator or point person should walk through both the old site and the new site to identify safety hazards and check that all entrances and exits have been secured.

During the move, your building may be at risk for theft simply because it is open and no one is around. Reduce the possibility of theft by having workers stationed at all entrances and exits. Have movers, volunteers, and library volunteers wear nametags, wristbands, and/or uniforms to be easily identifiable. If moving overnight or over many days, you may consider hiring extra security for both your old and new spaces.

Clean Up

Don't forget that you'll need extra time and personnel to clean when the move is over. Schedule extra recycling and trash pickups in the weeks and days before the move. If your library has paper records that need to be destroyed, shred these in advance. If you use cardboard boxes, arrange to sell them as soon as they are emptied, or if you use professional movers, request that they remove the empty boxes a few days after the move is complete.

Custodial staff may be needed at both the old and new locations during the move. You may want to hire temporary help or request volunteers. After the move, staff will need to "deep clean" the old space and repair any damage. The new space will require extra attention until everything is unpacked and the move is complete.

After the Move

After the move, spend a few hours simply unpacking your office and preparing your personal workspace for the future. Eventually, you will need to spend time shelf reading and ensuring that materials are in the correct order, no matter how smoothly your move went. You will also undoubtedly realize that you will need to make some small adjustments for growth space. If you have trained volunteers that helped you with the move, they may be able to help with these tasks.

Walk through your new space and note any damage caused by movers to carpet, walls, equipment, or furniture. Repair these items as soon as possible, or if using professional movers, submit the damage claims as part of your "punch sheet." Test all equipment and communication devices to ensure that they are functioning correctly in the new space.

If you have maps and other brochures that list locations, update them as soon as possible after the move. For weeks, you will get questions about your new address or phone number or new layout. Seize these moments as learning opportunities for patrons and invite questions about your new space.

To celebrate a job well done, host a small party in your new space. Invite everyone to walk around and experience the new layout. End with appropriate thanks to those who helped you with the move process and make a toast for many happy years to come. Most importantly, take a moment to give yourself a big pat on the back because your library move is over!

Part VIII

LIBRARY OVERVIEWS

CHAPTER 24

Making a Career-College Library Relevant

David Castelli

A career-college library is unlike any other, and so my comments in this chapter will have a bias toward that branch of librarianship. Part academic library and part special library, it falls in a void that is sometimes overlooked by professionals.

The mission of most career colleges is the transfer of the specialized knowledge and skills needed for entry-level positions to students wishing to enter a professional field. There are career colleges for automotive technologies, culinary arts, graphic arts, paralegal assistants, allied health professions, movie production, and more. Students enter the workforce prepared for their new career in less time than students who attend a liberal arts institution. Typical programs are eighteen to thirty months in length, compared to four to six years for a liberal arts degree.

As a rule these colleges are proprietary or for-profit, meaning they are businesses that provide education, rather than traditional educational institutions. Due to the focus of each institution, the library will stock only what is needed to support their programs, so the library will not have the depth and breadth of a typical academic or public library. The collection is so limited in its scope that in my area of the country our libraries are not eligible to belong to the local academic consortium, adding a facet of professional isolation to the job. The librarian often works alone or may have a student assistant.

I run a circulating library of about 1,200 titles and I manage a bookroom of textbooks for about 120 courses, including a collection of e-textbooks. Our current student population is approximately 820 students.

To be fair, I have two twenty-hour student assistants (who rotate in and out about every year), but I am the only MLS librarian for two campus locations. To be successful I have to do some cataloging, acquisitions, collection development, circulation, and reference, and be reasonably proficient in all of them!

It is a challenging and rewarding position. I believe it is necessary to think differently than librarians at larger academic institutions and public libraries. I have more opportunities to help undergraduates learn very basic college success and information literacy skills, those we assumed they learned in high school, and less opportunity to serve graduates in high-end research opportunities. From talking to other college librarians in my state and from my experience, I can say that many college students today do not have a working knowledge of a library, and some have never had a life-changing relationship with a librarian.

When I thought about it a librarian's duties boil down to (a) collecting and organizing information, (b) being relevant to our community, (c) making our services known through advertising and service, and (d) innovating to bring patrons things they didn't know were possible. It's a lot for one person to do, but that's the fun! You get to do all of these as you like, using the tools of your choice. When you see a student cross the stage at graduation, and you remember how your reference help made their success possible, your position comes into sharp focus.

Some Pros and Cons of Solo Librarianship

Solo librarianship means that you are on your own, with no teams to rely on and little if any outside help. The day-to-day decisions are yours, the hours may be long, and you may feel alone in the information world. The good news is that the benefits far outweigh any negative aspects to this career choice.

Being a solo librarian offers freedom to work as you feel is best. You can develop policies and procedures for your own library and your own acquisitions, collection development, and publicity methods. In my case I inherited a library that was not automated, not barcoded, and not used by students. The accreditation team would arrive in less than three weeks. It was time to dig in and rely on my professional training and experience to guide me.

Focus on the use of the materials. In my facility the library is an open alcove, adjacent to the lobby and the vending area. It is not secure as most librarians are used to, but it is open and inviting. While books do occasionally get borrowed without being checked out, this is offset by the increased visibility the library enjoys.

If You Find a Vacuum, Fill It

Collect everything you can to help your patrons. No one had begun to catalog helpful websites; I now add them to the ILS to keep them current and started using the Library of Congress Annotated Resource Sets as guides for our students.

In a career-college environment you run into many students who have not used a library in a long time, if ever before. For many students I am their librarian. I coordinate services with the local public libraries and refer students to the larger universities in town when required.

We had a need for instructor's resources, those ancillaries that publishers create to help teachers run their courses. Many instructors needed help getting the materials from publishers. We had no way to track them or to organize them. I made a new collection in the ILS and we now keep IR shelved by course prefix, and we include books and other media in the collection.

I collect material related to the curriculum at my college even if it is not directly part of the program of study. For example we train students for several allied health careers. I collect materials on diseases, emergency care, nursing theory, public health and administration, and insurance reform. In another example the graphics arts program had books that taught some theory directly related to the program, but most were focused on using the various applications. That is to say they focused on the buttons to click on the screen to get the desired results. I collected a broader mix of books including web design, managing graphic artists, entrepreneurship, licensing art, and so on. These are in a special collection for the graphic arts program and should serve instructors and students alike.

I look for helpful websites, including those of professional organizations. Students need to know that they can join these organizations and the benefits they can confer to someone new in the field.

I collect catalogs. A college receives catalogs on everything from turf management and parking lot design to uniforms and promotional gift items. I keep catalogs in my ILS in case they are needed.

Organize Your Library or Media Center

It's very hard to have a library that's not organized. I inherited a crowded bookroom lined with books and with a freestanding shelving unit in the middle of the floor. The first step I took was to organize my space. We circulate our textbooks every month, so regular access to the shelves is important. After removing the shelving unit and adding a worktable, I made a list of all the courses I could determine, then removed all of the books and reshelved the books by course.

Some of the trappings of traditional libraries were missing. For example, books did not have spine labels, and the shelves were not labeled. I ordered stock labels from Demco and labeled the shelves. In time the shelf labels proved less efficient than spine labels. Now books are simply shelved by their spine labels.

Once the bookroom was operating I was able to direct attention to the circulating collection in the library itself. I weeded books that were clearly obsolete and reordered titles that we should have. Judging by the property and discard stamps, many of the books were discards from local universities and from the Library of Congress. This collection was not barcoded at that time either.

ResourceMate was selected by the college shortly before my arrival. I like this product because it is simple to use, without the overhead that comes with elaborate ILS systems. Having worked for a software vendor for four years I can say that many single-branch libraries just want to catalog and circulate a book; they don't need all of the bells and whistles that are part of today's larger ILS systems. With the open-source ILS movement, my colleagues assure me there is open-source software that works as well as the one I use.

Acquisitions are done much differently than in a public library. Most often a textbook is chosen by committee or by a dean, and the librarian's responsible for stocking that title. While I am accountable for my purchases, I don't have to manage a budget in the traditional sense; I purchase what my patrons (deans and instructors) need. I do, however, suggest titles to deans and instructors if I feel they are better books, if they offer better ancillaries, or if I can get a better discount on that title.

Engage Your Students

Make your library a community center. Make your space available for one-on-one study or tutoring sessions and students making up tests. One year I had an extra pumpkin from my garden, and I was leaving town the next day. Rather than have it go to waste I brought it to the library and put a sign in front of it to "sign the library pumpkin." Within ninety minutes the pumpkin was covered with signatures, including some forgeries from sports and popular culture. Something so simple brought people into the library for a common purpose.

When new students pass by the reference desk, welcome them and check up on your current students. When students see you around town, be friendly and expect a hearty greeting in return. Develop a "rap" with each one; you will be surprised how far this will get you. Develop expertise in the MS Office suite so you can help with common questions. The more students who hang out in your library the better, even if they only come to plug in their laptop and update their Facebook; they will learn to come to the library when they need help. Allow small tutoring sessions and study groups and proctor exams; whatever the needs of your organization you are there to help meet them.

Advertise Your Services

Just like the public library, you should have a presence on your campus website. Be sure that your library is prominently listed online. Request an "Ask the Librarian" button for your college's home page or the library's site, if you have one. It helps if your PAC is searchable online, but some smaller systems have limited functionality in this area.

Take a cart of books from your circulating collection into a classroom, to let students know what you have for them. Many students lack library skills and are intimidated by the library, so you have to come to them.

On your receipts, print the hours of operation. Some students may not realize that the library is open certain hours, and they need to be aware of the hours you are available. Consider getting help from the public relations department at your school and design professional bookmarks, table tents, posters, anything to let busy students know you are available for them.

Serve Your Patrons

Look for ways to increase service to your students. For example, adopt e-books on your campus and give students instructions on how to use them. I send an e-mail message to every student at the start of every four-week module to make sure they know how to get their books, or even if they need a book, for their course. Now students have their e-textbook approximately ten days prior to the start of the course. For the past few years I have held an informal voter registration drive each September. I leave discarded books in our lunchroom for students to take, if they like. This not only helps me dispose of discarded books but gives the student exposure to a new topic for free.

Your time is likely to be quite flexible, and you will have time to offer ad hoc information sessions to your students. For instance, when you hear students struggling with the assignment from their course, offer suggestions of materials and websites that could help them. Often students are reluctant to ask for help, so approaching them with the help they need is appropriate.

You may have expertise in another area that you could offer a student. I help students who struggle with Excel assignments because I consider myself an Excel expert. Moreover, if I know someone is struggling, I can find an expert they need to succeed.

Develop New Systems and Services

Get to know the faculty at your institution. Often instructors don't know what the librarian can offer them. At my institution, I order review copies from publishers so the instructors can review the latest titles and select the best book for the course they teach. This is a great service to instructors and augments my relationship with the vendors.

I collect publishers' samples, database trials, and freebies wherever I can find them. Take advantage of instructor's resources and other ancillaries offered by the publishers. My experience has been that for many instructors these materials are difficult to find, and the websites they are available from are hard to navigate. Most of this material is available online only; the days when publishers would freely send CDs and other material are drawing to a close as these materials are online only. Once again, the more valuable you are to your patrons, the better!

Extend your influence by partnering with other organizations in the community. For instance, I have built a relationship with my community's adult literacy organization, and they refer their graduates to our GED tutoring program. In this way I gain more resources for our tutoring programs, have a source of a few referrals each year, and raise the consciousness of the college's library in the community.

Don't neglect professional development. Your campus or organizational leaders will be impressed by your interest in your continuing development and will be glad to fund these professional opportunities. Look for ways to get involved with your professional organization on the state or national level; even joining something as simple as a listserv in your area of interest often yields valuable advice. If you are lucky enough to live near one of the library schools offering MLS or equivalent degrees, be sure to stop by and meet your future colleagues.

Manage Your Time Well

Manage your time well. It's critical to your success and the success of your library to be as effective and as efficient as possible. Once you have determined your goals, be sure you leave enough time each week to achieve them. Beware of people and things that want to steal your time for less important things.

Remember the 80/20 rule: we tend to get 80 percent of our results from 20 percent of our input. You probably will find 80 percent of overdue books come from 20 percent of the patrons, and that 80 percent of the clothes you wear come from 20 percent of your wardrobe. The trick is to discover the 20 percent that really matters, and then guard that time and those activities jealously.

Do the most unpleasant tasks of the day first. Everything else will seem easy by comparison, and who wouldn't like a day full of easy tasks? When we put off unpleasant tasks in favor of something we like to do better, we procrastinate. A few days of procrastination lead to missed deadlines and catch-up days full of difficult, unpleasant work.

Check your e-mail once or twice a day. Most e-mail can be handled within this time frame, and you will avoid distractions caused by the ubiquitous announcements of cookie sales, weddings, and electronic greeting cards.

Develop a routine. Many people find the word "routine" loathsome, but I find it liberating. I find that things are easier, more orderly, and more efficient if I stay current with them every day. I arrive at work, break, and leave at the end of the day at regular times, and this forces me to stay focused and in touch with my department. It does not allow for many nonimportant items to make their way onto my workload.

Know Your Technology

When you are a solo librarian you have no other support. While that seems obvious the most daunting part for some people is that you are your own technical support. Some librarians approach the technical realm with care, while others are intrepid. I believe a healthy balance of both is in order.

Computer support is interesting to look at retrospectively. Gone are the days when one part-time computer guy could support your library. Today's public libraries need full-time IT teams to keep sophisticated networks, hardware, and software in good working order, and to keep the staff trained on new technological advances. At the same time, administrative personnel have been reduced, and each worker is responsible for his or her own administrative tasks. For the solo librarian there may be more technical things to know about, and be competent at, on your own, as a survival skill and as a way to offer more of the services your users have come to expect from life.

While some computer aspects have gotten easier, there are new wrinkles that you have to stay current with or you risk being left in the digital darkness. Here's what I mean: most everyone has to use a word processor like MS Word in their daily work life, so knowing Word is no longer a bragging point; it's a necessity. Likewise, knowledge of various e-mail systems is required.

Consider these more "advanced" situations that, not long ago, required special intervention:

- Know how to find and edit your IP address or DNS server.
- Know how to reset your library's router.
- Install virus checker and adware/spyware removal software.
- Know how to deal with a virus when one is detected.
- Know the features, benefits, and drawbacks of the major web browsers.
- Know how to delete cookies and your browsing history, configure your browser's security settings, and turn off pop-up windows.
- Have a familiarity with the current crop of wireless devices. As more people try to access library services with smartphone applications, librarians should be aware of their basic functionality. Sometimes the new technology will work seamlessly with the older in-place technology, and at other times they will not work so well together. More portable devices are sure to spring up every year or so, and librarians should at least be aware of what the devices do.
- Know your desktop applications. In this list include Word, Outlook, PowerPoint, Paint, Adobe Acrobat, basic Excel operations, Internet Explorer, Firefox, and Safari.
- Learn to identify RSS feeds and the tools used to read them.
- Troubleshoot a laptop computer that can't connect to your wireless network.
- Become fluent in the use of your ILS or OPAC and any reports it generates.
- Library uses for Microsoft Access, SQL, and HTML/XML applications may be explored by the more adventurous librarians.
- Learn to reboot your computer properly and to fix a paper jam or replace print cartridges in your printer.
- Know the difference between your computer's various ports. Can you tell the difference between serial, parallel, USB, firewire, and VGA ports?
- Can you identify the SD card, DVD, CD, and thumb drive, and know the pros and cons of each one?
- Since you will likely be doing some system administration for your location, are you familiar with the ins and outs of your ILS? Can you maintain the website/portal with your catalog?
- Brush up on your computer terminology and learn the technical names for things. This will come in handy when you need to call a vendor for support or have to make a trouble report to your helpline. Depending on your situation as a solo librarian, you may be part of a team or committee that makes system admin decisions, and talking the talk goes a long way.

Conclusion

When I go home each day I know that I have used all of my skills, as a dean and librarian, to bring the world of information to our students. Three years ago I never thought I could accomplish as much as I do in a single workweek, the position seemed so daunting. Today I continue to innovate, grow, and serve my library's population, and it's an awesome responsibility.

I routinely come across students from my college as I go about my business in town. I see students working at the local restaurant, frozen custard shop, or retail store. I came across a student in the parking lot of the local pharmacy and she introduced me to her boyfriend as "my librarian." As solo librarians, we get the chance, single-handedly, to show such students what today's librarians can do, and how much we can help them in all stages of life by connecting personally with them.

CHAPTER 25

The One-Man Band

THE SOLO LIBRARIAN SUPERVISING CIRCULATION, CATALOGING, COLLECTION DEVELOPMENT, REFERENCE, AND EQUIPMENT

Lois Kuyper-Rushing

No centralized music library or branch existed at Louisiana State University (LSU) prior to my hiring. Rather, the resources were interfiled in the library with all other subject matter. Services were dispersed. So I was also hired in order to create a music library.

Upon hiring, my duties included cataloging all music materials, working at the reference desk ten to fifteen hours a week, and handling all monographic collection development decisions. As a library faculty member, I was also expected to publish and become involved in service to meet tenure and promotion requirements.

Middleton Library at LSU has five floors. When I was hired, music materials were scattered throughout all but the top floor. Scholars and students retrieved scores and music books from the third floor. Journal articles and microforms were housed on the second floor. Reference and reserve materials came from the first floor. All video and audio recording were housed in the basement. The audiovisual materials did not circulate outside of the Listening Room in the basement, so if a student wished to use a score with a sound recording, the score had to be retrieved from the upper floor of the library. The student then descended to the basement to listen to the recording using the score. If the score was held on reserve, the complication possibilities were endless!

This highly ineffective arrangement had been identified by music faculty long before I arrived. A request had been made years before to create a space in which all the formats used by musicians could be housed and used together. In 1995, our relatively new dean, Jennifer Cargill, was able to commit space, time, and resources to the creation of a music area, which was called Music Resources. After designing and overseeing the creation of this space I became the head of the Pauline Mulhall Carter Music Resources Center at the LSU Libraries. This was a marvelous addition to the music program at LSU. I was thrilled to be a branch head, but designing the space and services added extra job duties to my already full plate.

My dream job had always included creating the perfect music library. I was determined to correct all the problems I'd seen in other libraries. My patrons would be able to find whatever they needed in the library catalog because the records input into the system would be accurate and every heading would be correct according to current cataloging rules. After finding materials in the catalog, patrons would easily find materials because the shelves would be in perfect order at all times. No patron conflicts would exist; I was certain we could easily resolve every disagreement easily. I was idealistic. I was determined. I was naïve!

My music cataloging, collection development, and reference services responsibilities continued. Duties as a circulation librarian would soon be added when Music Resources became a separate circulation point. I also became a supervisor for full-time staff, two graduate assistants, and up to twelve student workers. At this point it was quite clear to me that I needed to learn to delegate responsibilities.

Delegation of Responsibilities

The online *Cambridge Advanced Learner's Dictionary* provides this definition for the verb *delegate*: "to give a particular job, duty, right, etc. to someone else so that they do it for you."[1]

As I faced managing a completely new music library, I knew that I had to learn to delegate responsibility. The definition given above is not surprising, and the concept of a supervisor delegating responsibilities to staff members is hardly new. Nonetheless, learning to delegate can be difficult, and without this skill, the librarian "running his or her own show" will end up burned out and/or with a huge backlog of work to be done.

Three things are needed for a manager to run a successful organization. The first requirement is having someone to whom job duties can be assigned. In other words, a supervisor needs staff. A second requirement for a successful transfer of responsibilities is a set of well-defined procedures for various job duties. Finally, and most importantly, the supervisor must be willing to trust his or her staff to complete tasks without the supervisor's approval. This final step is the underpinning of successful delegation, a successful supervisor-staff relationship, and a well-run library.

STAFF

When the LSU Libraries began considering the possibility of a separate space for music, there was no staff assigned. I was hired as the professional music librarian, but support staff had not been considered. As I began planning the space and the services that would be provided, I realized that I could not staff the area alone. My new duties included cataloging all music materials, collection development, reference, and circulation—the last two occurring in the new space. The cataloging of music materials would require that I spend a significant amount of time in the Cataloging Department away from Music Resources (because cataloging tools were not yet online) while reference and circulation required someone on duty in the music area at all times. This fact alone convinced the administration that I would need staff to work with me in the new music area.

Full-time support staff may not be available to the librarian who is beginning his or her position in a small or separate library, or one who has identified a need for support staff. And, although I was allowed to hire someone in a staff position to help manage the library, I quickly realized that I needed to request help for other aspects of my job. For example, I realized that although I was cataloging the materials in a music format, I didn't have the time or the experience to catalog all the music books and serials for music. As I worked to organize Music Resources as well as cataloging all the music materials, the backlog of materials to be cataloged began to grow. I was feeling overwhelmed. I needed at least some part-time help from other areas of the library.

STAFF ASSIGNMENTS

Before a librarian requests either full-time or part-time staff positions, he or she must carefully choose the tasks that will be done by staff. Tasks must be clearly defined and precise rather than amorphous and open-ended. This will help the supervisor justify the need for staff. Also, having well-defined job duties is crucial when hiring appropriate staff or identifying existing staff who can help you. In my situation, I had to determine whether it was crucial for the full-time staff position candidates to have experience in the field of music. When requesting part-time help from the cataloging department, I had to determine what skills or experience I should look for in someone assigned to help with cataloging music materials.

Although most of these decisions will be determined by the pool of either applicants, it is wise for the supervisor to have an idea of what characteristics the "perfect" candidate would have. I hoped to find someone for the full-time position who was a "techie" or had experience with an online catalog, as well as someone with at least a rudimentary knowledge of music. Since staff in Music Resources would be handling its own circulation, and this is not an area of expertise for me, I needed someone who could function well as a circulation supervisor. The staff member would be the first person patrons interacted with when entering the music library, answering many of the initial and rudimentary reference questions.

The job was advertised, but the applicant pool was slim. Library staff positions are not well paid, and finding someone with technical expertise as well as familiarity with music is difficult at any salary. I needed to decide what my most pressing need was, and since I have a great deal of music librarian expertise, I decided to balance my abilities with a staff member who had technical expertise. I hired someone who was invaluable to me in setting up the circulation system, and who willingly passed the "musical" questions on to me.

Finding existing cataloging staff to begin working on music materials presented similar issues. The ideal person would be well versed in music cataloging as well as in name authority work. Music cataloging has a unique set of issues that differ from other materials. Various musical scores for the same music are often published by numerous publishers with titles in various languages. The title might include varying opus numbers and/or key statements. Even catalogers working on music that has pre-existing "copy" in OCLC must be able to identify appropriate uniform titles for music materials and perform authority work for these records.

Similar issues exist when cataloging sound recordings, yet there are even more issues with these materials. Questions like these need to be answered: "Does the main 'author' statement for a sound recording list the composer or the performer?" "Is there access given to every performer and every composition on the sound recording?" A staff member with musical expertise is helpful, but someone knowing the appropriate rules for music cataloging is even more important. How could this person be found from an existing cataloging staff pool of no more than ten people?

I realized early in the search that the ideal person, fully trained and ready to catalog music materials, existed within the staff. I was that person; I was the one who had been hired to catalog music materials. Realizing this, I knew that I would need to train staff to do the work I needed help with. I spoke with the head of cataloging and we identified two staff members who had some knowledge of music materials. These people were given a 25 percent job assignment for processing music materials. This, eventually, would ease my overloaded job assignment.

I began by training staff to process books on musical topics. They were already well trained on working with books with copy (from OCLC) in other subject areas, so the process was not new. My only addition to their current book cataloging procedures was to require them to check every call number for accuracy. Call numbers were carefully shelf-listed. Turning this aspect of cataloging over to them was easy, the training was minimal, and the amount of work lifted from me was significant. A supervisor will reap maximum benefit if job duties such as these can be identified: those that require the least amount of training and those that take a significant load from the supervisor's shoulders.

As I planned more training, I carefully scrutinized every area of cataloging. I determined what could be done by my new part-time staff. Cataloging training was completed in a year. After training was complete, staff were cataloging books, scores, and sound recordings with copy, and they were accomplishing most of the authority work needed. I continued to check the staff members' work until I felt confident of three things:

1. The newly assigned staff knew how to apply the procedures I developed and taught.

2. Staff could accurately catalog most of the items assigned to them.
3. Staff knew when to ask questions about an item.

TRUST

Perhaps the most difficult part of this process was allowing someone I had trained to do the work without my supervision. Work is only fully delegated when not only the work but the responsibility for the work has been completely designated to another person. The supervisor must believe in the training he or she has provided as well as the person to whom the responsibility is given.

In an article entitled, "The Micromanagement Disease: Symptoms, Diagnosis, and Cure," the author writes,

> People who micromanage generally do so because they feel unsure and self-doubting. Micromanagers, like many addicts and alcoholics, are the last people to recognize that they are hooked on controlling others. . . . Some areas are just too important and cannot be over managed, such as the recruitment of the best personnel or insuring overall customer satisfaction. But way too often the detailed-oriented boss loses the forest in the trees, becomes overly concerned with nitpicking details, and soon begins to micromanage subordinates.[2]

The successful manager must develop self-confidence and belief in his or her ability to identify the areas that need careful control. The next step is equally as important for the successful manager, and that is to learn to trust the work done by those who report to him or her.

After staff has been identified, duties for staff have been determined, and training has finished, the supervisor's job is not done. For a certain period of time, the staff member must be given freedom to do the job, find the areas of difficulty, ask for help, and learn how to solve problems. The supervisor must treat the staff person less as a trainee and more like a trusted colleague. During this period of time, the supervisor should be available for consultation, and the staff should be required to submit work that has been finished, but the trainee should be encouraged to do as much of the work as possible without consulting the trainer. The process is similar to that of a parent learning to trust an adolescent who is spreading his wings as he reaches for freedom and independence.

The supervisor must be diligent about checking the work turned in to him or her. This can be a most difficult assignment for the librarian who is extremely busy. If the backlog of items to be checked becomes too large, the trainee becomes frustrated. Mistakes are repeated and tend to become habitual. The learning process is interrupted. Work either stops or is done incorrectly, leading to time-consuming corrections.

Once training is accomplished and errors on submitted work are minimal, the trainer and trainee should have a meeting regarding the future. Each must feel comfortable concerning independence. The trainer must be confident that most of the work accomplished by the staff person will be done adequately well. The trainee must have confidence in his or her ability to perform satisfactorily. If either person does not have a high enough level of confidence, a decision will have to be made concerning the future. Should further training be done? Should the work continue to be checked by the supervisor? Should someone else be considered for the position?

This is a crucial point in the training process. If either party is not confident, the transfer of authority will never be complete. If the supervisor/trainer questions the staff member's ability to perform adequately, he or she will always question the work being done. The supervisor will tend to second-guess decisions made by the staff person, and will be inclined to "check up" on all the work being done by the staff person. If the staff person is not comfortable with the responsibility, he or she will not be able to move into independence.

When the trainee is handed the reins, he or she should be encouraged to consult the trainer at any point. Regular and frequent meetings should be scheduled so the staff member can accumulate questions to ask the trainer rather than consulting the trainer every time a question arises. These meetings can be scheduled less frequently as time passes, but should never be abandoned.

The organization gains a great deal when this process is done carefully and systematically. Primarily, the supervisor can relinquish these responsibilities, allowing his or her workload to decrease. Since the newly trained staff person is vested with the authority to make decisions concerning the work he or she is doing, he or she is prone to develop expertise in this area. In my situation, the staff members who were trained to catalog music books and scores several years ago have developed areas of expertise far greater than my own. Because the staff members have been given authority and the trust of the organization, they tend to "own" the work they do in ways that staff who are constantly watched and corrected do not.

Is anything lost in a process such as this? In my situation, there was both loss and gain. I had to give up the expectation of perfection in terms of music cataloging and authority work. As my plans for the perfect catalog became more flexible, my standards had to change. The staff to whom this work has been entrusted did not have the expertise, training, or background that I have. Twenty-five percent of their job is assigned to music materials, meaning they have only ten hours per week to spend on these materials. To expect them to construct uniform titles from scratch is not practical. Finding appropriate subject heading subdivisions is not something staff have time to accomplish. Authority work for every uniform title on every piece of music that comes into our system has to be entrusted to the automated authority control system. These were concerns that could cause a nervous breakdown for the librarian who expects or desires perfection.

Similarly, my expectations for flawlessly shelved materials were jettisoned after the first musicology papers were assigned and materials were flung far and wide in Music Resources. Staff members were busy each day with routine maintenance, projects, and assignments; there were times when we simply had to wait for breaks in the academic year before shelving problems could be addressed.

What I gained from this situation were happy patrons who didn't have to wait weeks or months for materials to move from the cataloging department's backlog to the Music Resources shelves. Requests for items that were awaiting cataloging declined immensely because items appeared on library shelves before requests could be made for these items. Although patrons occasionally point out cataloging errors to me, most patrons comment on the fact that they are happy to be able to retrieve items quickly. It has been years since faculty members requesting items have complained that the items are "stuck" in the cataloging department.

Ultimately I also regained my professional life. After relinquishing control over cataloging, I looked at other areas of responsibility I had, finding other job responsibilities to delegate. I trained either my full-time staff, part-time help from other areas in the library, or student workers or graduate assistants on various library duties. Having delegated these responsibilities, I am able to function as a professional librarian. I am no longer responsible for the day-to-day aspects of keeping the place up and running. Many of these duties have been relinquished for so long that I have to ask my staff questions about how it is done should I need to know. Now I focus on other issues. What is my vision for the future of the music library? How can I motivate this student or that staff member to be more productive in his work? What can I contribute to the university and the professional organizations to which I belong? What research can I do in the field of music librarianship? Without being able to trust the day-to-day work to my staff, I would never be able to fulfill my role as a professional librarian.

Notes

1. *Cambridge Advanced Learner's Dictionary,* "delegate," dictionary.cambridge .org/dictionary/british/delegate_2 (accessed November 23, 2010).
2. Richard D. White, Jr., "The Micromanagement Disease: Symptoms, Diagnosis, and Cure," *Public Personnel Management* 39, no. 1 (Spring 2010): 71–72.

CHAPTER 26

Working as a Solo Librarian in a Large Organization

RUNNING THE LABRIOLA NATIONAL AMERICAN INDIAN DATA CENTER

Joyce Martin

As one of the only special collection repositories within a public university library devoted to American Indian collections, the Labriola National American Indian Data Center holds both primary and secondary sources on American Indians across North America. The Labriola Center's primary purpose is to promote a better understanding of American Indian language, culture, social, political, and economic issues through use of its collections and expert reference service. The Labriola National American Indian Data Center has been endowed by Frank and Mary Labriola, whose wish has been that "the Labriola Center be a source of education and pride for all Native Americans."

Arizona State University (ASU) is one of the largest public research universities in the country, so it may be difficult to believe that I am a solo librarian. However, the Labriola National American Indian Data Center within the ASU Libraries has a staff of one librarian who is the curator of the center. As the curator I am assisted by student workers, unpaid interns, and volunteer support. The Arizona State University Libraries consists of eight libraries on four campuses located throughout the Phoenix metropolitan area. The Labriola National American Indian Data Center is located inside the Hayden Library, the social sciences library on the ASU Tempe campus. The Labriola Center is one of seven repositories within the Department of Archives and Special Collections. However, the Labriola National American Indian Data Center is the only repository with its own reading room. The mission and functions of the Labriola Center are also unique and lead the Labriola Center to essentially function as a library within a library.

Labriola National American Indian Data Center Staffing

The Labriola Center maintains a separate reading room within the Hayden Library that is staffed by the curator and student workers and unpaid interns, providing reading room hours of 9 a.m. to 5 p.m. Monday through Friday. I often hire student workers from within the ASU American Indian Studies Program, which is beneficial for the center since the students are familiar with specific research databases and resources needed to expertly answer reference questions while serving on the Labriola Center reference desk.

Interns from a nearby graduate program in information and library science are another source of student help that provides both a learning opportunity for a future librarian and a source of enthusiastic labor for the Labriola Center. Each semester I attempt to recruit an unpaid intern from the School of Information Resources and Library Science (SIRLS) program in Tucson, Arizona, to work in the Labriola Center. Connections to the local library school, including my alumni status, assist in intern recruitment. The students are able to receive course credit for their time and the center is able to have a short-term professional-level staff member at no cost; this is truly a win-win situation. The Labriola Center has had three successful interns so far and we have another intern lined up for the spring semester of 2011.

Labriola Center Curator's Responsibilities

Providing face-to-face, e-mail, telephone, and even the occasional snail mail reference is a large portion of a solo librarian's job. Even with the help of interns and/or student workers, I routinely spend multiple hours each day working on the Labriola Center reference desk, occasionally even spending the majority of the day at the busy reference desk.

While providing reference services is a large component of a solo librarian's job, it is certainly not the only facet of the position. Providing the vision and overarching direction for the Labriola Center, the curator performs onsite reference; remote reference; collection development; collection maintenance; bibliographic instruction; development; donor relations; grant writing and grant administration; supervision of student workers, interns, and volunteers; and much more. The curator also maintains relationships with relevant faculty and research centers within the larger university environment and maintains necessary publishing and service requirements critical to an academic librarian position. In order to succeed in such a multifaceted position, I needed to ensure my work methods were appropriate to the circumstances of being the librarian for such a library within a library.

Helpful Tips

Through my aspirations to be the most effective curator of the Labriola National American Indian Data Center that I can be, I learned three important things about being a solo librarian:

1. You cannot do everything by yourself—it is necessary to build relationships throughout all levels of the organization.
2. Make yes your default answer.
3. Be flexible.

TIP 1: BUILD RELATIONSHIPS

My first instinct when I began the admittedly slightly overwhelming job as curator of the Labriola Center was to attempt to do as much work as I could, as fast as I could do it. I became very good at prioritizing and working in an efficient manner, which is certainly necessary as a solo librarian. But I came to realize that even by working many additional hours each week, I was only able to take the Labriola Center so far on my own and I did not want myself or the Labriola Center to become isolated. The Labriola Center would not continue to grow dynamically and develop unless I changed my inward-facing work methods. Thus I began cultivating existing relationships (a strong foundation initiated by the previous curator) and reaching out to begin new ones.

One of the most rewarding aspects of being the curator of the Labriola National American Indian Data Center is maintaining close ties with the American Indian Programs at Arizona State University. Arizona State University has approximately 1,500 American Indian students and there are many resources, programs, and groups for American Indian students and faculty on campus, including the Special Advisor to the President on American Indian Affairs, American Indian Studies Department, American Indian Policy Institute, American Indian Student Support Services, American Indian Students United for Nursing, Center for Indian Education, the Indian Legal Program, and the Office of American Indian Projects though the School of Social Work. At ASU the American Indian programs are a close community often cosponsoring events together.

The Simon Ortiz and Labriola Center Lecture on Indigenous Land, Culture, and Community and the Labriola Center American Indian National Book Award are two examples of how building relationships with faculty and American Indian programs on the ASU campus has helped to promote and dynamically enhance the Labriola National American Indian Data Center. Professor Ortiz describes the lectures series this way:

> The Simon Ortiz and Labriola Center Lecture on Indigenous Land, Culture, and Community at Arizona State University addresses topics and issues across disciplines in the arts, humanities, sciences, and politics. Underscoring Indigenous American experiences and perspectives, this series seeks to create and celebrate knowledge that evolves from an Indigenous worldview that is inclusive and that is applicable to all walks of life. The Simon Ortiz and Labriola Center Lecture on Indigenous Land, Culture, and Community seeks to speak, act, offer, and share in order to assume responsibility for land, culture, community that is our world.[1]

The speaker series has provided the Labriola Center the opportunity to host such amazing individuals as Ned Blackhawk, Wilma Mankiller, Gerald Taiaiake Alfred, Leslie Marmon Silko, Peterson Zah, and Kathryn Shanley. The speakers have all presented an informal lecture in the Labriola Center to provide students and community members with an opportunity to ask questions and speak one on one. The formal evening lecture is presented at the Heard Museum in Phoenix, Arizona. The Heard Museum "explores American Indian history through the voices of Native people while celebrating the creative innovations of today's most masterful artists."[2]

Being a part of this speaker series has allowed me to foster closer relationships between the Labriola Center and the many cosponsors of the series, including the ASU sponsors (the American Indian Policy Institute; American Indian Studies; Department of English; Faculty of History in the School of Historical, Philosophical, and Religious Studies; Indian Legal Program in the Sandra Day O'Connor College of Law; and Women and Gender Studies in the School of Social Transformation) and the community partner (the Heard Museum).

The Labriola Center American Indian National Book Award was developed in collaboration with Distinguished Foundation Professor of History Dr. Donald Fixico. The Labriola Center Book Award is in its third year, and books submitted for consideration for the award are multidisciplinary, relevant to contemporary North American Indian communities, and focus on modern tribal studies, modern biographies, tribal governments, or federal Indian policy. ASU Department of History and American Indian Studies faculty make up the judging panel and the Labriola Center hosts the winning author to speak about his book at a reception in the Labriola Center.

The above two examples demonstrate the importance of building relationships with faculty. But it is also important to develop relationships with librarians and staff at the ASU Libraries, the parent organization, in order to successfully complete the day-to-day work of the Labriola Center. Much of what the curator of the Labriola Center does within the larger structure of ASU Libraries is persuading others to collaborate or assist the center on various projects large and small. For example, when the Labriola Center collaborates with one of the American Indian programs on campus to sponsor an event, if I would like to record this event, I must first make my case and gain permission from ASU Libraries before I can offer that service. I work with Bibliographic and Metadata Services to arrange for processing and cataloging of the Labriola Center books and with the preservation staff to maintain the existing collections. Even to set up the Labriola Center for an event, it is necessary to obtain assistance in moving furniture from the additional student workers who work for the Department of Archives and Special Collections.

Because I began to spend more of my time reaching out and building relationships and taking the time to teach others how to help, the Labriola Center has been able to accomplish much more. And I have realized this is a better way for me to function as a solo librarian.

TIP 2: MAKE YES YOUR DEFAULT ANSWER

This leads directly into my second tip, make yes your default answer. As the curator of the Labriola Center I am often approached by students and community members who are looking for a volunteer opportunity. And I accept every volunteer I can get; yes is always my default answer to a potential new volunteer. To prepare to accept volunteer help, it is necessary to have projects lined up and waiting for help to arrive, and it is also important to be willing to take the time to train a volunteer. Sometimes people think that it will take longer to train someone to complete a project (such as searching gift books in a catalog or placing call numbers on photographs) than it will to do it yourself. But in my experience that is not the case. Volunteers do bring a wide variety of skills and interests and it is important to do the best you can to match those skills with the tasks on hand. But I have found volunteers to be very eager to learn new things and able to pick up most tasks quickly, offering a fresh perspective and energy.

Volunteers for the Labriola Center have performed a variety of activities, from an ASU campus fraternity volunteering to move furniture for a special event in the Labriola Center to an alumnus of Phoenix Indian School starting a subject guide on Labriola Center resources on Phoenix Indian School. At the end of one semester I had around a dozen student volunteers within a two-week period that needed community service hours due to minor residence hall violations. They created a listing of photographs from the Kevin Gover Collection, with each student working on a separate box of photographs and one student compiling all lists. Every computer worktable and workspace was full of rotating volunteers.

The Labriola Center also has faculty, students, library personnel, tribal librarians, and so on approach the center with new ideas for collaborations, grant proposals, and special events. Be open to new ideas and see where things go before you move away from a project if necessary; in other words make yes your default answer. About a year ago, for example, the program coordinator for a tribal language recovery program contacted the Labriola

Center to inquire whether the Labriola Center could provide archival training to various staff and interested tribal members during their visit to ASU. I felt hesitant, but I said yes and then started looking around for help (see tip 1). I spoke with the assistant archivist with the Department of Archives and Special Collections and he was happy to present an archival training program that he previously developed. The Labriola Center had both language and culture history material pertinent to the tribe and the tribal members were able to examine this primary and secondary material during their visit. This initial meeting led to the Labriola Center sharing primary resources from the center's collection with the tribe. A few months later I also participated in a workshop held at the tribe's education facility. The Labriola Center is currently digitizing a set of audiocassettes for the community, which contains interviews with tribal members from the 1970s.

Being open to new ideas and new collaborations and meeting new people through an ever-increasing network of volunteers are great ways to build relationships while you build your library. Having a mind open to new collaborations led to the Labriola Center's involvement in such projects as the Labriola Center American Indian National Book Award, the collaboration with the program coordinator for a tribal language recovery program, and the completion of significant volunteer projects. However, the unpredictability of these new opportunities makes it necessary to be flexible.

TIP 3: BE FLEXIBLE

Once you begin building new relationships and taking on new (or rethinking existing) projects, adaptability becomes critical. As a solo librarian working with student workers and/or volunteers, it is important to be accommodating since these types of assistants often have many other commitments and priorities. It is also important to be open enough to be able to say yes when someone calls you up with a great idea for a speaker series, special event, or program when it benefits your library and your customers to do so. As a solo librarian it is important to be flexible not just with long-term plans, but with short-term plans as well, even when it comes to planning your day or even just a few hours in advance.

As curator of the Labriola Center I am very rarely able to plan my schedule in advance. If you know the saying "Life is what happens to you while you're busy making other plans,"[3] this is certainly true when you are a solo librarian. I am responsible for keeping the reference desk open from 9 a.m. to 5 p.m., Monday through Friday, and that has to be my first priority. When a student or intern calls in sick, which can occasionally happen on short notice, my original plans for the day must be set aside so I can cover the reference desk. I have become very flexible about working on writing projects and finishing paperwork at the reference desk knowing there will be frequent interruptions.

I have also developed three categories of meetings to determine how I handle a change in my schedule due to a student worker illness or sudden schedule change: (1) "absolutely must attend" meetings; (2) "important but not critical" meetings; (3) "if the world was perfect" meetings. For category 1 meetings, such as meetings with my boss, bibliographic instruction sessions, and meetings with faculty, I will go to all lengths to find someone to cover the Labriola Center reference desk so I can attend the meeting or provide the bibliographic instruction, including calling in whatever favors are necessary. For category 2 meetings, I will alert other Labriola Center student workers to see if anyone can cover the desk so I can attend my meeting, but if this is not possible I have to prioritize being on the Labriola Center reference desk over the meeting. Category 3 meetings such as optional trainings rarely stand a chance in the life of a solo librarian, but that is just part of being flexible.

Conclusion

Maintaining close relationships with faculty and student organizations on campus means the Labriola Center is very successful in finding qualified student workers. Staff and students are able to recommend their friends and classmates who are knowledgeable in American Indian Studies issues, making training students a much easier process. It is important to give student workers and interns flexibility in their schedule (as much as possible) and try to provide a great deal of autonomy. The student workers in the Labriola Center are required to take on a significant amount of responsibility, more than most student positions since they are assigned to specific reference desk hours, so it is important to treat them as the professionals they are. Most of the students who work in the Labriola Center stay with us for several years, so hopefully that means they enjoy their work as much as I do.

Working as a solo librarian within a large organization can certainly be challenging and also extremely rewarding. The three main lessons I have learned in my years as curator of the Labriola National American Indian Data Center at ASU Libraries are, first, that it is not possible to do everything yourself. It is important to constantly strive to foster and create positive relationships. Secondly, it is helpful to make yes your default answer in order to keep your library open to new collaborations, challenges, and opportunities. And lastly, when faced with the daily schedule changes and challenges, it is important to be flexible. When used together, these three principles will set the foundation for a successful library operated by a solo librarian.

Notes

1. Arizona State University Department of English, "The Simon Ortiz and Labriola Center Lecture on Indigenous Land, Culture, and Community," english .clas.asu.edu/indigenous/ (accessed November 22, 2010).

2. Heard Museum, "Heard Museum Brochure," heard.org/pdfs/10_General Brochure%20web.pdf (accessed November 30, 2010).

3. John Lennon, "Beautiful Boy (Darling Boy)," *Double Fantasy*, 1980.

Index

About the Editors
and Contributors

Eileen Boswell earned her MLS at the Catholic University of America in 2009. In her job as information specialist at the Community Transportation Association of America, she experiments with many free tools. She uses her blog, www.embeddedlibrarian.blogspot.com, to chronicle her adventures "working in the white spaces of the organizational chart," based on a speech by National Geographic's Susan Fifer Canby that she heard early in her library career. Eileen lives in Greenbelt, Maryland, where she spends her free time writing folk songs about librarianship, cats, and coffee.

Andrea Wilcox Brooks is the instructional services librarian at Northern Kentucky University at Highland Heights, Kentucky. She has served in this role since October 2010. Formerly, she was a library director at Brown Mackie College–Northern Kentucky, at Fort Mitchell, Kentucky. She obtained her MLIS from Kent State University in 2009. Andrea is a member of the Special Libraries Association, Cincinnati SLA chapter. She has appeared in the *Journal of Academic Librarianship* and is a volunteer reader for the Cincinnati Association for the Blind and Visually Impaired.

David Castelli has been the librarian and associate dean for the School of General Education at Stevens-Henagar College in Orem, Utah, since 2007. He obtained his MLS from Emporia State University and the MSM from Regis University. David is a member of the American Library Association, the Association for College and Research Libraries, and the Utah Library Association. He has experience as a reference and training librarian in public libraries and has done extensive training and implementation of ILS systems for a major software vendor.

Melissa J. Clapp, instruction and outreach coordinator at the Humanities and Social Sciences Library West, University of Florida, Gainesville, Florida, earned an MA in English from Northern Illinois University and an MS in Information Studies from Florida State University. She joined the faculty at UF in 2007. Melissa coordinates the libraries' mentoring program with the University Writing Program, working closely with the Dean of Students Office in library outreach. A recent publication is "Building a Participatory Culture: Collaborating with Student Organizations for 21st Century Library Instruction" in *Collaborative Librarianship* 3, no. 1 (2011).

Claudia J. Dold is assistant librarian at the Louis de la Parte Florida Mental Health Institute (FMHI) Research Library, a special library located on the University of South Florida (USF) Tampa campus. Claudia completed her MLIS at USF, with a special interest in creating teaching material to promote and enhance library skills. She has created two video series for graduate student audiences and recently began working on a new video series targeting the research needs of undergraduate students. She is regularly a solo librarian when the other librarian is away.

Virginia L. Eldridge, solo law librarian since 2007 at the Grayson County Law Library, Sherman, Texas, received her MLS from Vanderbilt University. She is a member of the American Association of Law Libraries, the Southwestern Association of Law Libraries, and the Texas Library Association. She recently contributed an article to *Legal Information Alert* 29, no. 3 (2010). Her current duties include running the library as well as working for the Grayson County District Attorney's Office. She is working with Laurie Selwyn to publish the first book on public law library administration.

Julie A. Evener has been the solo librarian at the University of St. Augustine for Health Sciences in St. Augustine, Florida, since August 2009. In that time, she has worked to improve library services and access for graduate students on two campuses and for distance learners around the country. Julie is a member of ALA, ACRL, the Florida Library Association, and the Northeast Florida Library Information Network's Continuing Education Committee. Julie has an MLIS degree from the University of South Carolina and a BA from Flagler College.

Barbara Fiehn, MS, EdD, is an assistant professor in library media education at Western Kentucky University. Following thirty years as a school librarian, consultant, and media services coordinator, Barbara taught in library media education at Minnesota State University at Mankato and Northern Illinois University. She has published automation articles in *Internet@schools* and "TQM-Continuous Improvement in the School Library Media Center" in *Educational Media and Technology Yearbook.* Articles are currently in press with *TechTrends* and chapters in *Library Management Tips That Work* to be published by ALA. An ALA member, Barbara's on the Intellectual Freedom Committee.

Jenny Ryun Foster, state law librarian for the state of Hawaii since 2008, obtained her MLISc from the University of Hawaii. Prior to her tenure at the judiciary, she was a solo librarian at a private college in Honolulu for eight years. Jenny also has her MA in English and has published online and in the *Hawaii Review*, as well as coedited *Century of the Tiger* (2003), which won the Hawaii Book Publishers award, called the Ka Palapala Po'okela, for excellence in literature in 2004.

Jonathan Frater is the technical services librarian at Metropolitan College of New York in New York City, New York. He obtained his MLS from Queens College at the City University of New York. While attending library school he worked in the Technical Services Department of the New York Academy of Medicine as a cataloger and electronic resources manager. Jonathan is a member of the American Library Association and New York Technical Services Librarians. He has appeared in the *Journal of Electronic Resources in Medical Libraries* (2007), and he has contributed to "The Resurrectionists," a digital exhibit at the New York Academy of Medicine (2007).

Lara Frater has been the technical services librarian at the New York City Department of Health and Mental Hygiene's Public Health Library since 2005. A graduate from Queens College's Library Science Program, she has worked in libraries since 1996 as both support and professional staff. She has twice volunteered for the MLA/Yale University's Core Public Health

Journal project and is a member of MLA and the New York Technical Services Librarians (NYTSL). She is also a published author of fiction, nonfiction (including the book *Fat Chicks Rule*), and poetry as well as a blogger (www.larafrater.com). She lives in Rego Park, New York, with her husband (who is also a librarian).

Jess deCourcy Hinds's awards include a Twining Fellowship for librarians to conduct research in Italy in 2008. Prior to becoming library director of Bard High School Early College Queens, she taught English with the City University of New York for five years. Hinds writes book and multimedia reviews for *School Library Journal*. Other recent publications include the *New York Times, Newsweek, Teachers & Writers Magazine*, and *Ms.* magazine. A graduate of Smith College, she received an MFA in writing from Brooklyn College and MSLIS from Pratt Institute.

Eva Hornung, solo librarian in a teacher education center in Dublin, Ireland, since 2001, previously worked for four years as a children's librarian in Germany. Eva holds a Diplom from Hochschule für Bibliothekswesen, Stuttgart, Germany, and an MLIS from University College, Dublin, Ireland, and is currently undertaking a part-time PhD with the University of Sheffield on one-person librarians and their perceptions of continuing professional development. She has chartered with CILIP, is an associate member of the Library Association of Ireland, and volunteers on one of their committees.

Cassandra Jackson-Ifie has worked in academic, public, and school libraries. Currently, she is employed at the Visible School-Music and Worship Arts College in Memphis, Tennessee. She serves as the administrative librarian. She earned an MLS degree from Texas Woman's University in Denton, Texas. In 2008, she was selected to participate in the Information Literacy Leadership Institute sponsored by the Andrew Mellon Foundation and Johnson C. Smith University. Sandy wrote a chapter for the publication *The Library Instruction Cookbook* edited by Doug Cook and Ryan Sittler.

Lois Kuyper-Rushing is the head of the Carter Music Resources Library at the Louisiana State University Libraries in Baton Rouge, Louisiana. She received her MLIS in 1993 and her doctor of musical arts in oboe performance in 1990. She has published in *College and Research Libraries*,

Journal of Academic Librarianship, and *Resource Sharing and Information Networks*. Her book, *A Thematic Index of the Works of Eugene Bozza*, will be published in 2012. She was awarded an ARTstor Travel Grant in 2010 to continue her research in France.

Holly Lakatos is currently the law librarian at the California Court of Appeal, Third Appellate District, in Sacramento, California, where she is a solo librarian. She previously worked as the director for public services at the Illinois Institute of Technology, Downtown Campus Library and as the access services librarian at the University of Texas, Tarlton Law Library. Holly graduated from the University of North Texas Library and Information Sciences Program and received the Mersky Spirit of Law Librarianship Award as chair of the Chicago Association of Law Libraries Community Service Committee.

Joyce Martin is curator of the Labriola National American Indian Data Center, Department of Archives and Special Collections, University Libraries, Arizona State University. She earned a master's in anthropology and museums studies from Arizona State University in 1997 and a master's in information and library science from the University of Arizona in 2007. Joyce edits the Labriola National American Indian Data Center Newsletter (www.asu.edu/lib/archives/spring2010.pdf) and holds memberships in the Arizona Library Association, the American Library Association, and the Society of Southwestern Archivists, where she is on the publications committee.

Kimberly Mitchell, reference and education librarian, Albany College of Pharmacy and Health Sciences, obtained her MLS from Simmons College. Kim has been a speaker at regional and national library conferences. She is the eBookshelf column editor for the *Journal of Electronic Resources in Medical Libraries* and a contributor to *The Medical Library Association Encyclopedic Guide to Searching and Finding Health Information on the Web*. She teaches drug information workshops for public librarians and is an expert searcher for the National Library of Medicine's Healthy People 2020 Information Access Project.

Valerie Nye is currently the library manager at Santa Fe University of Art and Design's Fogelson Library. She is coauthoring a book to be published by

ALA Editions in 2011 called *True Stories of Censorship Battles in American Libraries*. Valerie currently serves as a trustee on the New Mexico Library Foundation board. She holds a master's degree in library science from the University of Wisconsin–Madison, where she also worked for two years as a solo librarian for the Office of News and Public Affairs.

Rebecca Marcum Parker earned her BA in English and library science education and MA in literature from the University of Central Missouri. She has thirteen years' experience as an inner-city school librarian, currently at Wendell Phillips in the Kansas City, Missouri, school district. She is a member of the Isak Federman Teaching Cadre of the Midwest Center for Holocaust Education, the Missouri Association for School Librarians, and the Greater Kansas City Association of School Librarians Executive Council. She is a contributing author in *Library Management Tips That Work* (ALA, 2010).

Estelle Pope, library resources coordinator for Coconino College in Flagstaff, Arizona, earned her MLIS from Simmons College and an MA in theology from Boston College. She is a member of the American Library Association, the Association of College and Research Libraries, and the Arizona Library Association. She worked as digital library systems analyst at Boston College Libraries, systems librarian at Yale University Libraries, and systems/reference librarian at Southern Connecticut State University Libraries before arriving in Arizona.

Tatum Preston has been a solo librarian at the Birmingham Museum of Art in Birmingham, Alabama, for seven years. Prior to working as a librarian, she worked in both the corporate and nonprofit arenas as an AmeriCorps volunteer, an accounts-payable auditor, and a development associate. She has served in the Special Libraries Association as Alabama chapter president, chair of the Scholarship Committee, and secretary of the Museums, Arts, and Humanities Division. Tatum holds a BA in English from Davidson College and an MLIS from the University of Alabama.

Stephanie Renne is an independent audiovisual archivist for the Pacific Basin Institute at Pomona College. She obtained her MSLIS from the University of Illinois at Urbana-Champaign and is a member of the American Library Association (ALA), Society for American Archivists (SAA), and International Association for Sound and Audiovisual Archives (IASA). She has processed numerous archival collections, worked as an academic librarian, and is interested in issues pertaining to developing libraries and archives locally and internationally. In her current position, Stephanie has built a new facility on-campus and moved a collection.

Laurie Selwyn worked in a variety of positions ranging from young adult librarianship to reference and administration in academic, public, and special libraries including the New York Public Library Branch Library System, the San Antonio Public Library System (Texas), and the Grayson County Law Library (Texas). Selwyn, a frequent reviewer for *Library Journal* and *Legal Information Alert*, also contributed a chapter to *A Day in the Life* (Shrontz, Libraries Unlimited, 2007). Selwyn retired in 2007 from the Grayson County Law Library and earned her MSL in 1979 from Western Michigan University.

Carol Smallwood received her MLS from Western Michigan University and her MA in history from Eastern Michigan University. *Writing and Publishing: The Librarian's Handbook* and *Librarians as Community Partners: An Outreach Handbook* are 2010 ALA anthologies. *Lily's Odyssey* and *Contemporary American Women: Our Defining Passages* are new releases outside librarianship. *Pre-and Post-Retirement Tips for Librarians* is her twenty-fourth published book. Her magazine credits include *The Writer's Chronicle*, *English Journal*, and *Michigan Feminist Studies*; her library experience includes school, public, academic, and special, as well as administration and consulting.

Roxanne Myers Spencer, MSLS, MAEd, is an associate professor and coordinator at Western Kentucky University Libraries' Educational Resources Center. Spencer teaches collection management as an adjunct in WKU's Library Media Education Program. From 2004 to 2008, she contributed to an international school library exchange project with a private P–12 school near Barcelona, Spain, which led to her article, "Developing Library Classroom Children's Collections in English for a Catalunyan Private School." Spencer has reviewed for *School Library Journal*. She recently wrote about using an instructional design model for collection management and librarians' emotional responses to weeding.

Sandra O. Stubbs is the librarian in charge of the University of the West Indies (UWI), Mona, Western Jamaica Campus Library in Montego Bay, Jamaica, where she has pioneered library services since August 2008. Sandra obtained the master of arts in library and information studies, from UWI, Mona and is a member of the Library and Information Association of Jamaica. In 2010 Sandra received the ACURILEAN Star Award for Excellence in Research from the Association of Caribbean Research and Institutional Libraries. She has presented at conferences and coauthored three publications.

Rhonda Taylor received her doctorate in library and information studies from Texas Woman's University. She is an associate professor in the University of Oklahoma School of Library and Information Studies, where she teaches graduate courses in administration, multicultural librarianship, and organization of information, and her publications have these foci. She began her career in librarianship as a paraprofessional in an urban public library, with other paraprofessional experiences in academic library settings. As a practitioner, she served for a decade as director of a small liberal arts, denominational college library.

Cindy Welch is a faculty member at the University of Tennessee School of Information Sciences, specializing in literature, programs, and services for youth (children and teens) in public and school libraries. She has public library experience, at both branch and central locations; has consulted on youth issues with all types of libraries; and was previously deputy director at the American Library Association, for the American Association of School Libraries (AASL) and the Young Adult Library Services Division (YALSA).